When a mid-20s computer programmer seeks liberation by trading in his day job for a backpack and an unfamiliar roadmap to another culture in South America, he encounters not only beauty and inspiration but also colorism and uncharted territory, calling into question the decision that led him on his unconventional, enlightening path.

Until I Came Home:

A Sunset's Journal

Russell J. Earle Jr.

BENDING CORNERS
PUBLISHING

ISBN: 979-8-9913729-0-9 (Paperback)

ISBN: 979-8-9913729-1-6 (eBook)

ISBN: 979-8-9913729-2-3 (Audiobook)

Library of Congress Control Number: 2024917382

The following events are portrayed to the best of the author's memory. Some identifying details have been changed to protect the privacy of the individuals involved.

Book design by Katarina Naskovski.

Edited and formatted by MasterPieces Writing and Editing LLC.

Proofread by Elizabeth Leverton.

Printed in the United States of America.

First printing edition 2025.

Bending Corners Publishing LLC

#1607

4464 Devine St. STE M.

Columbia, SC 29205

www.RussellEarleJr.com

Acknowledgments

First, I would like to thank God for giving me the courage to take such an ambitious trip and the strength to stay the course and write about it, making those six months closer to ten years.

I would like to thank Erica L. James, my editor, for her outstanding work in helping my story take shape and for having patience with me. I would also like to thank James D. McCallister for providing me with tools and resources to help sharpen my writing and for introducing me to my proofreader Elizabeth Leverton, whose attention to detail and amazing suggestions strengthened my story even more. I want to thank Katarina Naskovski for her beautiful visuals and over-delivering on the graphic design, and my partner Mia Ulmer for her support and creative direction on the art cover. I love you, babe!

I would also like to thank my family and friends who have supported me over the years, staying on me about, "When's the book coming out?" Special thanks to my mom, Juvache' Belton, for introducing me to books and stories at an early age and for showing me how beautiful writing can be. And, special thanks to my grandmother, Jettiva Belton, for sparking the idea to write a book about my trip.

Lastly, I would like to thank all the unforgettable people I met along my journey. You made it worth every moment and that much more memorable. Thank you.

Contents

"Forward"

Where do I go from here?

My arms aren't wide enough to touch either side of the door frame.

A frame housing, a picture of two silhouettes whose shuffling feet are causing the foundation to rumble and roll.

I lose my breath yelling into this deafening room being unheard.

I start to question if I even hear myself.

The tears in the corners of my eyes are swept away from the speed of being pulled and shoved in directions I have no control over.

Where do I go from here? Is there any choice for my bullied heart?

Playing to my own tune that others wanted to pick on, I felt like an outcast as their fingertips calloused.

Anxiety built up from the stares of my community as I walked the runway of a culture birthed by trauma, praying not to trip.

My confidence was knocked down enough that it could pass for a pair of dirty jeans ripped at the knee.

The firm hand that picked me up from the ground like a baby carrot now points as sharp as a blade to a straight line.

A path so fixed and smothering, I worry if my development was deprived.

Needing something to follow, I trail behind the older kids, looking up to them with bright eyes, learning the game like a young assistant.

When I do not see clearly, my peers always have the answer when under their influence.

When I was with them I saw double, cussing and swearing we were grown.

My problem-solving muscle lacks strength because others lifted the weight.

Never needing to accept the challenge to think for myself.

Avoiding difficulties and barriers for them; being too tough to break.

Nor did I grow up with a tool belt around my waist. If something was broken, I didn't know how to fix it. What if I made things worse? Too afraid to try and repair.

Skills taught from lessons that extend further than turning a screwdriver.

And my communication is just as absent as my voice.

To avoid conflict, even someone as spoiled as me can put himself second.

Not wanting to inconvenience anyone. So being quiet comes easy to me.

However, I learned the ability to shift and form into whatever is needed to keep a peaceful environment.

To make others happy spread through my body like a disease.

For breaks, I quarantine with my imagination to keep myself company.

So much so, that my comfort in isolation is sickening. Weakening my emotions and my need to attach.

Where do I go from here?

Is it to televisions where I can have nightly thumb wrestles with joysticks?

Is it to hardwood floors where sneakers squeak feverishly to score baskets?

Maybe it's to do casual hookups with microphones because I like how amplified my voice sounds from speakers. Sounding braver than I feel at times.

Or is it to the number of lines evenly separated by the margins on sheets of paper?

Horizontal paths that are straight and fixed as the ones I've grown familiar with.

Though confined, I've always admired the places you can go with them.

They give me hope.

They make me curious about the things I read from them. A place to have new ideas and thoughts. A place to heal.

They make me hungry and give me nutrition. Growing from each line I visit.

They give me comfort and are relatable. They make sense to me.

I can be here and there at one time. They allow me to live multiple lives at multiple times.

They open my eyes to want to explore. Through them, I find an adventure that inspires me to want one of my own.

And even still, where do I go from here?

Signed,

A Chaser of Sunsets

Section 1: Manifestation

During the honks and horns, exhaust smoke forms from the pipes of traffic storms.

And when the defrost is on blast as you stare at ice crystal glass, there's something else that keeps you warm.

Your vision couldn't be much clearer in front of a toothpaste-stained mirror, though not sure of what they'll say.

Pulled from out of unseen matter, your hands began to gather around the shifting and molding of clay.

Transporting this precious cargo fueled by the burning sensation from the pit of your stomach.

You strive to connect these two points of imagination and reality.

Carrying your dreams like a newborn in the crease of your arms.

All the while hauling around responsibilities and others' uncertainty on your back.

But the magic of believing can lead you in directions only the heavens could have laid out.

So much so that at times moments and happenings seemed tailored just for you as if you were being rooted for.

Though you stagger and stumble, continue to be humble because one day they will see.

That transforming an idea into touch, doesn't require much, only a small amount of bravery.

1

Departure

I sat there in my tattered shoes, with the soles pulling away from the cloth. My unmanaged hair had grown down the sides of my face, across my cheeks, and around and under my chin. My mustache had grown so much that hair fell over my lips. My hair was tangled and matted, having not been properly washed in what seemed like forever. Colorful bracelets with unique patterns from different countries covered both of my wrists. And anyone who knew me could recognize the weight loss simply by looking at my face.

In each country I visited, I stitched the country's flag across the top part of my book bag, like a badge of honor. I had the Wi-Fi networks of all the airports and bus terminals I had visited still saved on my phone, like old contact numbers. In six months, I had traveled to seven countries and over thirty cities. Though I could not reach Brazil, I believed I had received everything I wanted out of the journey, something I could be proud of.

Over the past few days, I had experienced mixed emotions about returning home, confused about how to feel. I experienced moments of feeling excited about going home, and others feeling hurt that a beautiful experience would have to end. But the longer

I thought about it, the more grateful I became. I now sat in a terminal surrounded by other travelers preparing to embark on their journey. And there were things I could look forward to once I got home. Outside of being with family and friends, I would have a story to tell and share with others.

With home getting even closer, I boarded my plane to New York for a transit stop. I had never been to "The Big Apple" before and from the air, the city looked smaller than what I saw on TV. When I walked off the plane and saw the words "John F. Kennedy Airport" in English, I felt like Dorothy waking up at the end of *The Wizard of Oz.* "New York," "Welcome," and "Arrival" were words I did not have to think about when I read them. My brain took in words like water to a thirsty mouth, wanting to keep them a secret all to myself and to hold on to them like treasure. White people, Black people, Hispanic people, and Asian people wandered everywhere. I felt more of a culture shock now than when I had left six months before.

In the blink of an eye, everything had reset itself back to normal. No longer did I have to get my passport stamped. No longer did I have to check in with immigration. No longer did I have to exchange money. No longer did I have to worry about which direction I needed to go. From those profound words I now treasured, I knew where I was going. I was back home.

—

How in the hell do you tell your job you are quitting because you want to travel through South America? That question lingered in the back of my mind as I tried to enjoy Christmas at the beach with my family. As soon as Christmas break ended, I knew I would have to inform them, and my ninety-year-old great-grandmother gave me the courage to commit to my plan. We had finally convinced her to join us, after being reluctant at first to travel away from home.

There on the beach, I learned that my great-grandmother had never seen the ocean. The thought of her having never been to the beach astonished me, especially with her being raised in a town only a couple of hours away. Someone who had so much wisdom and knowledge was experiencing something new for the first time, something as common as the beach.

I thought about the era she lived in, which could have made something as simple as going to the beach difficult. Maybe the opportunities were not there. Maybe the situation caused a hindrance for something so minute, yet so important.

My great-grandmother sat before the body of water, a smile spreading across her face like a mother watching her child unwrap presents. "A lot of water," she said in amusement, never taking her eyes off the blue spectacle.

Upon hearing my great-grandmother's words, I knew the travel life was a life I needed to take advantage of because I might never receive another chance to. I wanted to take that leap because my family did not have an opportunity to do it. I wanted to do what felt good to me. And it was probably best to do it while it felt right instead of missing out on whatever was leading me in this direction. But first, I needed to turn in my resignation.

—

After multiple attempts at creating some explanation for my departure, I came up with nothing. I could not say I had found another job because I would have had to go into details about a job I did not have. Then I thought about saying I was making a career change, which, technically, was true. But it would not have made sense for me to quit if I did not have something else waiting for me. All the detours I tried to take, hoping to avoid embarrassment and judgment, led me back to one path: honesty.

The following Monday after my Christmas break, I drove to work, walked to my cubicle, turned on my computer, and typed up my resignation letter.

Greetings Mr. Todd, I just wanted to inform you that I am resigning from my position as Computer Programmer II for SCDC effective two weeks from this date. I am so thankful that you and Mr. Joey gave me an opportunity to work here in RIM. Being that this was my first job working in the programming field, it was certainly a blessing to gain some experience and to understand what it is like to work in a programming environment, and for that, I am forever grateful. I wish you and the department all the best.

Sincerely,

Russell Earle Jr.

I sat reading the letter over and over, making sure I said everything I wanted, how I wanted, with no mistakes. It's funny to think that just a few lines of words can change the course of your life.

Most of the department took the rest of the week off for New Year's Day. Ms. Angie decided to stick around, and there were never any dull moments with her. She was a chatty lady whom you could hear laughing from just about anywhere in the building. The office usually joked about her being talkative and never at her desk when needed.

Before I printed copies of my resignation, I eased around the corner of her cubicle and told her about my plans. Her monotone responses led me to believe she did not pay me any attention, but then her excitement grew with the more questions she asked. After hearing about my plans to visit countries like Colombia and Peru, Ms. Angie humorously poked out her bottom lip, wishing she could join me.

We laughed for a moment, and I strolled back over to my cubicle to print my resignation letter. After printing my copies, I typed an email to send to my supervisor, his boss, and the director.

The thought of sending the email scared me and excited me at the same time, knowing that once I pressed the send button, there was absolutely no way I could take it back. I also knew pressing that button would give me confirmation that this trip was going to happen. How could I not go after sending my resignation? With a single stroke of my finger, I would receive the one push I needed to take control of my life, even if only for a few months.

Before I knew it, I took one deep breath and hit send. A small "Message Sent" notification faded off my screen as smoothly as it had appeared. I sat waiting for balloons and confetti to fall from the sky, or maybe a nurse to enter the door to offer me a cherry popsicle for not crying after the painless prick of resigning. But nothing happened. Just the soft and subtle taps of Ms. Angie typing away on her keyboard.

I did not feel any different from before, just relieved that I had finally done it. Though unsure of what I wanted to happen, I expected something.

Anything.

This stillness continued for a while until Ms. Angie broke the silence.

"Russell say he 'bout to go to South America. I don't blame you, Russell. I wish I woulda done that when I was younger. It's good that you doing that while you're young because before you know it, you can be stuck doing work."

When Ms. Angie spoke those words, I felt terrible because I was sure others felt the same. However, her saying those words reassured me I had done the right thing. Maybe my decision would be worth it in the end.

—

As we entered the following week, and the year 2015, news of my departure spread throughout the department like fumes seeping out of a broken pipe. Before I knew it, I began receiving more traffic around my area, along with more questions.

"Really, you're leaving?"

"Oh, that's awesome, dude."

"What are you going to do when you get back?"

"So how would you like to work on the web application development team when you get back?"

Though it sounded like a good deal, I knew coming back

would feel like starting back at square one. I desired a different path.

At first, I was uncertain of my supervisor's reaction, as he only asked me, "Are you sure?" I thought I had no more worries until my director called me into his office unexpectedly.

Feeling like a student called into the principal's office, I sat in front of a large desk organized with stacked papers, my eyes wandering around the mahogany-furnished room. The director held an olive-colored folder in his hand, which I assumed contained my information, as he asked the same question I had heard before. "Why?" And just like everyone else, I told him the truth.

"Well, sir, I just wanted to take this time to travel a bit. And to be honest, I don't have any set date on when I'll be back."

"We would sure hate to see you leave," he began. "I've gotten nothing but good feedback from management and your coworkers about how much of a pleasure it is to work with you."

"Oh, yes, sir, I understand. It's been a pleasure to work with everyone, really. They've all been helpful. This is my first job in the computer science field, so I really appreciate the opportunity."

Something that once seemed like a monstrous hurdle to overcome turned out to be not that scary of a leap after all. My director only wanted to make sure that no issues within the department were causing my sudden resignation. He even offered his support if I needed anything in the future.

And before long, my days remaining in the States dwindled to two weeks. Two weeks dedicated to spending time with family and friends.

—

To prepare for my departure, I spent months surfing the web for information about the places I intended to visit and the people who lived there. I reached out to the Couchsurfing community and learned the ins and outs of being a couch surfer, mapped out a route of locations I wanted to visit, and took an eight-week Spanish course, where the instructor even gave me advice.

"Oh . . . you mean backpacking?" the instructor said after hearing about my travel plans. "That's something that my husband and I always wanted to do as well."

I had never heard the term "backpacking" before then. It excited me that finally there was a word for what I was doing.

"Yeah, I'm nervous, but I'm pretty excited for it. Do you have any recommendations on what's the best way to get around or places I should visit?"

Before I could even finish my sentence, the instructor ripped out a piece of notebook paper and started writing suggestions and places to visit. She scribbled down places like Buenos Aires, Salta, and Iguazu Falls and attractions like El Tren a las Nubes (Train to the Clouds) and Cerro de Los Siete Colores (The Seven Colors). She also jotted down her email address.

"Let me know the places you're trying to go; I may have family and friends in those places that will give you a place to stay while you're in the area," she explained.

Though I did not plan on traveling to Argentina, I could not help but feel joy and comfort knowing that someone would be willing to help me on my journey. I had questions about my safety and limited expectations. But this kind gesture from my Spanish teacher assured me I would be fine. All these new people I encountered, all reaching out to assist, were like gentle hands intertwining and knitting the fabric of my trip as it began taking shape right before my eyes.

And once my two weeks were up, I walked out of my job knowing that the only thing standing between me and South America was a one-way ticket—my ticket to a new world.

2

Disturbance

I have heard it is better to get things over with as soon as you can because the longer you wait, the harder it will be. Though that may be true, execution is execution no matter how soon or late it happens.

As I walked into the den to announce my travel plans to my grandparents, my mother accompanied me as my priest. My grandfather sat on the couch with his legs crossed while my grandmother reclined in her La-Z-Boy chair.

"Hey, what's up, gangbusters? How y'all? We didn't even hear ya come in the door," my grandmother said.

"We doing alright, just came over here to see what y'all was up to," my mother replied, walking over to hug my grandmother.

My grandfather uncrossed his legs to stand up. "Well, y'all caught me just in time 'cause I was 'bout to go over to the other house and feed my hound."

With my grandfather preparing to leave, I knew I had little time to talk. He walked back into the bedroom to put on some of his overalls as my mom and grandmother chatted while watching television. He took longer than usual to get ready while I wrestled with how to break the news of my departure. I could hear him poking around the bedroom. I heard dresser drawers open and close, and the clicks of the light switch as he entered and exited the bathroom. He finally came to sit down on the couch next to me as he started putting on his shoes. My mother grabbed the remote to turn the volume down, knowing I had to be ready.

As my granddad finished tying his shoelaces and stood, I hesitated to speak. He grabbed his hat and patted his chest pocket, making sure he had his pack of cigarettes before he left.

"Alright, I'll catch y'all later on."

By the time he could reach the corner, I let the words spill out, knowing there would not be a better time to tell them than now.

"Aye, Granddad, right before you go, I wanted to tell y'all something."

"Yeah, what's up, bo?"

I inhaled one deep breath and exhaled, letting the words go with it.

"Well, I've been planning on taking a trip at the beginning of next year. Something like a li'l vacation."

My grandmother looked at me curiously. "A trip to where?"

"To South America."

My grandfather took off his hat and scratched his head as he plopped down in the chair next to him. My grandmother chuckled hysterically as I sat and watched. Honestly, it sounded stupid after I said it. In my thoughts, it made perfect sense to me, but as soon as I spoke it, it seemed like all of my logic was gone. This substance called reality seemed to have dissolved the fantasy trip I had been planning for the past couple of months.

"South America? South America? Russell, who do you know over there?" my grandmother questioned. "You don't know anybody."

I hesitated to inform them about the people I had found on the internet.

"Well, I've gotten a chance to reach out to a few locals around the area. They gave me information about different places and what's going on. I think I have a good bit of knowledge to get around."

"Russell, you don't know what's going on over there! Anything can be happening, baby. Them people could be setting you up. And if somethin' happens to you, what you gonna do? You don't know anybody. We can't get to you. You wouldn't know who you could trust."

While my grandmother continued to spew out her thoughts, my granddad had said nothing yet. His eyes remained fixed on me and the matter at hand.

"And what about your job? You just gon' leave?"

If the TV was still on, I could not hear it. It would not have surprised me if the people on television had stopped themselves to hear my response. The only movement in the room was the whirling fan above us, sending down a breeze that was not cool enough to mollify the heat or the tension. I took another deep breath.

"I'm going to leave. I don't feel like I'm doing anything there. I'm not learning anything. And honestly, it just feels like I'm being babysat. I'm using nothing I learned in school to do what I'm doing at work. It just isn't for me."

"No, no, no, no. If it's your job you're concerned about, then see if they have any other positions open that you can apply for. But you just don't give up ya job, honey. You got people looking out for you, and yo' grandaddy out 'dere pulling strings to help get you a good job. And you just gonna leave?"

Strangely enough, my grandfather still had said nothing, but he began adjusting his chair and making sporadic taps with his foot, which I guessed was better than not doing anything.

"Shay, what do you think of this? What your son is telling us?"

My mom was so quiet that I forgot she was in the room.

"Yeah, well, when he mentioned it, I certainly expressed my concern about it. That's quite a distance to be from home not knowing anybody. And if something were to happen to him, it would take us a while to get to him."

Then she carefully added, "But, I do know that he is also a young man and can make his own decisions."

While my grandmother sucked her teeth and looked away with disappointment, abandonment had taken refuge in my grandfather's eyes. It seemed like he had left the conversation without ever entering it. Ever since I had been working as a computer programmer, I had always sensed that my grandfather knew I did not enjoy it. Every time we would see each other, he would ask me about the job, tell me how lucky I was, and remind me of when I used to push carts back at Walmart. It was his way of reassuring me I was right where I needed to be. He knew my mind would shift and sway, but he would still act as my harness, keeping me grounded the way taut ropes secure a hot-air balloon. But now, he appeared to have given up, finally letting go of all those efforts of clinging on.

"Well, how about we do this? I think you been at your job long enough to be eligible for a two-week vacation. Check with them and see if you could take some time off. Me and ya granddaddy got some timeshares you can use so you won't have to worry about spending all ya money. Then you can go down there and have you a li'l vacation time. Maybe a few days at the Sheraton or Marriott. I think that will be nice. That way, you'll still have a job to come to when you get back. How does that sound?"

Though impressed at the thought of her considering me going, I knew two weeks would not be enough to do what I wanted to do. Besides, they did not seem to grasp the concept of me not wanting to work there anymore.

"I want to be gone for longer than two weeks. I would be moving around traveling to a few places."

"Well, how long you planned on bein' gone? Where all you trying to go?"

I did not have an answer to her question. After all, how long does it take to find one's self? How long does it take to finally take in everything that you have dreamed about and longed for? Would time move faster or slower? How long is too long? How long is not enough? I answered long enough to where I could not keep the job and short enough to where it would not seem like forever.

"I want to visit a few countries but my goal is to go to Brazil, but as far as how long I want to stay . . . I guess like . . . probably . . . two months."

"Two months? You think you gonna be staying two months over 'dere? How you gonna get around? Where you gonna stay?"

"The basic essential things I need like food, a place to stay, and transportation is cheap there. If I need someplace to go, I could take taxis locally and for long distances, I'll take the buses. As far as a place to stay, hostels are inexpensive, but I would be saving a bit of money by Couchsurfing. There's a website for travelers to connect with others around the world and give them a place to stay for free and . . ."

"Let him go! I'm through with it!" my grandfather yelled as he shot up from his chair, reaching for his cigarettes in his shirt pocket. Our necks snapped in his direction.

I felt somewhat relieved that he had finally spoken. It was almost like the turning of a valve to release the pressure and tension in the room.

"Imma tell ya right nah, ain't nobody gonna let you stay nowhere for free, son. And you don't know the language that good.

You go over there and them people start to talkin' that shit, you ain't gonna know what to do. You gonna mess around and go over there and get yo' ass kidnapped. And if something happens to you, I can't get to you 'cause I ain't gettin' on no plane!"

I recalled a story that my granddad told me once about his first and his last plane ride. My grandparents had endured a terrible experience while flying on a crop duster in Arkansas. I imagined my grandfather clinching onto the seat, with his head stiffly leaned against the headrest going through air pockets of turbulence. While holding back a smirk, I remembered his words as if he had just said them.

"And I said right then and there, if the good Lord let my feet touch the ground, He ain't never gotta worry about me getting on a plane again. If I can't drive to it, I don't need to be there."

My brief moment of reminiscing ended as quickly as it had begun when I heard my grandfather's voice again.

"Son, listen, there is no place in the world better than here. It's people out there dying trying to get over here. Why would you want to go somewhere else?"

For a split second, I thought about the recurring headlines of Black males being killed by police and wondered if it was that much safer here.

"You planned on going to Colombia?" he asked, as if already knowing my answer.

"Yes, sir."

He left the room, looking at my grandmother. "Cocaine," he grumbled.

After my grandfather left, the maelstrom of questions and tension vanished with him. As we sat saying hardly anything, my grandmother made remarks every so often, like leftover winds from a dying storm. Once my mother and I finally left, I felt a huge amount of relief knowing that I had gotten a chance to tell them about my trip.

My grandfather's truck sat in the yard as we pulled up in the driveway shortly before night fell. I could imagine him sitting in his shop in the backyard, still trying to process the news he had just heard.

Simply put, I was unsure of what I was doing with my time. I wanted to feel like my time had meaning. I wanted to make some type of progress with something worthwhile, and I was not doing that there. Oftentimes, I wished my grandparents could see that. Throughout the years, I made most of my decisions based on what they said or thought I should do. I understood they wanted the best for me, but they based my life on their experiences without factoring in the present times.

It seemed as if they believed playing it safe was better than taking a chance, that somehow I would be more secure and financially stable by staying at home. In my opinion, security did not exist. I believed security and stability could change in a blink of an eye, so I focused more on the moment. Essentially, that is all there is. Tomorrow is not promised, and yesterday is just a memory.

During that time, I read more about self-improvement and a higher conscience. Though my mother and grandparents raised me in a Christian home, I began gravitating toward spirituality as opposed to religion about two or three years prior to my trip. Because I feared they would treat me differently, I had not mentioned it to many family and friends.

Being that I was raised in a Bible belt state—one of the multiple areas in the South where Christianity heavily influences politics and society—most people considered anything that differed from tradition to be blasphemous. It was not anyone's fault. Some people just carried on what others passed down to them.

However, I looked at religion like maps: one destination with several routes. I just believed in taking the path that resonated with me.

—

Between my continuous research, gathering supplies, and getting my shots, I spent the rest of my time with family and friends. I even received a gift from one of them. Reaching down into a striped gift bag, I grabbed what felt like a book of some sort. A gray leather book emerged as my hand reappeared, a travel journal with white text printed on the front cover that read, "All our dreams can come true if we have the courage to pursue them." Those words seemed to resonate with me more and more each time I read them.

Some friends even put together a going away party at Yesterday's, a restaurant whose logo included a naked cowboy with a beer in his hand reclined in a tub. Friends conversed, looking as though we were trying to recreate the *Last Supper*. Dishes of half-eaten burgers and devoured bowls of Apple Pie à la Mode cluttered the table, only to be washed down with mixed drinks. Ambient sounds of music played in the background of laughter and chatter that saturated the restaurant.

Witnessing everyone come together to see me off and wish me good luck felt pretty special. Each had unique stories about how we met, and everyone who said goodbye seemed a bit more unrealistic than the last. Their parting words felt like layers of my life being peeled back, and the pieces of who I was being broken down.

A few days later, I visited with my dad as he sat in silence watching my little brother and me play video games. I could still sense his concern about my safety on my last visit with him. When I told him a few weeks prior that I would be leaving, he mostly listened to what I had to say instead of offering me feedback. I gathered he knew I had made my decision, and he respected it.

My father and I stood outside in the cool night air as we prepared to say goodbye. When it comes to fathers and sons expressing their emotions, society believes that men are supposed to show masculinity and toughness when around each other. It seems almost like an unspoken "man law." And when we do share our feelings, we often dress them up as manly as possible, usually ending each sentence with the word "man."

Keeping with tradition, my father and I shook hands and embraced.

"Alright, I love ya, man."

"Alright, Pop. Love you, too, man."

My father stood outside for a while, watching as my car pulled off. And now alone in the car, man law was not in effect. The roads and streetlights became blurry as my eyes filled with water. Pretty soon, I would be leaving everyone behind.

3

Lifted

"So, how do you feel?" my mother asked as she reached to get what I assumed to be lint out my hair.

"I feel pretty good. I think I got everything I need," I replied as I watched people getting their bags checked and tagged by ticketing agents. Dressed neatly in their uniforms, they worked casually, tapping away on their computers and breaking only to lift luggage onto the conveyor belt.

"Yeah, I know you've been preparing for a while, ya know?"

"Yes, ma'am," I responded, standing there with my head down and my hands in my pockets, reflecting on all the planning that led up to this moment.

My mother stood in line with me, which helped pass some time. However, I was more concerned about her. I was anticipating that moment when she would burst into tears and cling to my neck while I attempted to walk into customs. But surprisingly, she was keeping her composure.

"Hey, how you doing, sweetheart? You got your passport?" the lady behind the counter asked.

"Yes, ma'am."

I reached into my jeans pocket, slid out my newly received passport, and handed it to the lady.

"Okay, let's weigh your bag, sweetie."

I swung my behemoth of a backpack off my shoulders and carefully set it on the scale. She printed off a tag and secured it on my bag, and I watched it travel along the conveyor belt beyond those dangly black flaps.

"Wow, so you're traveling to South America, huh? Do you know someone over there?"

"Oh, no, ma'am, I'm just going to go travel."

"That's amazing! I wish I could come. Well, you be careful, hun. And make sure to remember to pick your bag up in Aruba."

With my plane tickets in hand, my mother and I walked back over to where my grandfather sat. A sinking feeling started creeping up in my stomach; the only thing left to do was to say farewell. From planning to informing my family I was leaving, and even to putting in my two-weeks' notice, I thought about all the events that preceded this moment. And now I was sitting beside my mother and grandfather, staring at the security gate.

My grandmother decided not to come along for my departure. I believed it was her way of rebelling against my decision to leave, along with not wanting to watch her grandson go. On my way to the airport, she called to wish me good luck.

I could sense the worry among my mother and grandfather as we sat in silence. They waited for me to make the first move.

"Let's get a quick selfie right quick," I suggested. They both agreed.

The photo captured a family huddled in winter coats, wearing heavy smiles and uncertainty on their faces. As I stood up, throwing my backpack over my shoulders, my mother and grandfather followed suit. My grandfather and I shook hands, bringing it into a hug.

"Take care of ya self, bo."

"Yes, sir, I will."

I knew once I looked over to my mother to embrace her, water would start building in her eyes, triggering streams of warm tears down her face. She looked at me and smiled with her plump cheekbones and stretched out her arms.

"Alright, I love you, baby. Be careful, and we'll see you when you return."

I gave her a slight grin, proud that she kept it together.

"Yes, ma'am, I'll see you all when I get back. Y'all take care."

They stood around as they watched me walk through customs, emptying my pockets, taking off my shoes and belt, and walking through the metal detector. I looked back one last time to give my family a quick wave. I continued heading down the terminal until I could no longer see them, swept away by the flow of travelers.

After a few minutes of walking, I located my gate and found an available seat. Staring down at two plane tickets as I waited to board, I remembered I had not ridden on a plane since middle school. One summer, my mother and I took a plane trip to see my uncle, Willie, in Houston, Texas. The only thing I remember was how badly my ears popped and that chewing gum helps for relief.

"All travelers boarding flight 148 to Miami International Airport, please come to gate A9 for boarding," boomed over the loudspeaker.

That was my cue to go.

Boarding the plane, people stuffed their carry-ons in the overhead compartments as others patiently waited to sit down. I eased my way to my seat, taking out my iPod and headphones before packing my bags into the compartment. I scrolled down my list of music to play a song I had downloaded that morning, an acoustic version of Mali Music's song "Ready Aim." Those compelling and relatable lyrics mirrored just how I felt as I waited for takeoff—and I needed to hear them. While hearing the engine turning and building power, I gazed out the window as the plane glided carefully onto the runway. There was no turning back now.

I laid my head back on the headrest as I watched the stewardess perform safety procedures. The plane rocked and rolled down the runway, waiting for the others ahead of us to take off. Before long, I felt the power of the engine build stronger as we sped down the runway, preparing to head into the grey of the morning skies. And in one smooth motion, the plane lifted as we began ascending into the air.

—

My usual mornings lacked such excitement. By the time I finished brushing my teeth, I would typically be fully awake, staring into the mirror. Along with seeing toothpaste spots on the glass, I'd see someone who was still trying to figure things out. Someone who looked unsatisfied with how things were going, and who was preparing to head into a job that he did not care for.

I normally checked in on my mom as I headed back to my room. Her room was somewhat similar to mine. Baskets of clothes on the floor. Jackets and pants hanging off the chair and room door. Her dresser was not cluttered with CDs and books, but instead with makeup, hair care products, stacks of mail, and prescription bottles. As my mom lay wrapped up in faded covers, I could see only the worn nightcap on her head.

The house was so quiet that subtle creaks could be heard as I crept back to my room. Down the hall, the carpet had a discolored middle from being walked on over the years, a path I had traveled many times. The floors and now-tinged walls were all still the same, full of history, memories, and heartache.

Entering my room one day, I noticed it had gotten brighter from the rising sun, making the mess in my room more visible.

Notebooks and half-drunk water bottles lingered on the floor. My rug scrunched up against the dresser like it was about to be swallowed underneath it. Chargers and cords lay tangled and wildly connected to the surge protector by my nightstand. And my bed looked like the Tasmanian devil had endured a rough night of sleep. I gazed out my bedroom window so that my eyes could escape the unsightly clutter.

For the past couple of months, I had been spending more time outside. On the weekends, I would take a chair from my granddad's garage and place it directly in the sunlight. When my head was not constantly on a swivel checking to see if people were watching, I would close my eyes and savor the moment, lifting my face toward the sun. Even if only for a few seconds, the sun's warmth felt like a gentle cloak. A warm veil of protection from any viewer. If I was lucky, a soft breeze would come along and kiss me on the cheek to assure me it was safe.

Occasionally, I would take off my shoes and socks to feel the blades of grass between my toes. Sometimes I felt so disconnected from everything when indoors. It seemed as if I were missing out on so much. When the weather grew colder, I peered out of the window, anticipating the arrival of warmth's embrace like a loved one returning from war.

Before leaving for work, I would hug my mother, the final step before walking out the door. She would lift her head from under the covers and, though halfway still asleep, smile and kiss me on the cheek.

My mother has lupus disease, and the medication she takes often keeps her tired and weak. There have been times when I would leave for work and come back, only to find her still asleep. For as long as I can remember she has been sick, fluctuating from feeling good on some days to feeling bad on others.

—

One of the highlights of my day, I enjoyed my music most on the ride to work. My collection mostly consisted of Hip Hop and Soul, but at the time, I had only a few classic albums on rotation like Erykah Badu's *Baduizm*, Outkast's *Aquemini*, and D'Angelo's *Voodoo*—some of my biggest influences in songwriting and rapping.

When the topic of music would arise and I'd mention being in a rap group, I doubted people took me seriously. Probably because I looked more like a sales rep for Best Buy than the stereotypical image of a rapper. If you searched for a computer programmer on the web and clicked on Images, I would probably look like the first Black guy you found.

Ironically, I had been a computer programmer for about eight months and I still did not understand what the hell I was doing. I would come in, sit down, log into the mainframe, change one or two letters and dates in some coding, copy and paste, and submit. This would take about three minutes and for the next several hours, I would surf the web, either checking on my fantasy football team or jotting down thoughts and ideas.

I certainly did not take the job for granted, especially after working at Walmart for almost two years, but it seemed as if I were there to make others happy. I was withering away behind two mismatched computer monitors in a 70s-style, mustard green desk chair.

The only perk was that I sat next to a window where I could gaze outside from time to time. Even though it was not much of a view, I liked the fact that I could see the clouds drifting and the sky changing. I could have some actual sense of the day passing by instead of looking at the clock. Whenever the sun began setting, I could feel its warmth soothing my neck and shoulders, letting me know the day was about done.

And now, several months later, a new day was just beginning.

4

Turbulence

Stepping off the plane for the second time after a stop in Miami, I remembered that I needed to pick up my luggage in Aruba. Spanish now displayed across the majority of all signs as I went to locate my bag. I scanned around for familiar words like I was looking for someone awaiting my arrival. My hand grasped the phone in my pocket ready to use Google Translate, uncertain of my direction.

I followed the crowd, assuming I would be led to baggage claims. Instead, I found myself in line at immigration, scrambling to fill out the form the stewardess had handed us on the plane. Though all was new to me, my mind was elsewhere, wanting to get to my belongings. My search led me into a plaza, getting me caught in an intersection of flowing travelers. I would go to one place and get turned around by someone directing me elsewhere after showing my baggage claim ticket.

After going back and forth, I finally laid eyes on my Sasquatch of a bag coming around one of the conveyor belts. I felt better knowing that I had my bag now; but, I would feel even better once I found the next airline.

Having only an hour of free Wi-Fi, I used that time to

message my family. I also messaged my first Couchsurfing host, Jose, that I should be arriving in Caracas, Venezuela on schedule.

For almost three hours, I waited for my next flight as I sat on a bench by an outlet, charging my phone. I had never been out of the country before, and I still had to wait a bit longer before I could enjoy it. As I prepared to board, only enough light remained to make out silhouettes of clouds on the horizon from the engulfing darkness. Excitement filled my body like that of a child on the night before Christmas morning.

—

While in flight, the stewardess strolled down the aisle rolling a cart of refreshments. I remembered being warned against drinking water or ice from other countries because you could potentially get sick. I pointed at the apple juice on her cart and signaled to have no ice. She gave a nod and looked at the other stewardess.

"El debe supersticioso."

I did not know what her words meant but I could make out the word "superstition," which made me think, *What if it is just superstition? What if the water isn't bad for me after all?* However, I was still not comfortable taking the risk. I thought about how bad it would be if I ended up having an upset stomach on the first night of my trip.

A voice came over the intercom speaking in Spanish, which I assumed meant we were preparing to reach Caracas. I peered outside of my window and noticed lights off in the distance. The closer we got, the lights began elevating as they soon covered the hills of Caracas. Though this might not have been too much of a spectacle for some, I had not quite seen anything like it. And from the darkness, it looked like the lights were rising, hovering over the ground.

As we descended, I filled out my immigration form to turn in immediately after landing. Walking off the plane into the airport, I scanned around the unwelcoming terminal as I approached the dismal building. I felt a sense of abandonment as I entered the poorly lit building. I did not see any traffic outside, or even other planes for that matter. I walked down the halls of an empty airport to immigration.

There was not much chatter or much of any conversation. The short lines made for an easy wait as I approached the lady behind a glass window. Without speaking, I handed her my immigration form and my passport. She read my passport and glanced at me over the rim of her glasses. As she proceeded to stamp my passport with the word "Entrada," she finally broke her silence.

"Be careful," she uttered.

Slightly taken aback, I stood there as her words took a moment to register. As new thoughts pushed her words to the back of my mind, I walked to baggage claim to locate my backpack. There seemed to be only one conveyer belt active, as bags slowly crept around on the belt while people stood around. I checked for Wi-Fi to let Jose know that I had arrived, but for some reason, I could not pick up any networks. Catching my bag, I threw it over my shoulder and continued my search for a connection as I walked further toward customs. One guy around my age noticed I was confused, and he signaled me in the direction I should walk.

I spotted the area for exchanging money, but I remembered that I would not get the best rate if I did so at the airport. I also read that I should be aware of airport officials, who would try to exchange money using the black market. And before I knew it, an official had scoped me out, flagging me for my attention.

"Hola, mi amigo. ¿Dónde eres? Americano?"

I could make out that he said American, and I could not ignore him being that he was right in front of me.

"Yes, I'm American."

"Ahh, okay, my friend. You need Wi-Fi? I help you with Wi-Fi."

I wondered how he knew I was looking for Wi-Fi.

"This way, my friend. I help you get Wi-Fi."

He signaled another person around my age, but he was wearing green military-type attire.

"My friend help you with Wi-Fi. He can type in code for you."

The young official held out his hand as I cautiously handed over my phone. While he entered the password, the older gentleman turned to me.

"You exchange money yet, my friend?"

"No, I will later, but thank you."

"You hear of black market? I will offer more for your dollars. My friend, I give you fifty Bolívars for each dollar."

Fifty Bolívars? Hell, from my research I knew I could at least get up to 176.

"Oh, no señor, gracias." I turned my attention to the guy with my phone, suspicious of why it was taking so long.

"Okay, okay, my friend, seventy Bolívars."

I refused again. He went on until he reached 110 Bolívars, and at this point, I was just ready to go.

"Okay, 110 Bolívars is good."

Finally, my phone connected to Wi-Fi.

After making a low comment, the young official and I walked into an area that was out of the sight of people and cameras. He pulled out a roll of Bolívars from his pocket and started to count their exchange for one hundred dollars. Truth be told, I did not feel good about any of it. I held on to my bags, not wanting to put them down to get my money. The older official watched from a distance, seeing that the transaction went smoothly.

I knew I would have been able to get more if I had exchanged the money later, but their persistent pressure led me to believe my non-compliance might have stirred up some problems. And problems were the last thing I needed. My eyes bounced between the wad of cash and his eyes counting it. I tried to reason with myself by saying that either way I would be getting more money than the country's official rate. But I knew I was getting cheated.

The young official reached out his hand to make the exchange and at the last minute, I refused and turned away. The older official and I made eye contact as he threw up his arms.

"Hey, my friend, what is wrong?" he asked.

I walked away like I knew where I was headed but I didn't, being approached by three more officials to exchange money along the way. I refused them all without stopping until I reached the food court upstairs where I saw people gathered.

Up until that point, I would not have doubted I was in the airport alone, left to dodge money-hungry officials. The weight off my shoulders relieved me as I sat down, taking a break from hauling my heavy bag. My Wi-Fi signal was weak but strong enough to inform my mother and Jose of my arrival.

Employees wiped down counters and swept floors as food places began shutting down. I watched travelers read their papers while others scrolled away on their phones until I heard the buzz of my own.

"Hey sorry. I don't think I can come get you. I am on other side of town and city buses will stop soon. I have only enough time to go home."

Are you fucking kidding me? I thought. *Is he telling me that I'm stranded at the airport right now?*

"Please stay at airport for tonight. It is more safe to leave in the day," he added.

After the ordeal with the officials, I was ready to leave as soon as possible. I tried my backup Couchsurfer Yolangi just in case some bullshit like this happened. Besides, she worked for an airline, so I was sure she would be able to help me. While sending the message to Yolangi, the Wi-Fi signal dropped.

Using Google Translate, I queried various people in the food court asking if they knew the password. Back and forth I wandered through the food court, ping-ponging between this person and the next. Going anywhere except back downstairs.

Ultimately, I typed a message to use someone's phone to call a friend, having success with one cautious gentleman. Yolangi's phone rang as I desperately hoped that she would answer.

"Hello?"

"Hey, Yolangi, it's Russell! I'm here at the airport. Do you think you can pick me up? My first host can't make it."

Four guys in guerrilla military attire began advancing toward me. Though I pretended not to notice, my heart started racing as I could barely make out what Yolangi was saying. I deciphered the one part that mattered the most, however.

"I can't come."

Even though I kept my composure, my stomach churned with anxiety as the four men, now in front of me, reached for the phone. No longer able to pretend they were not there, I held up my finger to stall for time, trying to listen to the instructions from the other end, but my mind went blank.

As I began to grab the attention of the food court, Yolangi spoke, unaware of my situation. The calmness on her end of the phone compared to the tension on my side was tormenting. I could no longer keep the men waiting as one took the phone and handed it back to the gentlemen I had borrowed it from. The man who I assumed was the one in charge spoke to me in Spanish while I responded to him in English.

"What's the problem? What's wrong?"

After a brief pause, they signaled me to follow them. Knowing I was in a different country where I could not speak the language and did not know the laws, or anyone, I had no room for argument. Everything moved in slow motion as they led me into the bathroom and out of the public eye.

I heard no more noise from the food court, just silence and the ruffling of my bags being searched. I stood there thinking that maybe this trip was a mistake. Maybe I should have listened to my grandparents and agreed that this was a stupid idea. Three more officials walked into the bathroom, and now I stood before seven guys who took my bags, my passport, and my wallet. One guy opened my wallet to count the money I had.

My eyes remained on my bag, hoping they did not find the $2000 I had stashed in my secret compartment. A few of them fixed their eyes on me, showing no concern that I was a visitor. Though I was oblivious to the things they said, they continued speaking Spanish as if I understood. I stood there just watching, unable to communicate, do, or say anything. *Why did I come here? What am I doing?*

Unaware of how much time had passed, I stood, wondering what would be the outcome of this moment. I motioned my hands while speaking, in hopes that they would somehow magically understand me. However, they did not need a translator to see that I was confused. My squinted eyebrows and shoulder shrugs every ten seconds undoubtedly got the message across.

Out of the group, one attempted to speak English. The English was so bad that in a way, it mollified the tension.

"What your name? Where . . . wha . . . where you go?"

Every time he spoke, he straightened the top of his necktie, like he was unsure about what he was saying.

"Is there anyone I can speak to? Like a chief? Y'all got a chief?" I asked while raising my hand in a level motion.

Though it probably would not have made a difference, he understood my message and told me to "wait," which sounded more like "wet."

Strangely, I felt much calmer than when they first ushered me into the bathroom. I figured they would have done something to me by now if they were going to do anything. I could now hear faint noises of people in the food court, but no one had entered the bathroom since we had been there. *Maybe they have someone guarding the door?* I wondered.

As the other soldiers murmured among themselves, one seemed to never look away from me. With a face of stone and his hat tilted down, he was the one who approached me earlier to take the phone and, as of recently, confiscated my wallet to count my money.

Suddenly, the door swung open and a familiar face walked in. There stood the airport official who tried to pressure me to exchange money earlier. When I recognized his face, I burst out in laughter. The soldiers exchanged looks, baffled at my reaction. Confusion even chiseled away at the stone-faced soldier. To be honest, I puzzled myself laughing at a time like this. And like before, the official tried to exchange money, but this time more sternly.

"My friend, why you not want to exchange? We offer good price."

"No, sir, it's not a good price. I know how much the dollar is worth on the black market."

Once he noticed I would not budge, he stormed out of the bathroom. The other men returned my bags, my passport, and my wallet, with my money still inside. I gathered my things, and they cleared a path as I headed out the door, relieved to walk out of there unharmed.

5

Grounded

Though relieved to have my belongings back, I still had a problem. *Where do I go from here?* I wondered. I had no one to pick me up and no place to stay, and the likelihood of spending the night at the airport became more of a reality. Being trailed by green uniforms exiting the bathroom, I spotted a young girl with a backpack like mine. *Could she be a backpacker as well?* She might have just been there to catch another flight, but for me, I had spotted an angel wandering in public.

For a moment, I watched and waited until she found a place to sit. And naturally, she found a seat next to an outlet to charge her phone. I approached the stranger as if she were some guide sent from heaven.

"Um, excuse me. Tú hablas inglés?"

Through her black-rimmed glasses, she peered at me, neither surprised nor pleased. "Yes, I speak English."

Like seeing an old friend, I slung my bag to the ground, plopped down in a seat beside her, and told her everything. I was not even sure if she cared or not. I just knew I needed to talk to someone.

"Wow, that is scary. And you decided to come to Caracas for your first trip?" she questioned.

I felt like an ass yet again.

"Well . . . uhh yeah . . . but . . . it's just for a little while. I really would like to go see Angel Falls, though. So, where are you from?"

"I'm from New Zealand. I'm just coming from Madrid and I'll be catching a flight to Bogotá to meet some friends in the morning."

"Oh, that's awesome. I plan on heading to Bogotá once I'm done here. Have you been traveling for a while?"

"Yes, I've been traveling for two years."

"Two years? Damn, and you haven't seen the whole world yet?" She could tell her response surprised me. I dropped my head and then raised my eyebrows. "What about your family? Don't you miss them?"

"Yes, I do, quite often. After the first three or four months, I started to get homesick, but then after a while, it just became normal. However, it does get tiresome, sleeping in and out of hostels instead of your own bed. But in the next couple of weeks, I'll be headed back home for a break."

I listened to the experienced New Zealander angel named Nanako as we got up to search for a Wi-Fi signal. As exciting as it sounded, I doubted I could travel for that long. There would be so much back home that I would miss.

As we walked back downstairs for a stronger signal, I could see soldiers watching us. Despite occasional drops, we found a strong signal in an area that had a bench nearby to sit down. I sent messages to Jose for advice on my situation, and to my family saying that everything was going great. The last thing I needed was for them to worry.

Knowing I had someone there with me felt good. No longer did I feel alone, even if it would only be for the night. As I

33

waited for Jose to respond, Nanako mentioned she had not eaten since leaving for her trip, and by now the airport food court had closed. I reached into my book bag and pulled out the saran-wrapped sub-sandwich they served on my previous flight. It was the least I could do.

A few minutes later, I finally received a response from Jose. He recommended the hotel La Floresta in the La Floresta district and mentioned that I could get a room for a good price. He said that until I could exchange money in a safe place, I could use my card and just pay later. Not only did I feel uncomfortable using my card this early, I still did not know who I could trust to exchange my money. But at least I had some direction on where to go next.

Nanako and I sat at a table and propped up our bags beside us, making this our place of rest for the night. We passed time chatting as midnight approached. I even pulled out a deck of cards and showed Nanako a card game my mother showed me once. Before long, Nanako had laid her head down and dozed off. Tiredness had certainly taken its toll on my eyelids, but the urge to stay up and watch our belongings gave me enough energy to fight it. I thought about how my day had progressed since early that morning and how so much had happened. If that was what a day in the life of a backpacker was like, then there was no doubt this experience would be exhausting.

Though I no longer saw soldiers lingering around, I continued to stay alert despite nodding off from time to time. Each nod seemed to forward the night into dawn, bringing more noise and traffic with it.

Before going our separate ways, Nanako and I exchanged numbers and took a quick picture together.

"Thank you again for helping me, and I hope you have a safe trip. Whenever I get to Bogotá, I'll make sure I hit you up. Take care," I said.

She replied, "Thank you. Same to you and safe travels."

After meeting Nanako, I associated the airport with safety

and comfort. Now, I was heading back out into the wild. Black SUVs lined up outside of the airport waiting for customers to use their taxi services. Without trying to draw too much attention, I approached one driver standing off by himself.

"Hola," I said, grabbing his attention and handing him my phone. I pulled up the name of the hotel Jose sent me, hoping the driver knew where it was.

He stared at the phone, confused for a moment, then asked another driver what I had just shown him. Stepping back over to me, he nodded, handed me my phone, and opened the back of the SUV. As he loaded my bag, I pulled out my wallet and showed him some folded American dollars. He nodded his head again when I stuck up my thumb to see if he approved.

It was just after 7 a.m., and the sun had not quite risen over the hills that stood as backdrops for the structures we maneuvered around. Along the grooves of hills, shabby buildings and small communities sat bunched while somehow covering the sides of the hills. If it had not been for the clothes and towels that drooped over clotheslines, one might have thought these mini houses were abandoned. It was not until we reached the other side that we saw the golden sun rays cast over the slumbering hills of Caracas. The closer we got to the city, the heavier traffic became. Mopeds zipped between and around cars like lines of ants weaving through cracks.

Nearly an hour later, we pulled up to a tall, light green hotel, Hotel La Floresta. An extended overhead entrance stretched out from the hotel just before the start of the sidewalk. I reached into my wallet and pulled out a twenty-dollar bill to hand it to the driver. He turned back and held up two fingers, motioning for another twenty. I knew it was too much, but I gave it to him anyway. I was just glad to be somewhere finally.

From the looks of the hotel, I could tell it was one of the higher-end establishments. The gray marble tiles covered the walls and floors straight down the hall and into the lobby. Flowerpots and mirrors helped decorate the not-yet-busy hotel. I also noticed the hotel lights had not been turned on yet, as daylight brightened the undisturbed lobby.

"Si, Buenos días," the receptionist greeted me.

"Uhhh, si . . .um . . . un cuarto para . . . un noche por favor," I spoke cautiously, making sure I said the right words to request a room for only one night.

"Doce." He then repeated it holding up his index finger on one hand and two fingers on the other.

Check-in was at noon, which meant I had to wait four hours to get a room. Though I hated to wait that long, at least I had somewhere to sit down and relax.

"Wi-Fi?" I asked

"No Wi-Fi señor." He said something afterward, but I could not decipher his words.

I figured I could at least call Jose to let him know I was there. I pointed at the phone to let the receptionist know I needed to use it.

Hearing Jose's voice for the first time gave me some relief, knowing I could put a voice with the messages.

"That is great you are at the hotel. I get off work later today and I will get train to come meet you," he said.

"Okay, cool. I tried messaging you, but the Wi-Fi doesn't work here."

"Yes, the government has shut down internet in the country since the weekend."

"Shutdown the internet?" *Maybe that is why I had trouble getting Wi-Fi back at the airport.*

After he assured me that he would meet me later on, I felt better. But not having Wi-Fi during my stay here would be bad news for my folks.

For the next couple of hours, I sat and watched as people walked in and out of the lobby. Occasionally, I walked around to stretch my limbs. The glow from the vending machine in the back corner reminded me of my hunger. Digging into my bag, I pulled out some Fig Newtons I had packed for the trip. I washed them down with a bottle of water I had brought with me.

The non-circulating air gave the lobby a humid and uncomfortable feeling, not to mention the drifting mosquitos that started to make me paranoid and irritable. During my moment of discomfort, a young guy walked into the lobby and perched on the other end of the sofa. Maybe a year or two older than me, he sat with his legs crossed and phone in hand. I hesitated to say something because he looked as if he did not want to be bothered. But I had nothing to lose. I was alone and I did not know anyone. If anything, I would at least be able to practice some Spanish.

"Hola, tú hablas inglés?" I asked.

"Yes, I speak English," he responded.

"Check-in is at twelve, right?"

"Yes, sir, that is correct."

"Cool, thanks." I posed a couple more questions. "What's your name? Are you from Caracas?"

"My name is Ernesto and no; I am here visiting the university."

Before long, Ernesto and I got to know each other well. I told him about my situation and he was more than willing to show me around during my stay.

"You will be okay; I will watch out for you, my friend," he assured me.

Shortly after, his friend Ruben came to visit. We sat there, and Ruben felt just as welcoming as Ernesto. With our interesting conversation, I forgot about the uncomfortable humidity that lingered around us. We talked about everything from the history of Venezuela to the different dialects of Western and Eastern people to hip-hop. Ernesto even surprised me with his best Eddie Murphy impression from *Coming to America*.

37

I stayed one floor above Ernesto. As I entered my room, I might as well have opened the door to paradise. I did not care about the small box TV or the air conditioning that sounded like it struggled to blow out its stale air. I had a bed. Tossing my bags on the floor, I threw myself onto the firm twin-size mattress and closed my eyes. For a brief moment, I thought about everything that had happened, recognizing this was the first time I felt safe. The idea of me laying my head down in Venezuela had become a realization.

—

On the way to grab a bite to eat, Ernesto informed me of the do's and don'ts when walking on the street.

"First thing is, always stay close in front of us so we can keep eye on you. Next, do not speak. If anyone hears you, they will know you are American and might try something. If you need to ask or say something, say it low. And make sure you do not have your phone out while in the street," he explained.

Though in plain daylight, I followed his instructions as we walked out into the busy streets.

Looking ahead, I noticed enormous mountains that stood behind the city as though they guarded Caracas. They appeared so close that they seemed to be in the center of the city. As we continued walking, I realized just how thick the polluted air was. Breathing felt like trying to inhale with your face pressed against a wall.

Only a couple of blocks down, we passed Plaza de Altamira, a hotspot where people protested. While walking past, a gang of law enforcers lined up against the wall on mopeds, some with automatic weapons.

"Look. They are called by the people 'the Force of Oppression.' But please do not stare for too long," Ernesto warned.

The force reminded me of the officials back at the airport, but with more tactical gear. They wore dark green uniforms with black combat vests fastened over their torsos. Their dull, scuffed helmets hung off their mopeds, while others wore them loosely. We may have spoken here and there throughout our walk, but we spoke none when we entered the station.

The further we walked, the more the spaces in the crowd tightened as we advanced toward the howling sounds of the subway. The amount of silence in the station compared to the number of people there felt nothing short of bizarre. However, I noticed just how many beautiful women there were. A display of long, flowing hair and arrays of cream to pecan-colored skin surrounded me. Venezuela is known for having some of the most beautiful women in the world, and the people definitely take pride in that.

My awestruck eyes broke focus as a string of subway cars came hurtling down the track. As one side of the subway unloaded, we crammed into the other side, squeezing and shuffling our way into the cars. A few passengers managed to split between Ruben, Ernesto, and me, but I remained within eyesight.

The transition from the streets of Caracas into the mall was like night and day. People's moods shifted while touring up and down the four levels of lined stores. Even if for a moment, the people who turned into shoppers had escaped from the economic stress that awaited outside the mall doors. Still gazing at the many stores around me, and the women, I followed Ernesto and Ruben, stopping at one of the food establishments they both enjoyed. Because I could not recognize any words on the menu besides chicken and beef, Ernesto suggested an item for me: an arepa.

An arepa is similar to a taco, but instead of toppings being stuffed inside a hard shell, the shell is replaced with a thick bread made of corn flour. Tacos are one thing, but anyone who can scarf down more than one arepa is an absolute monster.

Ernesto ordered two barbeque arepas with cheese, one for me and another for him. For a drink, I tried one of their many fruit juices.

Being that I was in a different country, I wanted to do

something more exotic, in my mind at least, so I chose papaya. When our drinks came, I realized they used all-natural juices with no added sugar. At all.

Ernesto and Ruben conversed in Spanish every so often but mainly spoke in English to keep me in the conversation. We were laughing, talking more about Ernesto's obsession with *Coming to America*, when Ernesto asked me about the word "nigger." I was not shocked that he asked, but I was caught off guard by his curiosity. I automatically felt like the spokesperson for all African Americans.

"Well, the word 'nigger' was a word used during slavery to degrade black people. So it is a bad word to say."

"Then why black people say this to each other?" he questioned.

"In a strange way, it's become a part of the culture now. Though we know the history of the word, time has desensitized the meaning with the younger generation. Now, it's used among friends even in other races, which older people still get upset about."

"So I can call you 'my nigger'?" I cringed slightly when he said it.

"Well . . . not exactly." After explaining the rule for substituting the 'er' to 'a,' he somewhat understood.

We continued with our meal, and Ruben and Ernesto explained the severity of the economy while mentioning the "toilet paper situation." Toilet paper, among other items, was scarce in the country. Something I considered a basic necessity was practically a luxury there. I had heard rumors about their current affairs, but I could not have known how true they were.

After our meal, we stopped by one of the shops at the subway station to pick up a souvenir. Ernesto suggested a Venezuelan hat. There were two identical Venezuelan hats with one differentiating itself by having the number four on it. He pointed out the hat I should get, the one without the four.

"The number four stands for a date: February 4, 1992. Our last president, Hugo Chávez, planned and eventually was able to overthrow the president at that time, Carlos Andrés Pérez. So to all the people who like and follow Chávez currently, they take that as an act of triumph for socialism vs. capitalism. This is why they use the number on the hat. You have the number 4 next to the letter f for February. It's the fight they think they are doing against capitalism," Ernesto explained.

I did not know shit about politics but the more and more I listened, the more it sounded like Democrats and Republicans back home. Different names but ultimately the same game. Red against blue.

Adding to his growing list of good deeds, Ernesto exchanged money with me for the first time. With twenty dollars, I was able to get about 3520 Bolívar, which, in perspective, was about two or three nights in the hotel and three to four cheap meals. He also informed me about an app called Dolar Today that would display the black market price for the American dollar that day. That way no one would be able to cheat me out of my money.

I held the foreign money in my hand, staring at large unfamiliar faces that were not Jackson or Grant. Each bill increment was a different color from the next. Blue to orange, pink to green, each bill displayed a beautiful array of colors.

We did not go back out until later that night. Ruben had gone back home, but Ernesto and I went to a burger spot a few blocks down to meet up with another friend and her mother. Though Ernesto had to translate for most of the conversation, they seemed interested in learning more about me. Being in South America, not South Carolina, grabbing burgers and fries with people I had just met still amazed me.

During our outing, Ernesto invited me to come to his university the next day as he prepared to leave his teaching job and move back to Maracaibo, Venezuela. I agreed to go because it was not like I had anywhere else to be. Besides, from what I had experienced at the airport and gathered from his advice, sticking with Ernesto would be my best bet.

—

Arriving back at the hotel, I let my mind wonder about my first full day in South America. I tried to process how this new environment I had thrown myself into had begun bleeding into the fabric of what I had always known and called home. How certain aspects of getting here did not go according to plan yet still conveniently worked out, making the transition as seamless as the plane ride here.

Outside of standing halfway in and halfway out of the shower, shivering as cold water sprinkled down my body, I felt quite comfortable in my new environment. Wedged between a chair and the closet, I lay in bed looking at my backpack that contained everything I owned. The thought scared me, but knowing I did not have many possessions felt therapeutic. I could move easily if I wanted. I could venture to cities and countries I had never dreamed of visiting until now.

I envisioned myself touring unfamiliar streets, visiting local markets, exploring shops for handmade trinkets, and gazing upon vast green landscapes. Witnessing the end and start of a new chapter of my life amused me. I knew stepping out on faith and being unable to see where my foot would land would be complicated. Maybe I was crazy for being optimistic about the unknown, but I considered that people were so accustomed to associating not knowing with fear that they seldom took chances. Of course, this trip would be tough on my family and I, yet I understood that great things happen when great moves are made.

Before drifting to sleep, I thought about my family and friends and what they could be up to. I wondered if my grandparents were still talking about me making this trip. I wondered if my mom was doing all right. I thought about the craziness of all that had happened in the past twenty-four hours. From the airport to meeting angels from nowhere to help me when I was stranded, to wondering whatever happened to Jose, my Couchsurfing host.

As the once noisy streets dwindled to occasional passing cars, I had the feeling that I would have a long journey ahead of me. But for now, I would just take it one day at a time.

6

Connection

Ernesto and I met downstairs the next morning to head to Simon Bolivar University where he worked. His job was similar to that of a teacher's assistant. Students waited at the bus stop a few blocks down from our hotel as we approached to join them. Though around college kids, I still remembered Ernesto's rules, keeping quiet when out in the city.

Before long, we loaded onto the chattering bus and made our way to the back.

Even though I had not sat on a school bus since high school, the rattling windows and occasional head jerks from shifting gears still felt the same.

It took us about forty-five minutes to reach the university. As the scenery changed, the quality of the air changed along with it. The buildings and traffic that had once filled the bus windows were now hills and mountains. The hills that surrounded us created beautiful scenery, with the university as its centerpiece.

After grabbing something to eat, Ernesto and I walked around eating our cheese and ham burritos, finding ourselves in front of the Laberinto Cromovegetal. The Laberinto

Cromovegetal is a sacred garden designed in the shape of a bullseye with flowers and walkways making up the rings. With each level you complete in school, you can move up and walk around the level, "the ring," you just completed. When you finish all your levels, you can move into the center, which is considered your life's purpose or your goal. I stood there looking at the well-kept garden, wishing it was that easy to find purpose. I was still searching for mine.

For the next hour or so, Ernesto introduced me to a few of his peers. Everyone he introduced me to welcomed me, all curious to know about me. They were not too familiar with where South Carolina was on the map, or even about it in general. To make it easier, Ernesto told me to just say I was from Atlanta. I thought it funny that the whole world knew about the "A."

After walking around the campus, we came across a statue of Simón Bolívar.

"Hey, Ernesto, what's that say at the bottom of his statue?" I asked curiously.

"'The slavery is the daughter of darkness; an ignorant people is the blind instrument of its own destruction.' That is why Bolívar always wants the people here to learn, and study a lot to be free. To be free about our intelligence and not about fighting and stuff like that," Ernesto explained.

I stared at the statue of Bolívar as he stood with a robe draped over his uniform and an unraveled scroll in his right hand, thinking this was someone who realized that knowledge was power. Someone who understood that learning new things would expand your mind and set you on the pathway to freedom, the freedom I did not even know I was looking for at the time. Ernesto continued schooling me on Simón Bolívar as we headed toward the cafeteria.

We stood in line as students steadily came in and out of the cafeteria doors. The menu consisted of baked chicken, white rice, bread, bananas, and soup. Periodically, I would look around to see if anyone noticed me. Being the only black guy, I did not exactly blend in with the rest of the crowd, but no one seemed to care.

While at the school, I made sure to contact my family, since I could finally connect to a strong Wi-Fi signal. Opening my email, my mom was already at the top of the list waiting for my reply.

Hello son are you settled in? I was still waiting for a call from you. It is now 1:03 am Monday morning right here now. Call me please. I would like to thank your host for getting you. I am still awake so call me or the G-parents. We are waiting. Please send me a picture of where you are immediately if you can. Thank you.

I could tell by reading her message that my mom probably had the same anxiety NASA has when astronauts temporarily lose communications after re-entering Earth's atmosphere. Outside of leaving out details like I did not have dependable internet, I had to spend the night at the airport, and I was with someone who was not my planned host, I replied I was good. Putting emphasis on the good part.

Before heading back to the city, Ernesto escorted me to the IT department to help me find out the best way to Angel Falls. The thought of finally being able to gaze upon the towering fall felt eccentric.

We entered the lab as he greeted people sitting behind their computers. It started becoming a routine as I smiled patiently, preparing to say "Hola" as Ernesto began introducing me. Once Ernesto explained, a huddle of people gathered around a computer screen staring at Google Maps, using their fingers to point out potential routes.

After the wonderful insight, Ernesto and I departed as we headed back to the bus to leave for the city. I had met nice people, had taken a campus tour, and even received a brief history lesson. Everything felt good. As we approached the city, however, it seemed as if my blissful experience had stayed behind as the smell of pollution crept its way back through the open windows of the school bus.

A few hours later, Ernesto and I met up with his friend for food. The three of us sat on the patio of the restaurant, enjoying the warm night air while waiting for our meals. When our food arrived, I began feeling a bit nauseated from the smell of it. I tried to put something on my stomach because this would be my last meal for the night. I also did not want to seem rude for not eating. Shortly after, I started getting small chills and feeling fatigued.

"You okay, my friend?" Ernesto asked.

"Nah, my stomach doesn't feel too good," I replied.

"Okay, we head back shortly."

While they finished their meals, I sat through this awful feeling, desperate to make it back to the hotel. As soon as we returned, I hauled myself up the flights of stairs as Ernesto went to his room.

It was already nightfall as I sat up looking over my Venezuelan hat, still proud to have made the trip. I doubted that I would ever get a chance to meet Jose or Yolangi.

Buried in the bottom of my bag, I still had a small teddy bear I had bought for Yolangi because of her birthday, but at this point, she would probably never get it. After taking a picture of it and sending it to her on WhatsApp, I picked up my journal to write.

As I wrote, I could feel the nausea worsening. I began to grab my stomach and clench my shirt. It was bad enough that I had diarrhea as soon as I got back to the room, let alone the urge to vomit. Even though I expected my stomach would be messed up from getting adjusted to the food, after a while, weakness took over my body.

For the next hour, I would get up, use the toilet, and lie down. Then get up, use the toilet, and lie down. Before long, vomiting would be a part of this tormenting rotation. The stale air circulating the room seemed to contribute to my discomfort. I recalled being this sick once before with the same symptoms, which resulted in my grandmother driving me to the hospital in the middle of the night due to dehydration.

As I struggled to carry myself to the bathroom, my body felt heavy and my joints started aching. I found it difficult to keep my eyes fully open as I leaned against furniture while navigating through the small room. I drank the last half bottle of water I had, which seemed to do nothing but tease my dry mouth. Trying to find comfort in the fetal position, I wrapped my arms around a pillow and held it tight. It even felt challenging to reach for my phone, which laid just in arm's reach, to send Ernesto a text.

He replied saying stores had closed at this hour and he did not have any water himself. He also mentioned he would be returning to the school early in the morning but would have Ruben check on me. I thirsted for water so badly that I started to drink out of the faucet using the purification tablets my uncle had told me to buy. I hesitated to use them because the truth is, I did not know how to use them. And if the food or water had caused me to be sick in the first place, drinking the faucet water could have made it much worse.

Though concerned for my safety at the airport, nothing compared to how scared I felt for my health at that moment. There was nowhere I could go, and the only people who could truly help me were over eighteen hundred miles away. There was no late-night ride to the hospital in my grandmother's Cadillac. I was on my own. But as sick as I was, I knew better than to tell my family, just like I knew not to tell them about the airport encounter.

Having survived the night, I woke up the next morning feeling disoriented. I felt much better after practically shitting myself to sleep. As promised, Ruben messaged me to check on me, saying he would stop by later to take me to get food and that there was a canteen close by that I could go to.

Parched, I dragged myself out of bed, forced my shoes on my feet, and headed downstairs to the humid streets. I wanted to move as quickly as possible just in case I needed to use the bathroom, lethargically making my way from corner to corner. The vendor had a variety of drinks and snacks, but I wanted only one thing: water. I bought two forty-eight-ounce bottles of water and some crackers, and I drank half of one bottle by the time I reached the hotel. As soon as I arrived back in my room, I messaged Ruben and went straight to sleep.

Ruben came to get me for lunch later that afternoon. I hardly had any type of appetite, but I knew I needed to get my strength up. We walked to a food court a few blocks down, which made me uneasy about my irregular bathroom schedule. Just the smell of food seemed to make me nauseous. All the restaurants and food spots seemed to blend, except for one particular one. One that I never thought I would be so happy to see in my life: McDonald's.

I usually tried my best to avoid fast-food restaurants, but at that moment, it looked like a safe house. It took me a while to eat as Ruben watched me struggle with a Big Mac, medium Coke, and Yucas fries, a tougher and less greasy version of the fries back home. Even though I did not finish it all, I was satisfied with what I ate.

"Once you are done, I will take you to one of our local grocery stores. That way you can see how bad the economy here really is," Ruben said.

Though I had already been convinced, we visited a store nearby, which offered more proof of the economic devastation in the country. As I watched people on a continuous hunt for goods, it seemed as if more wandering shoppers occupied the aisles than the scarce goods.

Ruben mentioned they typically visited multiple stores to get what they needed because people would buy loads of one item when in stock. I thought about how easy we had it back home. We could shop from a wide selection of goods, ask an employee if they have any more in the back, and sometimes have the luxury of listening to music over the intercom. Witnessing the complete opposite in a neighboring continent certainly was an eye-opener for me.

Undoubtedly, Ruben, as well as Ernesto, followed politics

well and enjoyed talking about it. He also discussed how he was familiar with racism toward People of Color in the States. I always wondered what the rest of the world thought about the United States (U.S.). And to hear from someone on the outside looking in confirmed that others see the truth. He even poked fun at realizing the presence of white privilege in the U.S., which showcased his sense of humor.

Though the next day would be my last full day in Caracas, I honestly enjoyed my short stay. Outside of diarrhea and the thick polluted air, I had a fairly good arrival. I was lucky to meet Ernesto and Ruben and to receive their help. I considered them my friends.

—

Later, Ruben and I went up to Ernesto's room to hang out and to receive more advice about my next stop, Puerto Ordaz. In mid-discussion, we began hearing people banging pots and pans outside.

"What's that?" I asked.

"President Maduro is about to speak," Ernesto replied.

"Yes, when the president prepares to talk, neighbors alert each other this way," Ruben informed me.

"It is no problem, my friend," Ernesto said assuringly.

"We can go out so you can get a better look," Ruben said.

I agreed, and we walked downstairs as the banging continued. I pulled out my phone to record the spectacle, until Ernesto warned against it.

As we exited, I noticed people in the complex next to our hotel leaning outside of their windows, banging pots and pans, filling the night with sounds of metal colliding. From what I understood, the president's speech would be equivalent to the State of Union Address back home.

We returned to Ernesto's room as he pulled up a live audio stream on his phone. We sat patiently as President Maduro began speaking. As he spoke, Ernesto quickly dissected and explained the situation.

"There are three different types of exchange rate. The official rate, the black market rate, and . . ." Before he could finish, the president began discussing the current value of the Venezuelan dollar.

For the next few minutes, I understood nothing as the president spoke. I could only go off of the disappointing expressions on Ernesto and Ruben's faces. They would speak to each other in Spanish, asking each other questions with uncertainty.

"So, what is happening?" I asked.

"The economy is getting worse, my friend," Ernesto replied.

The president did not address the black market rate, almost to avoid informing the people.

They listened a bit longer and then decided to stop listening. From my standpoint, I was merely a spectator, someone observing this economic war from afar while they lived it. It was crazy to come from a place where people often blow money and spend it on meaningless things. But there, our dollar was valued and appreciated. People bought into the dollar almost like an investment. As the value of the Bolívar decreases, the value of the dollar increases over time.

Years ago, Venezuela was once considered one of the most prosperous up-and-coming countries in South America, and possibly in the world, until a change in leadership caused what had begun as promising to turn tragic. The typical story of a good guy turning bad. Power, greed, and respect were what it seemed to come down to toward the fatal end of Hugo Chávez's presidency.

A good majority of people believed his death was a conspiracy and that the government was keeping a close watch on the citizens. Any government that shuts down your internet and controls your communication with the outside world comes off as suspicious. I believe Ernesto wanted me to know the situation in Venezuela was real and only getting worse.

I felt terrible seeing them in this situation, knowing how helpful they had been to me. Ernesto said that the people would protest at the end of the week and would probably riot. Luckily, Ernesto and I were both leaving before anything began.

The next day, Ruben and I both accompanied Ernesto on his last day at the university. It was a bittersweet moment for him. We made our rounds as Ernesto said his farewells and turned in his last bit of paperwork. I saw a few of the people I had seen the day before, even some from the IT Department. I enjoyed visiting the university, simply because the people were helpful and the air was much cleaner. I wondered if the air was better in Puerto Ordaz, and if the people were just as friendly. While I did not know what to expect, I loved going wherever the ride would take me.

We left the school for the last time and headed back to the hotel for some rest. This would be the last time I would see Ruben since he lived across town. I thanked him for everything and for showing me around. Later that night, Ernesto and I met up with his friend and her mother for dinner. They already knew about me not feeling well the day before, so they took me somewhere I might feel more comfortable: TGI Fridays. I could believe a McDonald's in South America because that shit was everywhere. But TGI Fridays?

Ernesto translated the conversation as they wanted to know about the places I planned to visit and my safety. He had already made his concern for my well-being clear and encouraged me to leave as soon as I could. Luckily, Ernesto's friend ended up buying my plane ticket to Puerto Ordaz. We exchanged money discreetly under the table as we waited for our food.

As you mature and study the behaviors of others, you learn not to put yourself in dangerous situations. Ernesto and Ruben were my guides during the infancy of my trip. I listened to and followed what they told me to do and not to do. They also shared some good news. The internet would be back up for the weekend, which could not have come at a better time.

For the rest of the evening, I wondered how things would be at my next destination. I knew it would not be another Caracas, so I figured there may be some positives: less traffic, which meant cleaner air; and less population, which meant less crime.

Ernesto and I would head to the airport the next day. It felt good knowing that I would be traveling to my next destination. It would have been nice to see more, but I knew it would be best to go. Besides, the timing felt right.

The beautiful morning complimented the way I felt as we made our way through the streets of Caracas. We approached all the homes and shacks that decorated the hills of the outskirts of the city. Though I knew the poorer people of the city lived there, the setting still looked beautiful as the morning brought out the variety of colors on the homes. Before long, we arrived at the airport and found ourselves awaiting our departure.

I reflected on my stay and how a few turns of events led me to meet people like Nanako, Ernesto, and Ruben. Though my next stop would be Angel Falls, they were the real angels to me, random people who did not have to help me, but did. While I had only known them for a short time, it hurt knowing I had to leave these amazing people behind.

Though we had known each other only for a few days, the friendship between Ernesto, Ruben, and me seemed like it had existed for years. Ernesto and I said our goodbyes as my plane arrived, and I thanked him for everything he and Ruben had done for me. Ready to face the next phase of my journey, I could only hope to meet more outstanding people like them.

7

Layover

The mountains that once grabbed my attention stayed behind in Caracas as the flat plains covered the city of Puerto Ordaz. Along with the mountains, the people appeared to have disappeared as well. My assumption of Puerto Ordaz not being a big city was more than correct.

As I roamed around the airport looking for a Wi-Fi signal, the too familiar "wandering" look slowly crossed over my face. My search came to an unfortunate halt as I eventually learned there was no Wi-Fi, again. I did not feel as stranded this time being that it was still so early. Like before, I pulled up Google translate and put it in front of people's faces.

One lady allowed me to use her phone to text my Couchsurfing host, Romel. He informed me he was still at work and would not be back home until 4 p.m. He also told me to take a cab to his apartment when it got closer to that time. The cost would be ten American dollars. I was thankful for the heads up.

With about four hours to wait, the only thing to do was to play the waiting game. My mind raced with thoughts about my new host and whether we would get along. Technically, this would be my first official experience with a Couchsurfer host. Ernesto and

Ruben just happened to find me stranded and decided to help me out. But this meet-up was planned. If things did not go right, then it would affect my decision to meet up with another host. Though Couchsurfing would help me save money, I would much rather have my safety first.

As 4 p.m. approached, I became nervous. I considered the airport a safe haven, a public place with food that had everything I needed. Leaving it felt as though I would have to start over from scratch to rebuild my confidence. But I knew I could not stay there forever.

Taxi drivers waited outside for passengers as I headed out the door. I knew better than to pay forty dollars this time. I showed one driver ten dollars and the address, and then we were on our way. The taxi driver tried sparking up a conversation, but there was not much I could say; Google Translate helped me communicate for most of the ride.

When we arrived at the complex, I realized Romel failed to mention that he lived in a gated community, to which I did not have the access code. The driver called Romel from his phone, and Romel told the driver that he would be home shortly and instructed him to drop me off. Though hesitant, I followed his instructions, grabbed my belongings, and watched the taxi drive off.

It was not long after when a car came to trigger the gate open. I trailed behind the car as the gate wiggled stiffly as it opened. Once inside, I walked down the main entrance street, passing the brick complex buildings. The community seemed so quiet that if it were not for the car letting me in, one could have mistaken it for a deserted property. Unsure of which building Romel lived in, I sat on the curb of the sidewalk and waited for him to return home.

I could hear a few birds chirping as I sat peacefully in the evening sun. A park sat in the middle of the complex with swing sets and slides under a tree, casting shade on a portion of the park. On the other end laid a great patch of dirt where the grass had been worn from what could have been kids playing fútbol. I glanced around to look at the buildings across the park from me; they resembled project buildings like the ones back home. I could see clothes and fabric hanging from inside some of the caged windows. I could faintly hear air conditioners running, protruding out of some of the windows. The area felt like a warm place to be, though such a contrast from Caracas, as the fresh air proved evident in this suburban area.

As I sat, residents rolled by in vehicles looking curiously at me, along with the backpack that was about as big as me. I noticed a young girl walking who had just entered through the gate toward the entrance. As she walked, staring down into her phone, I assumed she was just leaving school from the book bag that clung to her back. *Maybe she knows Romel.* I thought it best that I should at least try to ask her, so I whipped out the Google translator on my phone.

I caught her attention as she walked closer. She smiled slightly, flashing her braces, and began reading my phone. She texted back to the translator saying she was not familiar with Romel or where he lived yet offered to call him. I spoke to Romel as he confirmed they were around the corner. After I hung up, I thanked her for her help. I wish I could have chatted longer, but she just smiled, nodded, and walked to her building.

As soon as she turned the corner, Romel and his roommates pulled up to the park in their jeep. I grabbed my bags and walked over to greet them.

"Hey, Russell!" said the one who I assumed to be Romel. He looked slightly different in person than in his profile picture. The photo showed him clean-shaven, and he appeared somewhat taller. Yet, he still had a wide grin similar to that of a car salesman.

Romel introduced me to his roommates, Ronald—and to Ronald's girlfriend, Maria. Everyone welcomed me with open arms. Once inside, Romel showed me around the apartment and placed my bags in the room I would be staying in. He mentioned he had another roommate, Alex, who was still at work. In the meantime, the three of us sat around and talked until sunset.

56

From the window, you could feel the warm air from the sun setting, which gave the apartment a nice feel. And like the sun, I got settled as well and decided to take a quick shower before we went out to eat.

Back in Caracas, I had to deal with mostly cold water, and if I was lucky, it might have been lukewarm. But now, the situation was slightly different.

"Okay, Russell, so let me explain about the water issue. There is a problem with the water here at the complex where it does not run all the time. So we have a system put in place," Romel informed me.

He led me to a large barrel of water in the kitchen, the water supply for him and his roommates. I peeped into the wide barrel as I waited for him to explain this "system."

"If you want to use water, depending on your need, you take a bowl, bucket, or cup, and get water. For showers, use the bucket with a cup so you could dip the cup in the bucket to pour on you for the shower."

"And what about using the bathroom?" I asked.

"If you needed to use the toilet, you would use it like you always would, flush, fill up a bucket of water, and pour in the tank for the next person to use."

Shortly after Romel schooled me about the water routine, I put it into practice. I did not question or judge anything because I knew I had to be open-minded when traveling, especially with Romel being kind enough to let me stay there. I just thought to myself that for me it was temporary, but for them, it was common for the water to act up from time to time.

Once I finished my "cup" shower, I used Romel's phone to message my family. Though there was no Wi-Fi, Romel had a temporary hotspot that he would turn on so that guests could have internet, but only occasionally.

Shortly after my family check-in, we left to get food. We

sat outside at plastic tables surrounded by food trucks. It looked like a hangout spot people would go to after work or to grab a quick meal with friends. Even though a couple of days had passed since I had gotten sick, I was still not one-hundred-percent. However, a few bites of a burger proved I did not have a problem getting my food down.

As we dined, I learned Romel worked in forestry and Ronald was his boss. They were quite entertaining as we conversed in the warm night air.

"I've hosted travelers all over. My last guests were a wild bunch—guys from Scandinavia. But you are the first black guy. So you can say we are both experiencing something new. I am quite excited," Romel commented.

"Oh okay, that's what's up. Yeah, this whole trip has been quite the experience for me, so I understand," I replied.

After we finished our meals, we picked up a few beers from the local store and headed back to the apartment to listen to music. When we arrived, Romel's other roommate, Alex, was already there. And like the rest, he was just as welcoming. Alex dragged his words and spoke much slower than everyone else. I spoke to him and found out that he played rugby for a local league.

The night ended great with everyone drinking a few beers and listening to some music. Romel seemed to enjoy alternative rock music and wanted to know my music of choice.

"What kind of music do you enjoy, Russell?" he asked.

"I enjoy any genre of music. A good friend of mine and I make music as well. We've been making music for about four years."

"That's awesome. What music do you make?"

"Hip-hop music."

"Of course, you make hip hop," he replied, almost like he was not surprised. Even though I brushed it off, his stereotypical comment made me feel a bit sideways.

That night I laid on an air mattress on the floor of Romel's room trying to get used to strangers snoring, and to my living with them temporarily. I did not know Puerto Ordaz existed before this trip, but there I was staying with a resident and his roommates in one of its communities. Who knew there were actually people in the world who would open their doors to travelers? Still, I did not feel like a traveler yet. As I stared up and let my eyes sweep the ceiling, I could not help but think of myself as a fraud looking for refuge. Just needing a place to stay. I was grateful for their hospitality, but I made sure I kept all of my things close before shutting my eyes to fall asleep.

The next morning, I woke up feeling refreshed, and was the first to take my bucket shower. I took the time to write in my journal while I sat in the main room on the window seat. For the first time, I felt like I could relax. No heavy pollution or loud noises from traffic. Just occasional cars passing the complex.

We ended up leaving the apartment and picking up one of Romel's friends, Brian, from the airport. Romel, Brian, and I went to the main park in Puerto Ordaz: La Llovizna Park. Within this park dwelled a man-made waterfall and small monkeys that swung from trees. Kids to adults reached out with pieces of crackers and bread, hoping to lure the monkeys to them. Romel handed me a piece of cracker he had, and I stood waiting with my arm out toward the trees. Then I caught the attention of one monkey as he swooped down, flipping himself from the vines. As the monkey made his way toward me, my mind began creating crazy scenarios. *What if he is not coming for the cracker? I hope he doesn't try and jump on my head or pull my hair. What if he spits on me? Do monkeys have fleas?* I tensed up as he positioned himself in front of me. As his tiny fingers grabbed the corner of the cracker, he looked up to make eye contact, as if to make sure it was okay. As soon as he took it, he dotted back up the vines and found a nice branch to sit upon and nibble at his treat.

Despite it being a scorcher outside, we had a pretty great time. I found out that Brian planned on going to Angel Falls the next day. Romel booked the same travel package for me that Brian had. A three-day and two-night stay in Canaima would not cost much of anything, and being that it was the dry season, it would be even cheaper.

The contrast between Caracas and Puerto Ordaz was strong. Outside of the population, and the traffic, it felt like things were not as tense there compared to the bigger city. This first came to my knowledge later on that day when we went out to eat. We decided to visit a rooftop restaurant that sat atop one of the many buildings downtown. The dress code was casual though the only thing I had anywhere close to that was a pair of blue jeans and a solid, long-sleeved shirt.

We met up with five of Romel's friends who all had nowhere near the same extrovert personality he had. Throughout the night, one guy tried to strike up conversations with me. We would chat, but not for long. I instantly felt embarrassed when he introduced himself as Gustavo, who I had initially reached out to online before making the trip. Gustavo referred me to Romel, because he could not host me at the time. He had agreed to host someone else prior to my arrival.

—

Every morning I made it a habit to journal about what happened on the previous day. I saw it as my time to reflect on my day and to have some time to myself. When everyone finally awoke one morning after I finished journaling, they planned to take me on a boat tour.

The highlight of the boat ride was the river itself. Two rivers, the Orinoco and Caroni, came together but technically did not merge because the Orinoco contains saltwater and the Caroni contains freshwater. While the boat guided us between the non-merging rivers, the contrast between the two was like a never-ending dance as they pulled and tugged each other back and forth. The Orinoco was a solid light brown that felt warm to the touch, while the Caroni was a cool black. Like school kids we went from one side of the boat to the other, letting our fingers submerge, bewildered at the two different temperatures.

With our itinerary instructing us to bring swimwear, we would receive a chance to swim at a nearby beach. Even though I was not a big swimmer (for one, I could not swim, and for two, I realized I was pretty insecure about my body), I figured I would join the fun, not letting my skinny frame and hairy chest rob me of my joy. Out of the group of ten, I found myself chatting with a girl from California who had come to Venezuela to visit her parents.

It felt good talking to someone from the States. We enjoyed our time as we all got into the water and socialized while drinking beers and listening to music. It would have been cool to talk to my new friend a bit longer, but we stayed there for about forty-five minutes before we began heading back to get food.

Everyone sat around the table with stuffed stomachs full of spaghetti, and we chatted for the rest of the time.

Then, randomly, Romel took a piece of bread, reached over to my plate, sopped up the leftover spaghetti sauce, and ate it. He even had the nerve to look around at the table like, "Oops . . . you caught me."

At that moment, I realized Romel was a little too comfortable and carefree. I knew he was not normal. Don't get me wrong, he was an awesome guy and certainly one of a kind, but I thought that shit was nasty.

I looked around to see what everyone else thought. Though no one addressed the matter, I noticed the slight embarrassment on their faces as they could see I was thrown off by Romel's antics.

Once back at the apartment, they began setting me up with the Angel Falls tour for the next day. I had some American dollars on me and I paid Ronald in cash so that he could use his card to pay for my tour. "Adrenaline Venezuela . . . Tierra Mágica" was written on the voucher in colorful letters. While I could not read the voucher, I could see where it said I would be staying three days and two nights in Canaima, which included three breakfasts, two lunches, and two dinners.

Angel Falls was my reason for going to Venezuela. Back when I worked in my cubicle, I looked at the image of Angel Falls often, and now I was finally getting a chance to see the real thing.

The night ended with Gustavo coming over and I got a chance to hang out with him and some of his friends. Gustavo's friends must have still been undergraduates, because they looked younger than Gustavo and me. They all could speak good English. And just like everyone else I met, they were curious about where I was from and, strangely enough, wanted to learn more about the word "nigga." I understood their interest because I had probably been the first African American guy they had ever met. Since my arrival in South America, I had spoken on this subject three times, with Ernesto, Romel, and now Gustavo's friends. This whole time I had been under the assumption that everyone was knowledgeable about the word, not realizing it was something they probably heard on TV and in music and wondered why it caused conflicts.

We stayed out until close to midnight, playing Frisbee in a neighborhood park. They even offered me some marijuana they were passing around. Though I was not a smoker, I figured why not. After all, I was hanging out with some Venezuelans in Puerto Ordaz, playing Frisbee. We laughed and talked about music and even the music that I did back home. I can admit it was not too bad of a night, though I regretted needing to get up at 5:30 am to get ready for my plane ride to Angel Falls. So before long, Gustavo and I left his friends and he dropped me back off at Romel's apartment to prepare for the next morning.

Gazing out of the window, I sat along with a few others, watching small planes land and take off as we waited for ours. We eventually found ourselves squeezing into a small aircraft, packed tightly just like the luggage behind us. The language barrier did not stop us from understanding we felt like sardines in a can, concerned for our safety. For at least thirty minutes, our plane growled and bellowed its way until we reached Canaima National Park located in the southeastern part of Venezuela around midday. Everyone else's faces reflected mine, thankful to finally have our feet back on land as we gathered our belongings. I chuckled thinking no wonder my granddad felt the way he felt about planes.

The air felt thick as we strolled toward the shelter where other arrivals waited for guides to provide information. Even with my hat on, my eyes still felt the need to squint from the humidity of the Amazon heat. The large thatched roof of the shelter immediately gave me relief from the intense sun as I walked under it.

While standing there, I noticed locals had small trinkets and handmade necklaces displayed on wooden tables. And sure enough, it attracted wandering tourists. I also spotted a large wooden map hanging on the wall with the words "Mapa Topografico Parque Nacional Canaima" written above it. The map showcased the vastness of the park, labeled with engraved landmark names and pictures that detailed mountains, camps, and waterfalls.

I scanned the area for the tour agency Romel had signed me up with, but I did not recognize any logos or signs around. Every tour guide seemed to wear the same outfit: polo shirts and khaki shorts. And like all the other times when I did not know where the hell I was supposed to be, I went straight for my Google translator. I showed it to one woman who looked like a tour guide, and she politely escorted me to where I needed to be.

The woman introduced me to the person who would guide us. I would have never guessed that he would be our guide. He wore a T-shirt with the word "Wicked" written across it, basketball shorts, a drawstring backpack, and a pair of sandals. Because of the heat, I could not say that I blamed him.

Nine more people joined the group, and we headed off to where we would be staying. We rode for a few minutes on a bus down a dirt road as the heat came along with us. I regretted wearing my cargo pants as they began sticking to my legs from the sweat. We drove through small village communities made up of short houses and buildings all covered with either tin or thatched roofs. Outside of a few vehicles lingering around that looked more like old military jeeps, people either walked or drove mopeds. It started feeling like the South America I had imagined, the South America I had seen back home on television, with large leaves and plenty of humidity.

It took us about ten minutes to reach our destination. The layout reminded me of a summer camp retreat, where people had small living quarters that were spread out. The smell of freshly cut grass lingered in the air. Out of the ten of us, four of us were around the same age and the rest were older couples ranging from their late forties to late fifties. The conversation was minimal as people mainly conversed with their travel partners. Shortly after, we were instructed to break off into our rooms and to reconvene later.

For the brief intermission, I scoped out my empty room with two beds, a table, and a bathroom. I appreciated the small space more than anything, having a room to myself, until I spotted a twelve-inch lizard that clung above the shower wall. Then and there, I decided I would not be showering that night as I put my bags on top of my bed and walked back outside. *Welcome to the Amazons.*

Our first tour would be to the Canaima Lagoon, located in the backyards of the local people, whose grass we cut across to reach the sandy lagoon. We approached the copper-colored water that served as the foundation for three palms that stood close to the shore like greeters. Further out into the lagoons stood two waterfalls, Salto Ucaima and Salto Hacha. The waterfalls looked like they were bursting out of the surrounding trees. You could even hear the water crashing down to the lagoon below in the distance.

Though everyone spoke in Spanish, taking pictures broke the ice for people to interact as we took turns smiling for the camera. Shortly after, we headed toward boats resting further down the shore for our next destination on the other side of the lagoon, Anatoly Island.

It took us about ten minutes to cross the lagoon as we passed the Ucaima and Hacha waterfalls. Water rushed over the moss that hung off the top of the fall like wet hair.

Reaching the shore, we wasted no time beginning our trek through the island. Our guide alternated between speaking Spanish and English as we maneuvered through the woods. He stopped every so often to explain things about the island.

During our trek, he walked up to a plant and ripped off a leaf. "If you run out of toilet paper, be careful not to use this leaf."

When he crushed the leaf, ants instantly started pouring out of it, almost like a magic trick. He also shared a story about how the woods were protected and watched over by the people who had been out there for many years. You never saw them, but they were always watching you. The more he talked about "them," the more I realized he was talking about spirits protecting the island. Yet, I kept peeping and listening in case he was serious.

We continued walking until we found ourselves at the top of a viewpoint of the island. The fallen twigs and leaves that once crackled under our feet had now led us to an open space of rock and stone. We stood in awe gazing at the amazing scenery of mountains in the distance and the dark blue lake right below us. My eyes roamed in all directions, guessing which way Angel Falls might have been as I stood on the uneven ground of rock. Excitement rushed through my body, knowing that the next day I would finally see it in person.

After snapping a few pictures, we walked to a nearby lake for a swim. During our swim, I chatted with the young couple in our group, Maria and Kurt, about their travel plans. Maria was from Venezuela, and Kurt was from Belgium. It was nice to know there was someone with whom I could have a conversation.

Upon reaching our last stop, I realized our guide had saved the best destination for last.

"If you not want things to get wet, leave here, please."

Are we getting in some water? I thought.

"Please take off shoes and turn socks inside out so you not

slip on rocks."

Turn our socks inside out? What the hell?

We did as instructed and began following the guide around an under passage of stones. The further we went, the more we had to bend and maneuver our way around large, damp rocks. It seemed like a scene from *Tomb Raider* as we eased between illuminated stones that reflected from the puddles of water we threaded through. We could hear running water but did not know where it was coming from. We followed each other curiously as we made one last turn around a wall of stone when we realized we came out directly behind a waterfall. Everyone's eyes lit up as we encountered the exotic sight. We stood in the mouth of a waterfall as the strong waters rushed over the lip of stone above us.

Carefully, I stepped on the slick slabs of stones and moss like I was tiptoeing in a giant's den to explore the watery cave. We took turns sitting in one spot toward the edge for a nice massage where the water fell blissfully.

While conversing with Kurt and Maria during dinner about the fun we had, our guide told us we would be going to the disco that night. Though we referred to it as "the club" back home, I was all too familiar with the scene. All my friends knew I was the last person who would want to go to the club because I hardly ever enjoyed myself. Most of the time, people just stood around and drank while watching other people stand around and drink. When you did say something, the other person could not hear you, and you realized you could barely hear yourself over the music. Unexpectedly, I ended up enjoying myself as we drank, danced to salsa music, and got to know each other more.

It amazed me how fluent Kurt was in Spanish. It came second nature to him as he translated my words for others. Kurt was in school for his Ph.D. in philosophy. Even when he was explaining to the group—in Spanish—why he enjoyed the subject, I could tell he was passionate about it. That was one of the biggest reasons I took this trip, to reach the potential of passion he had, hopefully. Whether my passion be for music, writing, or anything, to be honest.

Even among such beautiful people in a beautiful country, I felt like an empty shell just drifting along without any substance or a genuine sense of purpose to anchor me. Hell, anyone could do anything, but not everything was meant for everyone. I just needed that one, whatever it might have been, wherever it might have been.

8

Takeoff

The next morning, we woke up around 7:30 a.m. for breakfast to prepare for a long trip to Angel Falls. Though I knew it would be a long trip, I did not know what we would have to do to get there. We arrived at a small area that had wooden boats drifting in water, as ropes anchored them to nearby trees. Two more guides awaited us as they prepared for our trip, securing our bags and items under a large tarp upon our arrival. They even prepared lunch for us, storing the food containers along with our belongings. Soon after, we all piled into the boat, strapped on life jackets, and drifted further and further away from land.

My choice to sit toward the back of the boat might not have been the best idea as water constantly slammed against my face. Thirty minutes of such torture felt suffocating as I had to put my head down a few times to get air. Eventually, we reached some land where we had to walk temporarily while our guides went around because the river had begun flowing in rough parts. This detour gave me not only a much-needed break but also an opportunity to finally enjoy the trip.

For the next hour, we saw only sunshine and mountains in the distance with clouds hovering above them, as though someone had painted the mountains steaming at the top. We walked scattered in one direction on a beaten path through an open field surrounded by hills. Everything felt so good that I even took my shirt off to enjoy the weather even more. A few of the older guys followed suit, basking in the sun's rays.

When we reached the river, we spotted the helpers waiting patiently for our arrival to continue on our journey. And just like before, I had to struggle for air as water flung in my eyes and dripped down my face. The further we advanced, the harder it seemed to travel as we fought the current upstream. Now and again, the belly of the boat would rub and bang against the rocks, causing the boat to jerk. One of the helpers in the front of the boat tried his best to guide the boat away from as many rocks as possible as he poked and jabbed his paddle into the shallow water.

After another two hours of riding, we stopped on a little island for lunch. Considering we had already traveled for about four hours, I could see some tiredness in the eyes of the group. And we still had another two and a half hours to travel. As soon as we finished lunch, we were off again to tackle the river.

The river was so low at times that we would hit the rocks below. We encountered a few instances where we had to get out of the boat and help push it over the rocks that caused us to get stuck. Despite being in Amazonian water, our guide ensured us that we were safe. All the guys would get out of the boat on either side, push the boat a few steps, and hop back in as swiftly as possible. The cool river came up to about mid-thigh level but quickly lost its crispness as we moved our legs to pedal over loose rocks. It was not until after we had been in and out of the boat that I realized I still had my phone in my pocket. Luckily, it was not seriously damaged, but I could see where it blurred the lens in my camera for quite some time.

We continued upstream maneuvering our way around large boulders, focusing more on the high clifftops around us. With each large cliff we approached, I imagined Angel Falls being just on the other side. The boat struggled to get through the last stretch as the motor revved and roared, shuffling stones underwater with its propeller. Then, like the ending to a stressful adventure, our guide pointed to a humongous cliff that sat right under the sun like a marker waiting to be found: Angel Falls.

The towering rock stood boldly, almost proud to be revealed to newcomers. Majestically, the stream of water that fell high above the top of the fall turned into a fine mist before it could reach the bottom. Though the waterfall was not as strong, it was unquestionable that the mere sight of the fall was nothing short of unforgettable.

It would take us another hour and thirty minutes of hiking before we reached the viewpoint. My shoulders felt tender and sore from being exposed to the sun during the long trip. Strangely, the pain felt good as we entered the thick, shaded jungle. The sun fell just enough behind the fall that there was not any heat making the hike more difficult.

The once togetherness of the group stretched further and further away as the hike started to take its toll on us. Climbing across fallen logs, stepping on bulging roots, and trudging over mounds of dirt tested everyone's endurance. As large leaves decorated the walls along the ever-changing path, I found myself pulling away from a few people until I was alone. Sweat began beading across my forehead and chest as I took deeper breaths, but my energy remained consistent as I stepped on large stones to reach the next hill of dirt. I felt good. So good that I admit I did not acknowledge my carelessness. Still having my shirt off, I could have exposed myself to malaria. But in that moment, I felt great. I did not have any worries or any problems. The air was fresh, the trees were rich and green, and my body craved more.

Normally, I would have been at work, trying to decode some computer program I did not know shit about. Or trying to see how many hours were left before I headed back home. But instead, I decided to travel a nearly seven-hour trip by boat and land to visit the largest waterfall in the world. I would take that experience over computers any day of the week. It felt like freedom.

In some ways, I felt guilty because my family never had the

opportunity to experience such freedom. My grandparents and mother were already parents by their mid-twenties, so traveling to new worlds might never have been an option. The main focus for my grandparents was probably just maintaining as a Black couple in the prejudiced South in the 60s. As for my mom, just taking care of me as a single mother was more than enough. I felt blessed upon having that realization. In some weird way, I felt like this trip was something I had to do. I felt like someone had to see the other side, life outside of the norm, for us to progress as a family. If no one made that leap, then how would we ever move forward?

—

By the time I reached the top of the viewpoint, I could hear the group up ahead. I walked out onto the stone cliff that stuck out high above the trees, still having to look straight up to behold the captivating waterfall. As others began approaching, photos had already begun as we posed with the waterfall behind us. I had arrived.

I stood in front of something that I had only imagined and seen in pictures before. Now, I could share a picture with it. My desire to be here had finally materialized into reality. My sore shoulders from the harsh sun were now soothed by the coolness of shade from the monstrous fall. I could hear the pleasant sounds of echoing escaping from the mouth of the fall as the water slapped against the rock below. Even the watery fragrance of Amazonian air filled my lungs, as it too brought life to all those pictures I once saw before.

An hour passed as we gazed at the fall. Layers of discolored stones constructed the face of the fall, while vegetation covered its sides down to the trees surrounding its feet. The fall set back in a half-cylinder shape from the water, carving out the mountain of rock over time. The water fell straight down into the Devil's Canyon, a dip at the bottom of the fall created from years of pounding water. Even though I stared down into the Devil's Canyon, at the top was quite the opposite. I had reached Angel Falls.

On the way back down to the boat, the sun had set, putting us well into the evening. We pulled out our cell phones for light as the night set in. The flashlight on my phone came in handy until it abruptly rebooted itself, thanks to the water damage from earlier.

We stood engulfed in darkness when we got back down to the river, having to walk across it to reach our camp on the other side. The frigid water came up just below the knee as we carefully made our way across. Some had to hold each other by the arm to keep their balance as the rocks below shifted and slid under our feet. The LED lights on our phones and our voices were our only allies as we migrated to the other side. Outside of Angel Falls in the distance, and the subtle noises of a flowing stream and chirping insects, we fixed our ears on each other. I would be lying if I did not say I listened out for other movements as well.

After several minutes of wading in the water, we reached our campsite. Before then, I hadn't a clue where we would be staying. But when I saw we would be sleeping in hammocks just under a tin roof, the first thing I thought about was animals ripping our asses to shreds while we slept. Of course, I knew not to expect some resort; we were in the middle of the jungle after all. However, the realization of having to sleep outside in the Amazon, with no walls, indicated it would not be an easy night.

Spent from our adventure, we approached a lit shed structure with about twenty hammocks that hung side by side from the pillars that supported it. With only a table for eating, an extra table for our bags, and a wooden bench for sitting, this would be our home for the night. And after the trip we had, I think everyone just cared about getting some rest.

As the lights went out, only a few flickering candles remained, lighting up a pathway to the outhouse. I lay there with my eyes open, taking in the moment. Hammocks wobbled and rocked as bodies tried to get comfortable in their drooping beds. Angel Falls sounded like faint white noise being overpowered by the sounds of insects and what I assumed to be bats.

Though I lay awake thinking I had heard something in the

woods, I also thought about how I never imagined I would be there. The day had worn me out, but I could not stop thinking about how surreal this was. It all just felt peaceful. Even though I was out in the open sleeping with total strangers in the thick of the Amazon, I had no worries. I had no place I needed to be or to go. I just needed to be there. And it felt good.

I mostly slept through the night, but I woke up occasionally just to make sure I did not have a snake under my ass. Sure, I was at peace, but I did not forget where I was.

The following morning, I stood in a small patch of an open area next to our camp to catch one last glimpse of Angel Falls. I could see the fall behind the trees with the sun glaring off its face and a cloud that hugged the fall on all sides. Everything seemed to be over so fast. Even though we endured this long trip only to spend a moment around the fall, I enjoyed the time we did have. I did not have to look online for pictures any longer. I now had one of my own.

Relief set in once we returned to what I guess we considered home. We were proud of achieving our goal of witnessing Angel Falls and persevering through the tiresome journey to get there. Before making my trip back to Puerto Ordaz, I made arrangements with Romel to be picked up at the airport. Kurt and Maria said they would be in Puerto Ordaz for a night before heading back home, and they suggested we all meet up. Before long, I found myself back where I first landed a couple of days prior.

As I arrived back at Romel's crib just after 6 p.m., my bag felt heavy and my feet dragged as I entered the apartment. With the apartment empty, it gave me some time to chill and think about the trip. I unpacked, took a bucket-water shower, and then went outside to enjoy the last bit of the sunset.

I sat outside of the apartment writing in my journal and reflecting on how in a blink of an eye the trip to Angel Falls was over. From the experience to the people I encountered, all were incredible.

Shifting my focus, I thought about my next stop and how I did not have a CouchSurfer lined up. Instead, I had a recommendation about a hostel in Bogotá, Colombia. I sat a while longer in the warm weather as the last bit of sun fell behind some houses. Then the girl who helped me the first day I arrived caught my attention as she walked back home. We made eye contact and smiled at each other.

"¿Cómo estás?" I asked.

"¡Bien! ¿Cómo estás?" she said cheerfully.

"Bien."

After that phrase, I was stuck, wishing I knew more Spanish. I could only smile at her as she turned the corner of the building.

Early the next morning, I caught a taxi to the Orinokia Mall to pick up a phone card for my phone so that I would not have to rely solely on Wi-Fi to communicate. I kept the Google Translate app open as I walked up to different people, asking if they had any phone cards. When I did not have any luck, one employee from a store I visited helped me connect to the Wi-Fi in the mall, where I could at least get in touch with my family and friends.

Having spent my entire day at the mall walking around and going back and forth to the food court, I should have known at some point I would need to use the bathroom. I did not realize the impact of my dilemma until I found myself searching multiple stalls for toilet paper. Not even empty rolls remained to give me the slightest bit of hope that paper had at least once been there. At this point, paper towels would have been feasible but, of course, there were only hand dryers.

Eventually, I spotted a janitor nearby, knowing that might have been my best chance to score some paper. "Señorita. Papel? Papel?"

This middle-aged lady walked over to one of the custodial storage rooms, where she kept her bag, and pulled out a small ball of toilet paper. Because items like toilet paper remained scarce, it was quite generous of her to give some of her paper to a stranger. It blew my mind that this place had electronics everywhere but did not have simple necessities like toilet paper.

While I was at the mall, birds had made their way into Romel's place and were shitting away. I entered the apartment as fans blew and cleaning product fumes met me at the door. Romel's usual smile was nonexistent as he carried a pail of water and a rag to wherever bird droppings were in the kitchen and on the couches.

"Damn, what happened?" I asked, taking in the scene before me.

"Birds came and crapped all over the place, Russell. The window was left open."

"I made sure they were shut before I left," I replied, but I doubted he believed me.

"Russell, please make sure that you close the windows or birds will come and crap over the place," he cautioned.

From his tone, I could tell this was not the first time this had happened.

My concern about bird poop went out the window when I discovered I would be stuck there for five more days. Though the airport workers went on strike for better pay, I needed to leave . . . and soon. Outside of the bird-crapping incident, I hated feeling like I had worn out my welcome.

—

For the next few days, I tried to find something to occupy my time, making another trip to the mall and hanging out with Gustavo whenever Romel was at work. We ended up finding a store that had SIM cards for my phone. With the SIM card, I could call Kurt and Maria, the couple I had met in Canaima.

About an hour later, my SIM card stopped working. Eventually, I realized the water damage my phone had experienced back at Angel Falls permanently messed up my network connections. Though I could still rely on Wi-Fi, it limited my options for communicating.

While I was waiting for time to pass until later that night, Maria and Ronald returned to Romel's house. Ronald was kind enough to pay for my ticket to Bogotá, Colombia in exchange for U.S. dollars. I paid about fifty dollars for a one-way flight to Bogotá in three days.

Jose from Caracas told me about one hostel in Bogotá called Musicology Hostel, which sounded like my kind of place. Even though I never met Jose, he never disappointed me with places to stay.

Later that day, Gustavo, Romel, and I met up with Kurt and Maria at an outside restaurant. Seeing those two again delighted me. We sat around, drank, and shared our stories about our trip to Angel Falls. We laughed and continued to drink well into the night until we said our goodbyes. Kurt and Maria were catching a flight to Spain the next morning. All in all, they were a great couple and, even more, amazing people.

Before heading to Colombia, I spent a good bit of time writing, listening to music, and enjoying the weather outside. Every so often, I would see the girl who had helped me, and we would wave and smile. I made sure to remember to thank her before I left.

One day, I spent an entire day with Romel's roommate Alex. He had a rugby game that day, and he invited me to come out to see it. I met his teammates, and everyone was welcoming and entertaining. They joked about me joining the team, knowing I had the body mass of a tenth-grader. The closest I ever got to a contact sport was football, and that only lasted a practice.

I had enjoyed my time in Puerto Ordaz with Romel and his friends, but honestly, I was excited, if a little anxious, about leaving. The time had come for me to see something new. It seemed like I was stuck in one place again.

As time dwindled, I decided to write a note for the girl who had helped me when I first arrived. I told her I appreciated her help and gave her my contact info to stay in touch, with the help of Google Translate, of course. Having learned that she stayed with her grandmother in an apartment below Romel, I put the sticky note on the door. Right before my departure, I noticed the note was gone. Hopefully, she received my message.

Gustavo, Romel, and I arrived at the airport an hour early, so we hung around and chatted. I spotted one obvious backpacker as he hauled his backpack, wandering around with his phone in hand. I imagined I looked the same when I first arrived. Gustavo and I watched him walk back and forth, clearly in need of direction. After thinking to myself that I would have wanted someone to help if that were me, I approached the disoriented traveler.

"Hola, you speak English? You good? Need some help?"

"No. Thank you. I'm fine," he responded, but his turning in circles said otherwise.

I walked back to Gustavo.

"What do you think he will do next?" Gustavo asked.

"Go get something to eat," I joked. We both shared a good laugh.

When it was time for me to depart, I thanked the guys again for everything they had done. It felt good to be walking to the plane. I was unsure which excited me the most: the thought of leaving, the thought of going somewhere new, or having the free will to go. I did not have to go to Bogotá; I could have gone somewhere else. But either way, it felt good. And this time, Bogotá, Colombia was the destination.

—

The radiance from the full moon reflected on the thick silver clouds that stretched far beyond what my window could display. This breathtaking scene even made me change my playlist on my iPod. I played D'Angelo's *Voodoo* album for old times, which made me reminisce about the times I would play it while driving back home at night. The drastic change of not having a schedule now made me somewhat miss my old routines. Crazy enough, it made me feel like I had more responsibility now than when I was back home. Beyond paying the few bills I had and trying to take care of my own, my current experience made me feel like I had a greater weight on my shoulders.

When I arrived at the airport in Caracas, I was prepared and ready for what the night would bring. Though fully aware from my first time there at night, strangely, I made light of the situation. Just like before, few people roamed the airport. Luckily, they allowed me to sit in the waiting area at the gate. I sat alone surrounded by empty seats only with my backpack and book bag keeping me company.

Things felt much smoother and calmer this time around. I knew my luck had changed when I had no problem connecting to Wi-Fi.

A bag of Doritos, a bottle of Sprite, and my headphones helped me settle in for the night. The only person around was the janitor cleaning the bathroom further down. I wondered if they had toilet paper in the stalls.

Eventually, I started dozing off while thinking about my time in Venezuela and how rough things had begun. But meeting characters like Nanako, Ernesto, and Ruben; "the girl"; Roman; and Kurt and Maria had made it enjoyable. It made my experience in Venezuela beautiful. I realized Angel Falls was not the only angel I had met.

As my eyes blinked heavily, I wondered if Nanako was still in Colombia, who I would meet next time, and what would come of my next trip. Whatever came next, however, I would have to wait for it.

Section 2: Uncertainty

Blindfold dark, it's hard to tell apart, the distance between my hand and my nose.

On a path so sure, with sight once pure, now I can only hear the shift of my clothes.

My breath gets short-winded, while my heart is suspended, unsure if it will come down.

Each step cautious and firm, I tread light with concern, to make sure I'm still touching the ground.

Like a spinning top losing its momentum, my trust wavers, causing my eyes to cross and my thoughts to turn green.

Nights I used to sleep in rooms alone, now I share with others and a second guess.

My judgment is being challenged like an unruly court.

With the scrunch of my brows, I tilt my head confused at the betrayal of my reassurance.

Aren't those the sun's golden rays I'm chasing after?

Or are those headlights set on high beams coming head-on?

There's a blemish in the sky, that I hope passes by, for it will cause my plans to be fickle.

I dreamed of pearl-shaped doves, drifting high above, but should I plan for their downward trickle?

9

Dismay

With the radiant sun giving off the perfect temperature, the weather reflected how I felt about the next chapter of my trip, optimistic and anxious. As I flew over Colombia, the plentiful mountains grabbed my attention. Beautiful green hills and valleys sculpted every inch of land, seeming almost artificial as I gazed out my window.

When I made it to Bogotá, it felt entirely different compared to Venezuela. Maybe it was because I had arrived early, but people seemed to have a good energy about them. Based on the things Colombia got associated with back home, my knowledge boiled down to two things: cocaine and prostitution. While I was not naïve enough to think that was all there was to Colombia, I just knew I would not have any problems if I did not put myself in any sketchy situations. And it did not take long for me to see "situations" outside my taxi window. In broad daylight, we passed a corner where a group of women were clearly selling their bodies. One woman displayed her breasts as her areolas peeked out through her fishnet shirt. The driver and I noticed simultaneously, and he looked back at me and gave me a slight chuckle.

While trying to observe every corner now, I noticed how much graffiti covered the buildings in the city. It made the streets come to life with its vibrant styles and designs. And since my driver got lost finding my hostel, I got a chance to see plenty of it.

After some time, we pulled up next to a building with a string of doors and windows that stretched down the block, uncertain of which one my hostel stood behind. Each block seemed like one long building, separated by shades of red, white, green, yellow, and blue to differentiate each place. Every window had protruding bars with wooden doors on the inside. I noticed Spanish roof tiles covered every building as I looked down my declining street.

Looking above one of the doors, I spotted a wooden sign that read "Musicology." I rang the doorbell and a girl's voice came through a small intercom.

"Hola! You have reservation?"

"No, I would like to book a room if I could."

"One moment."

A few moments later, a young girl with a soft smile greeted me at the door. "How are you? Please come in. My name is Samita."

"Hey, I'm Russell," I replied.

Samita was Colombian and one year younger than me. I found out that, along with going to school, she helped manage the hostel in the evenings.

The hostel had a mini courtyard in the center of the dorms that surrounded it.

Along with hammocks that hung from the pillars supporting the hostel, stools and tables decorated the courtyard, with a broken fountain as the centerpiece. The hostel even had a hostel cat, a yellow-eyed black cat who did not mind strolling its way in and out of rooms if the door was open.

Each dorm room had a genre of music labeled at the top of each door. I noticed a few genres like Rock, Pop, and Blues etched in small boards of wood, each painted a different color. Samita assigned me to the Jazz dorm. *Maybe I should listen to more jazz,* I thought as I read the sign.

I would have never guessed just how far the hostel stretched, having yet another courtyard down a small hall that led to the dining area. Pictures of musicians hung on the walls of the hostel: a psychedelic yellow and orange drawing of Jimi Hendrix; a photo of Bob Marley playing a game of fútbol; and a big head animation drawing of Mick Jagger and Keith Richards, to name a few. Quotes from artists like John Lennon were written below black-and-white photographs of smiling children.

Are all hostels like this? Do they all feel this refreshing and inspiring? Will the people reflect that as well?

The guests appeared scattered throughout the hostel. Some sat at tables as they conversed, while others read and relaxed in hammocks. I was unsure where they were from, but one thing was for certain: they damn sure did not look like me. I could tell from all the loose clothes and bare feet that they were comfortable and in their own worlds.

I walked into my room to find a guy at the bottom of one of the two bunk beds. It looked like he had not moved in a while as he looked up and gave a brief nod from behind his laptop. I spoke to him, but from the shake of his head and the shrug of his shoulders, I think his English was just as good as my Spanish. Therefore, we both settled for just an "hola."

After setting my bags down on the hardwood floor, I gave my eyes a moment to sweep the room. Besides a bathroom, a wall mural of a jazz musician playing the trumpet, and the two bunk beds, that was it. There were markings etched in pens and sharp objects on the wooden frame of my bed, showcasing the various names and countries of previous travelers. Now, I could leave mine.

Once settled in, I ventured out to explore the city. It had been my first time being out alone since I began the trip. I observed the people, the streets, the environment. All so unfamiliar. All so new. That unfamiliarity sent a flash of energy to my steps as I lengthened my strides. The idea had not hit me until then that I was a foreigner, a role I never had before. How would I be treated? Would people even notice? Would they care? As my mind wandered with questions, I wandered into a nearby plaza.

People were scattered about with loved ones and taking photos while flocks of pigeons strutted their way toward any stranger tossing corn. Column-styled buildings surrounded the plaza, and a statue of Simón Bolívar stood as its centerpiece. I plopped down on the monument steps, giving myself a moment to take everything in, comfortable with how much safer I felt in Bogotá than in Caracas.

Though I felt safer, I should have known that a plaza of that size would be a hotspot for street hustlers. And sure enough, I got into a hustle, getting beat out of ten dollars' worth of pesos by some dude performing magic with paper clips. If that was not enough, he even left the paper clips for me to keep. After that fiasco, I cut my outing short and took my ass back to the hostel.

While the cold showers made my body tense, I was thankful I did not need to shower out of a bucket anymore. I was more thankful for knowing I would not experience problems finding toilet paper. However, I found it peculiar that they recommended not flushing it there. It was more beneficial for the pipes over time, and it helped them last longer. But whoever had to empty the trash must have hated their job.

When I heard that the hostel served free breakfast, I figured I could save a little cash, which was always good. I entered the tile-floored dining area to find people already getting their morning breakfast: a modest spread of coffee, tea, milk, bread, jam, and fruit. After grabbing mine, I found a seat at a table where a group of guys discussed where they were from.

"We were trying to escape the cold, but Bogotá is feeling like Montana right about now," said a sandy-haired guy with glasses.

"Montana, huh? I can damn near say the same for Colorado," said another who looked like a shorter version of the first.

"You guys from the States, too, right?" said the curly-haired baby face of the bunch.

"Yeah, man—from Georgia, and my dad came down from Minnesota. We just got in from Medellin last night," said one guy with messy hair who looked closer to my age and seemed to be the most experienced in traveling.

As they appeared surprised at how many people were from the States, their eyes eventually worked their way down to me at the end of the table.

"What 'bout you man? You just get in?" asked the baby face.

"Yeah, I got here yesterday, too. I'm from South Carolina. Just got done coming from Venezuela," I replied.

The dad from Minnesota snapped his neck in my direction. "Venezuela? Holy shit. What the hell were you doing there? That place is in shit right now!" he exclaimed, in his khaki dad hat.

Everyone's faces expressed the same questions. They looked at me as if I did not get the memo, which I did not.

"Venezuela, bro? What made you go there?" questioned one with an accent that I could not interpret.

"Yeah, man, that's hardcore. You're crazy for that shit," replied the son.

"Well, honestly, I didn't know. This is my first time backpacking, and I planned to just start at the top and just work my way down—" I began.

"Wait a minute; wait a minute."

I waited.

"You mean to tell me on your first backpacking trip, the first place you decided to visit is the most dangerous country in South America? Should I ask which city you were in?" said the dad.

"Caracas."

"FUCKING CARACAS, VENENZULA?" he replied, though it might as well have been the entire table.

After explaining my desire to visit Angel Falls and how meeting Ernesto and Ruben helped me out, they still were not sold on the idea of going to Venezuela.

"You're one badass man. I've couldn't have done that shit. Not to see a waterfall," the dad said, still perplexed.

"Damn. Yeah man, you're a wild one for that, bro," added the messy haired son.

Is Caracas really that bad? I thought. *Should I have been a lot more on edge than I was?* If there was ever a time I was glad that ignorance had worked in my favor, it was then. Had I been more conscious and knowledgeable about where I was, I might have attracted the attention and trouble I was trying to avoid.

Troy, the dad from Minnesota, his son Ty, and I clicked pretty well as we continued to share our experiences. Hanging out with actual backpackers felt like I had finally tapped into the community. I messaged Nanako to let her know I had made it to Bogotá, but she had already moved on to her next stop.

After breakfast, a few of us planned to go on a graffiti tour. Before heading out for the tour, I returned to my room to use the restroom and found a random girl sleeping in my bed. She looked exhausted as hell, so I decided not to bother her.

A few others and I walked the streets of Bogotá a few blocks over to the meetup spot of the tour. We arrived at our destination with tourists already waiting for the tour to begin. To my surprise, as the tour guide spoke, I realized he was not Colombian, but American. He had been studying graffiti in Bogotá for some time and was also a graffiti artist himself, making a living

85

off the tips he made from his tours. This guy had figured out a way to make a living doing what he loved to do and had reached a point that I could only wish to get to one day. But how?

The graffiti tour had to be one of the most artistic experiences I had taken part in. Artists from all over the world came to Bogotá to add their work to its walls and buildings. Even business owners paid for supplies to have artists deliberately put graffiti on their stores, hoping to attract customers.

Detailed murals from indigenous people and political artwork on the side of old construction sites captured my attention. I spotted pieces of street art that stretched the entire block down the walls—and some that even told stories. One of them showed what appeared to be a wealthy man being carried on the back of a more brittle and less fortunate man, symbolizing the challenges of the working class. But nothing caught my eye more than a mural painted in one of Bogotá's narrow alleyways, an Indigenous woman looking up to the skies. Her thin lips, high cheekbones, and soft eyes reminded me of my great-grandmother. A scarf covered her head, showing just enough of her jet-black hair underneath with a gold ring pierced through her septum. The elderly woman appeared full of wisdom as she stared upward, looking as though she could see things beyond our vision. The spiritual artwork of the paintings captivated me and left me appreciating art even more.

When we arrived back at the hostel, we were exhausted, though not enough to go to sleep. However, I did notice the girl who had occupied my bed was not there anymore.

Meanwhile, I decided to go relax in the small lounge toward the front of the hostel. I considered it the activity room because it had a TV, a computer, and even a library of books in a corner. It had no chairs, just cotton floor mats and a few piles of blankets. We all took some time to relax there, and while doing so, we struck up a conversation with three girls from Germany and Australia. That is when I found out I had an "accent."

"Where are you from? I haven't heard anything like that before," said the reddish-blonde-haired girl.

"Yeah, I love your accent," said another who was pale-skinned with blonde hair.

"Right? It's so smooth, yeah," replied the first girl.

I never thought of myself as having an accent until they brought it up. When I thought about accents, I thought of foreigners speaking English. As I considered it a bit more, I realized that was probably their first time meeting a southern Black guy from the States.

Smiles crept upon their faces as I continued speaking. At this point, I was talking just to be talking as I slowed down and dragged my sentences, slightly exaggerating to give my newfound accent more swag.

Before long, a spark of attraction happened between me and one of the girls, Anna. I always wondered why being from different places creates a stronger attraction between two people. Was it just curiosity? Or was it that something new meant something exciting?

The hostel offered a salsa class one evening that we both attended. Even though I had never done salsa dancing before, Anna was good enough for the both of us. She made me feel comfortable as the swing of our hips and steps synchronized as one.

"You're a fast learner, I see," she complimented.

"It's 'cause I have a good teacher," I replied.

"Ha, well thank you, but you move very smooth. You seem like a natural to me, yeah."

"Just trying to be like you, that's all."

People could spot the smiles on our faces from across the room as we bashfully looked down at our feet whenever our eyes met.

As the night ended, we found out that we were staying in the same room, and that the girl who had slept in my bed earlier was one of the other German girls from that day. With all the variables in place, the question came down to how one would try to smash in a room occupied with two other people and be discreet about it. Anna lay on the top bunk as I lay on the bottom, wondering if I was being too naïve to think she thought the same.

—

I strolled back over to Bolívar Square to sit and people-watch one day. The steps I sat on led into a building that people were coming in and out of, so I thought I would take a look inside. I walked into the building and realized I had walked into a church. Its painted pillars stretched as far as the wooden pews, heading down to the pulpit. Chandeliers hung down from pearl-painted ceilings, their gold frame matching the painted gold tops of each pillar. In the very center, there was a dome structure in the ceiling with paintings of Jesus performing miracles. Workers were renovating parts of the church as power drills echoed and bounced off the walls. I noticed a few people sitting down in the pews, and I took a moment to do the same.

As I sat there, I could not remember the last time I occupied a church pew. The stern, upright benches lined up in its columns and rows were all too familiar. It had been a couple of years since I had last been to church, but strangely enough, it felt like revisiting an old friend. Growing up, many of my Sunday mornings consisted of me trying to get out of going to church. Days of singing in the children's choir and going to Sunday school all seemed like a faraway memory now.

Though my religious views had changed over the past couple of years, I appreciated my upbringing in the church. I sat back and spread my arms across the top of the pew, relishing this time in church again. I was thankful that God had seen me through this far, even though my intentions were still on sinning before Anna left.

Our attraction still held as Anna and I joined a few others to go to a salsa and reggae club later that night. As we shot smiles at each other, using the moves we had learned in class, our chemistry still appeared to be on point. When we finally made it back to the hostel, it was about two in the morning. We stayed up for a while talking and laughing at a few moments that had happened throughout the night.

On Anna's last day, we spent just about the entire day together, along with another traveler, Ally. Ally had heard about some gourmet restaurant she wanted to try that took us all day to find. During our "tour" of the city, it seemed as if Anna and I grew closer as we continued learning more about each other. I even found out that she was Russian.

Along with being in theater, knowing how to play the guitar, and speaking five different languages, Anna blew me away with her many talents. It made me wonder what the hell I was doing with my time growing up. Her willingness to be silly made me like her even more. As I played some rap music by one of my favorite artists, Big K.R.I.T., Anna posed with her arms crossed, giving her best B-Boy impersonation, and began dancing the crip walk. We laughed until we were out of breath.

After we gathered our composure, Anna came and sat next to me on my bed.

"Hey, I want to give you something," I said.

"Yeah?"

I reached down into my backpack and pulled out the teddy bear.

"This was supposed to go to my Couchsurfer for her birthday, but I didn't get a chance to give it to her. I want you to have it."

"This is sweet," Anna said. "Wow, thanks. I will call him Russell."

If I could have blushed, I would have.

"I have a small gift for you as well," she continued.

"Really? What?" I asked curiously.

She reached down into her bag and pulled out a small seashell.

"I found this on the beach of Cuba. I've never seen one this perfect before."

I sat there in awe of Anna's kindness.

"Now I can say I have a piece of Cuba. Thank you. This is perfect," I replied. Though I expected nothing in return, her desire to return the gesture made her gift more valuable.

Like a thorn in my side, one of the receptionists had also taken a liking to Anna. Every so often, he would snoop around to check on us. Though capable of speaking English, he would speak in Spanish to Anna, cutting me out of the conversation. Though she would reply, I thought, *Ain't no way I'm going to get outdone by a nigga that has a hairstyle like Elvis Presley.* While fighting for Anna's attention, I learned I needed some time alone after I received a message from my grandmother that my aunt Mary had passed away.

It felt like a punch to the stomach. I kept reading the text over and over, trying my best to process what I had just read. It had been a little over three weeks and my biggest fear had come to fruition: losing a loved one and not being there to support my family.

Motionless, I sat on the edge of my bed, chilled from the cold that came with the night. I did not want to call home. I did not want to hear the hurt in my grandmother's voice. Guilt washed over me because I was away from everything. As I sat and listened to music alone, being by myself felt fitting. Even Anna's company would not have been enough to lift my mood. I did not want to do anything but sleep.

I slept until I awoke from the opening of the room door and the shuffling of bags. I did not have to look at the clock to know the time had slipped into the late hours of the night. I figured Anna must have still been getting her bags together before leaving in a couple of hours. Then I noticed another pair of feet moving across the room. It did not take long for me to realize Elvis was still at it. I lay still, waiting for the movement to stop, as the only source of light came from the opened door like a wide flashlight. I could hear a few murmurs of Spanish right before the door shut. Then I heard the creaks of the ladder as the two pairs of feet climbed up to the top bunk. After a brief pause, the sounds of kissing followed.

My stomach felt like it had sunken into a ball of fire as I lay there, trying not to breathe too hard. My heart wanted to leave the room, and it would have had it not been blocked by the lump in my throat. It was like all that time, all that flirting, everything, had just been swallowed into a black abyss like the pitch-black room we were now in.

Sounds of subtle shifting and soft kisses burned my chest as I listened with humiliation. Before long, I could hear the crinkle of plastic being torn as I heard the opening of a condom wrapper. My arms and legs felt restless from keeping still for so long. If there was ever a time that I wished I could teleport or disappear, it would have been then. I hoped like hell that my roommate would bust in through the door from his long night of partying.

But to my surprise, Anna did not want to go all the way. Maybe she feared the bed would make too much noise. Or maybe she just did not want to. To get some relief, I gave in to the uncomfortable feeling as I moved about as slow as a sloth to bend my limbs.

For the rest of the time, I remained awake as daylight began creeping between the cracks of the door. Shortly after, I could hear them climb their way back down the bed, gather her luggage, and walk out the door. I planned to lie there until I was certain all the commotion had ceased. While I was still pretending to be asleep, Anna returned to the room and placed something down on the side of the bed. Truth be told, I did not want to speak to her or see her, nor did I want her to leave without me telling her goodbye. I may have been childish for doing so, but I did not know what to do. So I did nothing.

I lay there for some time disappointed, not only because of what all had transpired but also because I knew I lacked the confidence to take a chance. My petty situation made me think deeper than just "losing the girl" to another guy; it made me question my hesitation to take chances in life. *What makes me retreat and give up so easily at the slightest resistance? Why am I comfortable at times with not even trying? Is courage what I'm after?* This weighed on me, along with still being saddened by the news of losing my aunt, not even being brave enough to get over my guilt and give my grandmother a call. I was hurt about everything, the hurt of people leaving and never seeing them again.

When I finally decided to get up, I looked over to the side of the bed and noticed Anna had left me a note.

> *Hey Russell, It was nice to meet such a nice person like you. Thanks for everything you taught me and take care. I'll take lil Russell with me and show him the world. Enjoy your journey and always believe in the good. Anna :).*

For the rest of the day, I drifted along, going wherever my feet would take me. I wandered to the plaza where fútbol fans hyped themselves up for an upcoming game and later found myself staring at street artists performing, not appreciating anything I came across. Most of the day I spent alone, walking around. The day reflected how mine went: cold and gray.

10

Insecurity

One thing I could say about Bogotá was that it had plenty of frosty mornings. While heading to breakfast, I walked with my arms tightly folded as the nipping cold searched for exposed skin to give goosebumps to. Some of the same guys from the U.S. met back up at the same table as I talked to Ty and his dad, Troy, about their plans for the day. Most of the people I hung with the day before either had other plans or had planned to go to the graffiti tour. Ty and his dad would head out later for Cali, Colombia, which would also be my next stop.

Before leaving Bogotá, I started enjoying the social experience of a hostel, being around other travelers who made my stay welcoming and fruitful. Talking to the people around me and seeing how helpful they were to a new traveler like me comforted me. Though it was not the best of days, I felt blessed to be there. Everyone I spoke with seemed to make the night easier to endure.

The morning of my departure began like any other morning, chilly with cold showers along with new and old faces at breakfast. Most of the people I had met upon my arrival planned on leaving the same day as well. From the time we spent together, it almost felt like graduation, while the newcomers were like freshmen, eager to explore the unfamiliar city.

I had met so many people from different places in just a few days: France, England, Australia, Germany, Scotland, Italy, Japan, Canada, and Denmark, to name a few. Amazed to see all these people under one roof, I concluded that my first hostel was a pleasurable one. Though far from a luxury, its warm welcome from its guests did enough to mollify its cool mornings.

—

By now, I had learned that depending on how far your next destination may be, it might be better to catch a night bus. That way, you could spend the night on the bus and have a full day the following morning when you arrive. Plus, you would not waste money on a room for half a night. With these thoughts in mind, I wandered down the lines of bus services, scanning unfamiliar words in search of trips to Cali, Colombia. A couple of people were helpful enough to direct me to where I needed to be, since I still could not read signs. From there, I bought a ticket and sat with the rest of the travelers awaiting our departure.

About an hour and a half later, the bus pulled up. Its workers wasted no time loading bags and luggage inside its compartments below. I sat next to a window and put my headphones on as the half-empty bus eventually began making its way to Cali, Colombia. As the bus leaned and swayed, I thought about my past couple of days in Bogotá. At one time, I was unsure if something like this would even happen. I no longer felt the anxiety of the unknown; instead, I felt comfort and contentment as I watched streetlights become trailing spots being outrun by rural darkness. I had no idea where I would end up or when I would have enough of traveling. I just knew I wanted to keep going.

Other things crossed my mind, along with thoughts of my family and friends. It surprised me that I thought about my job and if anyone else would decide to leave. While I still did not have the slightest idea of what I would do when I returned home, I figured I would find out whenever that time came.

Though my luggage occupied the bottom of the bus, I still carried the baggage from the other night with me, the fiasco with Anna. I could only say I was a work in progress. Maybe taking this trip was a step in that direction. It was not long before the sounds of my music and the humming of the bus had me dozing off to sleep.

We finally arrived in Cali around 6:30 a.m. while cab drivers awaited us outside. My cab driver and I later pulled up to a blue and white building, and I realized the hostel was just as discrete as my last one. Upon walking in, I noticed some similarities, like hanging hammocks and a quaint courtyard. After checking in, I learned I would share my room with some familiar faces. Ty and Troy were still sleeping as I entered the room. It felt good knowing I knew some people there.

Breakfast began shortly after, so I made my way to get some grub. The hostel had an outside portion with a swimming pool, an open bar, and a small stage for performers. Since no one had woken up yet, breakfast had been untouched as I approved the fresh spread: cold milk, cereal, fresh-squeezed orange juice, grapes, pineapples, melons, passion fruit, bread, and hot coffee. Everything was laid out neatly on a long table right beside the closed bar. Ty came down to breakfast not long after.

"How was the trip, man?" Ty said, widening his eyes, still trying to shake off his sleep.

"It wasn't too bad. I was glad that I took the night bus like y'all suggested," I responded.

"Yeah, man, you want to save as much money as you can. Things are cheap, but it doesn't mean your ass can't go broke."

He was right. I had done pretty well with my spending thus far. But because things were not as expensive, I could see how easily someone could spend loosely.

I asked Ty about his plans for the day, and he informed me about a yoga class scheduled at one o'clock, and a salsa class scheduled for later in the day. I had always wanted to try yoga, but

I never took the time to go. As far as the salsa class, it was not a question that I would be attending. Anna crossed my mind while I thought about salsa and how well we did as partners. I wondered if she was enjoying her time in Cartagena.

Eventually, yoga class rolled around and, to my delight, our yoga instructor was fine as hell. She wore her long, black hair wrapped up in a bun with a plum-colored bandana tied around her head. Her sports bra revealed her flat stomach as her spandex hugged around her thighs, giving her the perfect yoga body.

Out of nine people, Ty and I were the only guys. There were few guys, or people in general, who I knew that practiced yoga. I had not heard about yoga until my late teens. Growing up, the only things my peers and I were into were rap videos, wrestling, sports, video games, and mischief. My friends deemed any activity that looked like it was for women or involved wearing spandex and moving your body peculiarly as feminine and "gay." Nothing of any sort ever entered our circle or was even considered as a conversation topic. However, when I was twelve, I took gymnastics for a couple of months and never told my friends. I did not want them to think I was weird or soft.

After class, I met a few people around the hostel, including this guy from Luxembourg, which I had never heard of before. He was a cool and curious guy. He was into hip-hop and even enjoyed some of my group's music that I shared with him. I understood his curiosity because I doubted many Black people were hanging out in Luxembourg. Eventually, he asked me if I smoked, and I could see where his questioning was leading.

Outside of my recent encounter with Gustavo's friends in Venezuela, I had not smoked weed since college. I considered myself a novice smoker compared to the rest of my colleagues. However, my smoking run ended one night during a session as we sat around in a circle, slouched in saucer chairs, playing music from only one working speaker. By the end of the night, I felt like Smokey in the movie *Friday*, running down the street in his underwear. Though I was not outside in my underwear, I felt exposed and trapped in hell somewhere. My smoking days were over after that shit.

The salsa class began around 7 p.m. My excitement was evident, at least to myself anyway, as I was the first one to arrive in class. Before long, the class grew, and I was in a room full of ready dancers. Then, unexpectedly, the salsa instructor came jolting into the room as if he had been drinking Red Bull and coffee, going straight into salsa. Everything seemed to be in one motion. Even the music seemed to start by itself. As he moved his feet swiftly, his arms moved effortlessly and smoothly, like his joints were greased with butter. We all stood around watching like school children, dumbfounded as he danced.

After about five minutes, he finally slowed things down and began teaching. If anyone thought they knew something about salsa, they were quickly humbled, including me. Salsa was something I knew I wanted to continue doing. It was real dancing. In the only clubs I had ever been to, the only move you needed to have was just the slight balance needed to not fall while a girl twerked on you.

We had practiced enough to feel confident putting our moves to the test and decided to go to one of the more notable salsa clubs: La Topa Tolondra. Our optimistic minds chatted as we moved collectively, eager to test our skills and have a good time. As we strolled toward the nightclub, the sounds of horns and bongos trickled out of the entrances and onto the street. A graffiti design of a woman playing with bongos colored with yellows and oranges covered the entire face of the building. Fans fixed in areas of windowless walls suggested it could be as hot as a sweatshop inside.

The rising sounds of music as we entered softened our confidence. The air felt thick as we migrated our way through the wall-to-wall crowd. Feverishly, the crowd moved and swung as partners remained in sync with their counterparts. Their moments were so precise that if there were ever a misstep, it would go unnoticed, as their moves conformed and flowed like a river around a rock.

I walked straight to the bar and ordered a drink, overwhelmed by the scene. The rest of my classmates had the same idea as we stayed huddled in a group, like shivering kittens trying to stay warm.

The red light that radiated off the sweaty faces of dancers intensified the scene and for a moment, it felt as though it affected the temperature altogether. The music had possessed their bodies in a way that they never appeared to bump into other couples on the floor. Almost as if they knew each other's movements, the crowd danced as one body.

Their outfits looked like something from a musical, or a mobster film, with guys wearing pinstripe pants and suspenders. Some even wore brim hats to match as women donned long dresses and skirts that scrunched at the bottom. One lady looked as beautiful as a swan in a pure white dress with rhinestones that shimmered as she twisted and spun. All I had on was a burgundy long-sleeve shirt, khaki shorts, and a khaki football cap. Luckily, I was not alone. Everyone from the hostel wore some type of street attire.

Slowly but surely, we found the confidence to dance with people more on our level—ourselves. One or two guys built the courage to dance with experienced dancers, sporadically looking down at their feet, trying their best to be loose and not clumsy. But the dance was short-lived once moves became repetitious, or someone stepped on a few toes.

Though I applauded them for their bravery, I stayed in my lane. I danced with one of the girls in my class from Argentina. We danced for one or two songs, but for the rest of the night, I sat in awe of how advanced the professional dancers were. Their footwork was so fluid and light, that they could have defied the laws of physics and danced their way up the sides of walls. Disappointment began sinking in as I spectated, not being able to have fun and dance like I wanted to. Not being able to participate and enjoy myself like everyone else felt horrible. I could have given it a try, but the fear of being embarrassed was stronger than my will.

I hated feeling this way. I hated missing out on something special and simple like salsa, being too scared to make a mistake because I was not good. Sadly, I had been that way for the longest time. I could have taken many more chances if I had just given things a shot. That was what I was looking for. Truly being free and not caring what others may think. And that was something I did not have.

As the night went on, I wondered if anyone else felt the same as a few people next to me looked on in a trance. Though I could argue that making this trip was an act of being free, deep down, I still felt like a fraud. For the rest of the night, all I could do was just look on, order another drink, and nod my head to the music.

11

Exploration

One of the more adventurous things to do in Cali involved taking a day trip to San Cipriano, a remote place in the middle of a natural reserve. It was not so much about the destination itself as it was about getting there. The stories I heard about Las Brujitas (Witches) de San Cipriano, which involved riding on wooden carts, hurtling down abandoned train tracks, and risking the chance of meeting another oncoming cart, intrigued me.

During our search to find what bus would take us to this destination, Ty, Troy, and I learned that to get to San Cipriano, we could not take a normal bus but a "Colectivo" instead. Colectivos ranged from small buses to large vans, which were inexpensive ways to travel to far destinations. As long as you had enough people to fill the vehicle to cover the cost, it would make the trip.

We were all excited about the trip yet unsure of what to expect. It took us about three hours before we reached the drop-off point. A trio of dark-complexioned men awaited us as we unloaded the bus. Had I not known where I was, I could have sworn the tall, slender men might have been of African descent.

I had seen no one remotely close to my complexion since I began my trip. Remembering that South America had a variety of shades, I quickly checked my naïve thoughts. I found it interesting, however, that it took this long to see someone of my complexion. But why so distant from everything?

The three middle-aged men greeted us as their yellow eyes showed neither excitement nor enthusiasm. We followed the men down a dirt road while they asked us questions for the sake of being polite. When they directed questions toward me, though, they seemed a bit more interested. Maybe they were as surprised as I was. They spoke with a heavy accent as we continued along our path between the stone and tin roof shacks.

During our stroll, we passed one or two families standing outside of their homes, their eyes following us. We held their attention so long that they could have gone back inside and drawn us down to our socks. I wondered how many people they had seen walk down this same path. Did they believe their homes were just something fun for foreigners to visit? How did they feel about us being there?

We eventually reached the train tracks where others waited to ride the "Brujita," but not as backpackers. They were men and women with their children waiting to board, as if expecting an actual train. Ty and I had heard about the Brujita back at the hostel, but seeing it in person was more unreal than hearing about it. Instead of waiting for the Brujita to arrive, we found that they were setting it upright in front of us. Three men, including one of the older guys that met us, carried over a large sheet of wood that had train track wheels attached to the bottom. A wooden bench sat on top of the large rectangular board that could fit about five adults and maybe three small children. The back right corner of the wood had a cut-out for where the engine would be. And that engine was a motorcycle.

They placed the front part of the motorcycle on top of the board, keeping the back wheel on one track to make the Brujita move. Outside of sitting on the motorcycle to keep it steady, there was no other way to keep the bike secured. It looked like some shit straight out of *Indiana Jones*.

As the older gentleman straddled the motorcycle and started the engine, I was not sure if I began feeling excitement or anxiety. He let off the break and began turning his wrist back to give the Brujita gas as it began inching down the track. It rode heavy and smooth, as if being pulled by a magnetic force. As the Brujita's speed accelerated, it sounded like the clicks of a roller coaster before it took the first drop.

For the next three miles, there was nothing but the sight of trees, the flapping of clothes, and the roaring of the motorcycle's engine. I sat between two large women who gave me cover from the blinding wind. Every so often I would lean forward enough to see where we were headed and then lean back. I could imagine how it must have been for Ty and Troy, who sat up front.

It was not until the third mile that we could see another Brujita heading straight for us. *Ahh hell. Now what?* I thought.

The only way for either vehicle to continue going was for one to be taken off the track to allow the other one to pass. We ended up getting off, but the quick break was pleasant as they disassembled and reassembled our Brujita back on the track.

It was another mile before we reached San Cipriano. Our time there felt brief as we walked through the San Cipriano Natural Reserve, escorted by one of the local teenagers. While we toured the community, kids ran around in diapers, wanting to stop and talk to us. I watched them in awe, unsure if they were saying anything at all, as their Spanish masked the words in their youthful voices. It looked like they did not require much to be happy. They seemed to find the most joy in simply kicking a ball around, wearing smiles as big as their hearts.

I tried taking a photo with one child, but he dashed off, repeating, "No, no, no." I was sure I had not been the only person to ask for a photo before. I also would not doubt his family had told him not to take photos with the "visitors," which I could understand.

The conditions of their community were what we in the U.S. would consider a third-world country. Though they lacked technology and resources, I could sense they had everything they needed. Often I felt like the people who lived in secluded areas were better off. Yes, it appeared to be harder work, but it seemed as if the benefits were more rewarding.

We stopped to eat at a place that was nothing more than an outside shed with picnic tables. Two stoves and a deep fryer served as the kitchen, while three ladies took our orders and cooked right in front of us.

One of the women's sons had gotten into trouble shortly before, and his father had just heard about it. It eventually led to the little boy running around crying while his father chased him with a belt in hand.

Whether you are from South Carolina or South America, every parent and child knows the language of an ass whipping. The little kid even ran behind his mother's legs as she cooked our food. When his dad finally got a hold of him, he gave him a few licks while speaking to him in Spanish. Other kids giggled at him sneakily, having taken a break from kicking the ball around to watch.

We made it back to Cali around 10:30 p.m., which did not feel like a long trip since I slept most of the way until a sudden jerk of the vehicle awakened me. From what Troy said, our driver had been hauling ass during our trip back.

Once back at the hostel, I reached out to a few of my loved ones, and they all asked the same question: "When will you be back?" Truthfully, I did not have any idea. I figured I would know when it felt right to go back. And I did not feel anywhere close to being ready. It had not even been a month yet. As long as my legs could continue moving, and my stomach could hold up, I would leave the thought of returning home, back home. And maybe at the airport restroom in Venezuela.

When Ty said he almost got robbed outside of our hostel, however, I considered leaving Cali.

"Soooo some guy just tried to fuckin' rob me outside of the hostel!" Ty exclaimed.

"Bro, what the fuck? Just now? What the hell happened?" I asked, trying to process the situation.

"Ha, yeah, dude had a knife and all asking for my wallet. I think he may have known I was American. Must have heard me speak."

"Did you tell your dad?"

"Yep, said I should have kicked his ass. We just kinda looked at each other for a long time, and when he realized I wasn't going to give it up, he kinda walked away. I thought the shit was funny myself."

Following Ty's incident, I contemplated what my destination would be after Cali. I remembered someone saying that I should visit Popayan back when I was in Bogotá. It seemed more off the beaten path, giving me a chance to meet some indigenous people.

—

On one of my last days in Cali, a few of us decided to go to Cristo Rey, a viewpoint at the top of the city. We flagged down a taxi, standing there with our book bags and bottles of water in hand. Our driver was a young guy in his twenties. Though the rest of my companions spoke Spanish well enough to hold conversations and to exchange laughs, something did not sit well with me about our driver. I was unsure if my instincts had kicked in, but his cool demeanor seemed like a front.

We had arranged for our driver to drop us off at our destination and pick us up when we were done. As planned, once finished, we called the driver, but he did not answer. We tried a few times and still received no answer. We eventually found a guy with a pickup truck to give us a ride back, along with a few others. As we rode down the curves of the hill, I could make out one of our group members saying something, even though the wind muffled his words.

"I sure hope we don't run into that taxi driver, 'cause if so, he's going to be pissed," he said.

Almost as soon as the words left his lips, we spotted a taxi speeding up behind us. The taxi driver had driven up beside us in oncoming traffic, talking aggressively through his window and throwing his hands up in the air. He sped past us and stopped his car, which stalled us and everyone behind us. The taxi driver got out of his car and walked up to our truck driver, arguing with him and the rest of us.

A line of cars began forming behind us, honking their horns. Some drivers stepped out of their cars, baffled about the sudden stop. One curious driver behind us got out of his car as the angered taxi driver headed back to his.

"He is saying that we shouldn't get back in the taxi because the driver is irate and may try to follow us," a tall, slender guy from Canada said.

"Well, what are we gonna do? Should we just stay in the back of the truck?" asked one girl, the worry apparent in her voice.

"Damn, how'd I know this would happen?" the Canadian replied.

Suddenly, the taxi sped off, and we left shortly after.

As we continued, the curious driver signaled our driver to pull back over on the side of the road. One of our group members translated what the curious driver said after talking to him for a while.

"He suggested that we swap cars, you guys. Just in case the taxi tries to come back. We could at least throw him off if he tries to follow."

"Let's do it," we agreed.

As we unloaded from the truck, the curious driver's wife and three children exited from his vehicle. None of us realized he had his family with him until then. We piled into the car while the family loaded up in the pickup truck, realizing the man wanted us to swap cars for our safety. While riding in the car, we looked out of our windows, making sure we had lost the taxi driver. A group member continued to translate as we did so.

"Well, looks like our curious driver is a police officer. What's the odds in that, right?"

I did not know, but I was glad the odds were in our favor.

—

As I prepared to leave the following day, I hung out with Ty and Troy one last time before they left for Ecuador. And like always before a departure, a common trend of sadness seemed to occupy the space of what was once good company, a feeling I doubted I would ever shake.

I also decided to give Couchsurfing another try. In Bogotá, someone had recommended visiting Popayan before leaving Colombia. I became skeptical when my soon-to-be host messaged me that I needed to get off at another bus stop before reaching Popayan, yet I agreed to do so.

Luckily, I had a seat close to the bus driver. Before dozing off, I told him to wake me at the exit before Popayan. As soon as I closed my eyes, it seemed like I had to open them again, as the bus driver did as requested. Still skeptical and half tired, I just motioned him to continue to Popayan at the last minute. I had already booked a hostel ahead of time in case things felt weird, and I still had a couple of snacks in my bag that I could stretch until the next morning.

When I arrived in Popayan, which is more of a large town than a city, traces of sunlight still decorated the sky. My hostel was located upstairs in one of the buildings that rimmed the town's plaza. I checked into the quiet hostel, surprised at the number of older occupants that made it feel more like a retirement home. As part of my routine, I messaged my family to let them know I had made it safely. I also messaged the Couchsurfer host, Ikari, that I had planned to go to Popayan instead.

106

Within seconds of sending the text to Ikari, I got one back saying he was in Popayan. I was unsure if I should have felt lucky that he was there or annoyed that I would have been stuck if I would have gotten off at the earlier stop.

Ikari agreed to meet me down in the plaza and show me around. Little did I know, he would bring two of his friends with him.

12

Disruption

Once we finally met, Ikari introduced me to his two comrades dressed in all black. They stood behind Ikari, one on either side of him like henchmen. They gave me the impression they knew Ikari—his real name was Jefe which means "boss" in Spanish—called the shots and they were his goons.

"Russell, can you put my book bag in your room? I don't want to have to carry it all around," Jefe said.

"Yeah, that's cool," I agreed, not thinking much of his request.

After taking his bag up to my room, we set off to see the town.

The town's plaza, along with the people in it, felt warm and tranquil. A feeling of respect moved throughout the atmosphere. Even some level of understanding exceeded laws and regulations. The town felt safe. Families had their children out as their laughs chipped away at the bulwark I had up when I first arrived. So much so that as we explored the plaza and other parts of the town, Jefe and his gang did not seem half bad. I did notice that Jefe had these subtle shakes that I thought to be strange, but besides that, things appeared to be smooth.

One goon had packed some homemade brew, what I assumed to be equivalent to moonshine. We poured up some while I got to know the group more.

"Oh, y'all do music, too? What kind?" I asked.

"Gothic rock. I do the lead singing," Jefe said.

Maybe that explains all the black, I thought.

"He plays the drums, and he plays guitar," Jefe continued, pointing at each of his goons.

"That's what's up. I'll have to check out y'all music. I can let you listen to some of mine as well."

We took one or two more shots, and the "liquid courage" started kicking in, which causes people to feel comfortable and to show their true colors. Jefe's once-chilled disciples had become loose and annoying as we now made our way through the park. They were obnoxious, talking loudly and laughing like hyenas at any small comment. And they continued to drink.

Despite the annoyance, I still tagged along with the boss and his goons, and we ended up at one of the goons' houses. They cut on their music and drank some more. My half-tipsy mind stayed on alert and tried to make the best of the stale-temperature house. Posters decorated the walls of bands I had never heard of, along with images of satanic symbols. Just as I thought I had found some stability in my feelings, Jefe had to go against the grain. Jefe had a locket on the chain he wore around his neck. He took off his chain, grabbed his keys, and carefully opened the locket. Then he scooped out a hit of cocaine with the tip of one of his keys. The rest of the clan followed suit as they inhaled the white powder through their nostrils.

"Woahhh, hahaha," said one goon.

"Fucking good, man, hehe," said the other one.

"It's a party now, right? Haha," Jefe exclaimed.

I knew what would soon follow, being all too familiar with that same feeling I had growing up as a kid. That extra person who is there that you cannot see. The one who likes to come around when you are outnumbered and vulnerable. It is your acceptance, your credibility, and your need of wanting to fit in and not disappoint.

"You want to try?" Jefe asked.

"Oh nah, I'm cool. Y'all got it," I responded.

"Try."

"Nah, I'm good. I'll just stick to the drinks, ha."

"It's good; you will like. Try."

"Ha, nah, I'm fine."

I could feel all their eyes on me like lasers.

"Don't worry. This is purest form of cocaine from here. It is not tampered with like in the U.S.," he continued.

"I'm cool, bro. Let's pour up some more drinks, though," I replied, hoping to change the subject, which worked for a while.

As the night progressed, one of Jefe's disciples got a bit too relaxed. He put his arm around me and rubbed my shoulder like he had popped some ecstasy. I got up from the couch and suggested we all have another drink, though I barely took sips from the cup. I focused on contemplating my exit.

They finally got fucked up enough to where they did not offer me cocaine any longer. I sensed restlessness from one goon as he adjusted himself on the couch and began rubbing his face, as if trying to regain focus.

"I feel you don't want to be around here," he said.

He was not wrong, but I played it off. "If I didn't want to hang with y'all, I would have been left. Right?"

"Yes, yes, that is right."

"So it's cool, man; I'm having a good time."

Though my response made them less suspicious of me, I surely plotted to get the hell out of there, and it appeared to be working. I also questioned if I wanted to try Couchsurfing again. I knew it would be a risk, but how many more people would place me in this situation? How often would this happen?

The time had now gotten closer to 1 a.m., and the once childish hyenas had turned into tamed children as they slowed down, slumped from their fun. But Jefe seemed to be unscathed, keeping his composure.

"We plan a trip tomorrow to head to the river. Want to come? You can stay tonight, and we all go tomorrow," he suggested.

"Well, there's a few more other things I wanna do tomorrow, but I will let you know," I said, knowing there was not much to do in Popayan. I did not give a damn if all I had planned was just sleeping; I was not trying to go anywhere with them.

When the timing felt right, I took advantage of it and escaped into the night, retracing my steps to the hostel. Though slightly tipsy, I kept my focus clear on making it back to the hostel. I thought about that night, hanging with Jefe and his boys, and how glad I felt to be out of that place.

Back in the plaza, the laughter of children that once tickled my ears had fallen silent, leaving behind nothing but deserted benches in the orange-colored plaza lights. I thought to myself, *If I ever saw those dudes again, it would be too soon.*

The floor creaked as I entered my dorm, gently turning on the light, trying not to awaken the others. I walked over to my bunk bed and remembered the bag Jefe had asked me to hold for him. *Fuck*, I thought. I would have to see the boss and his goons again.

Hot water shot on my back the next morning as I enjoyed my first hot shower in a while. I stayed as long as I could, savoring every moment while trying not to hog all the hot water from my still slumbering roommates. While getting out of the shower, I spotted one older man peeping from under the covers, revealing only his eyes and partially the bridge of his nose.

I moved with ease, trying to be respectful of other guests, but my cautiousness was not enough for old school. His eyes stayed glued to me while I moved, delicately unzipping and shuffling around bags. My concentration broke, and I looked his way as he scoffed, still unsatisfied with my carefulness. Had I been any quieter, I would have levitated off the ground. Seeing I could not please the old man, I carried on until I left the room.

The plaza had livened since the day before as I looked out one of the hostel windows. People made their way through the plaza while pigeons tiptoed around messy eaters in search of crumbs. Mornings had always been my favorite part of the day. The time of a clean slate and another opportunity to take advantage of the day.

After getting a bite to eat, my rejuvenated spirit changed once I got a text from Jefe, asking if I could drop off his bag. *Fuck.*

Within a matter of minutes, I found myself back with the boss and his boys, still clearly fucked up from the night before. They invited me to the river again, and I passed on their offer, again. They did not give me much hassle this time as I made my stay short and walked back to the plaza.

While watching people carry on about their day in the plaza, a vendor selling bracelets walked up to me and eventually gave me one for free. Wearing bracelets was a common trend amongst backpackers, equivalent to earning stripes or badges of honor. In theory, the more bracelets you had, the more places you had been. Travelers solidified their experience that way. And now I had two.

During my roam of the city, I stumbled upon an artist performing street art. I watched as he created beautiful paintings with spray paint and a blowtorch, amazing drawings of lifelike planets with lush trees and waterfalls falling off into the background of vast space. I stayed and watched him complete three full paintings, thinking about how much practice and dedication he must have had, hoping I would find my purpose and gift the way he had.

As I saw it, I had been experiencing a void for the longest. I was twenty-five years old, still living at home with my mother, still not knowing what to do in life. I wanted to do something that would make me proud. Even while on the trip of a lifetime, I still felt empty and would give anything to know what would be the right thing for me.

—

Upon returning to my room, I noticed the old man had already packed his bags and left. My other roommate still had his bags there, but he had left the room. Then I noticed my bags, which seemed out of place. I dashed across the room to check my bags; someone had tampered with them. I dug down into one of my pouches where I kept my money, snatching out a white envelope. I peeled through my money and, sure enough, I had come up short, $400 to be exact.

The heat started building in my face as my jaws tightened. Anger filled my body so much that my head hurt. I counted my bills again slowly, convincing myself that maybe they were there. Maybe I just counted them too fast. After all, they were crisp bills, so they were probably just stuck together. I counted again and again and again but still arrived at $400 less.

It could have been anyone: the housekeeper, the old man, or the other roommate I had not met yet. Anyone. And I had no proof to convict anyone. I did not even bother reporting it to the receptionist. I even tried to make myself feel better by saying at least they just took some of it. They left me with $600 instead of taking the full $1000. They could have taken all of it, but they didn't. Looking at the glass as half-full was still not enough to make me forget that my pockets were half-empty.

From that moment on, I carried my money with me everywhere. That pleasant feeling I had when I first arrived had now disappeared. All those cheerful laughs and good people had become a decoy for the real bullshit. My missing roommate had become the number one suspect merely for being the first face I saw after the infraction.

I mentioned my money being stolen and watched his reaction as we left for food, trying to get a feel for who he was. He stated he did not see anything suspicious, and that he would have to check his things when we returned to the hostel. His reaction seemed genuine, and his surprised facial expressions looked convincing.

Though I knew I would not find out who stole my money, I still tried to make the best of my stay. The no-longer suspect, Eric, and I took a day trip the following day to Silvia, a town close to Popayan.

I had never seen indigenous people in uniform until I visited Silvia. Men wore what looked like a dark blue, almost purple, one-piece outfit with long sleeves and bottoms that came down like a long skirt. They also wore a black poncho draped over them, with pink stripes and a red scarf. To top it all off, they wore black brim hats like old mobsters. The women wore something similar but in reverse: black dresses, blue tops, and a black satchel hanging down from their shoulders and around their bodies.

Foothills comprised the landscape around the city of Silvia. Beaten paths laid their way across its uneven and jagged hills. I noticed small farms peppered about in the distance, and I spotted a farmer tending horses.

It was not long before Eric and I were staring two horses right in the face. Neither one looked good for any work as they looked old, one of them almost sickly. The old farmer threw on the beaten saddles and fastened them, and Eric and I carefully mounted the horses and traveled uphill.

Up and up we went around curves and twists, going over rocks and through the mud. My worry for my horse was equivalent to that of a car with the gas hand below E and being nowhere near a gas station; but despite their condition, the horses moved effortlessly over the terrain. Outside of just holding on, there was not much need for guidance. They just took us.

At the top of the hill sat a lake and a stunning view of distant hills and valleys. We could even see the town of Silvia below. A few Silvian women relaxed by the lake, all sitting down as they conversed closely, as if they were sharing town gossip.

Neither Eric nor I could speak Spanish well as we approached the women, hoping by saying "photo" and mimicking a camera with our fingers they would understand our request to take a picture. From the shakes of their heads, we understood, too.

After returning the shockingly reliable horses to the farmer, Eric and I returned to town and tried once more to get a photo with a local. One man finally allowed us to take his picture, though, from his body language, he was unenthused. The unsmiling short man stood awkwardly with his arms dropped by his side as he waited. I felt bad that this probably happened often when tourists came to visit. It made me think of the women at the lake and the kids in San Cipriano. Could it be that they felt like their culture was being seen as a show? Like something on display?

"Gracias señor. Gracias señor," I said to the man. He gave a slight smile and went on about his day.

I regretted not knowing more Spanish. I knew it affected my experience. Being an outsider, I felt like I had something, some reasons for wanting to communicate and share with others. Back home, striking up a conversation with a total stranger was not something I did regularly. But there, I felt like I had something valuable, something worth sharing, even if I did not know exactly what it was. I could not put my finger on why I did not have this same feeling back home. After all, the people of Popayan were just like us.

13

Awareness

During my last couple of days in Popayan, I traveled to San Agustín, which housed the largest pre-Colombian archeological site in Latin America. It excited me to have a room to myself. As soon as I walked in, I threw my bags down and sprawled across the bed, relieved to have my own space and privacy. At least I knew I would not steal from myself.

While exploring the town, I strolled down a dirt road, passing makeshift houses of brick and tin. There was nothing special about the neighborhood until I came across some wall art. The art displayed stone artifacts floating out of the atmosphere and into space. It looked good enough to be on a wall somewhere in Bogotá. I walked further and spotted some graffiti that spelled out "Hip-Hop" with the word "Conscience" in Spanish under it, and above it "San Agustín art is not vandalism". Seeing this art confirmed that we are more alike than we are different. While we may be unable to communicate by language, that does not mean we cannot connect in other ways, like through music. Or even through something like basketball.

After spotting people hanging around a park a few streets over, I walked over to a roof-covered area as a couple of people sat on bleachers chatting away. On the other side, I saw a guy shooting basketball by himself. I walked over and stood by the goal and flicked my wrist.

"I can shoot?" I asked, hoping he understood my gesture.

He nodded, and we took turns shooting the ball.

It felt good playing basketball again; it used to be everything to me. Growing up, I would play every chance I got, during rain or even late hours of the night. It did not matter to me. Until that point, I could not remember the last time I picked up a ball.

Before long, the stranger and I started playing one-on-one. I missed the exhaustion of playing defense and trying to go after a loose ball. Checking the ball up and taking the ball back to the three-point line to reset. In that moment, I forgot about being a foreigner or even being in Colombia.

As time passed, the lights under the roof slowly came on. When I began to leave, the guy asked me, in Spanish, if I would be back the next day. I told him I would be leaving, in the best way I could, of course. We shook hands and nodded, and then I left.

Between the graffiti and playing basketball, it made me think again about how I wished I could speak Spanish and how I figured I had something valuable to share and receive. I finally realized that something was appreciation—to have a love for the encounter and the experience.

—

The next morning, I ventured to the archeological site located two miles away. The walk there felt better than coffee. Early morning dew and beams of morning light found their way through clouds over the distant hills, so gorgeous that I stopped to take a picture. I thought about how my grandmother and I used to take morning walks on the weekends, delighting in the morning humidity and southern air.

I spent about an hour and a half at the site, amazed at how well preserved and detailed the stone artifacts were. An adventure filled with recognizable carvings of birds, jaguars, and people concluded with a vast view from a hilltop.

Though gone for a day, it felt good to be back in Popayan. I met two more travelers from Minnesota, and they planned to leave for Ecuador the next day. Knowing I had done all I could do in Popayan, I decided to tag along. The trip would be a sixteen-hour bus ride.

Roads and hills were the only things between me and my destination as we drove around curves both high and low. I might have played almost all the music on my iPod: Big Krit, The Weeknd, D'Angelo, Alex Isley, Janelle Monae, and so many others. We made one stop for food that cost me more than I had expected: it left me with a bag of Doritos and a half bottle of water for dinner.

As we approached Ipiales, a city near the border of Colombia, we discussed if we should cross the border. I had heard it was never safe to cross the borders at night. There had been stories of people coming on and robbing buses as they stopped to go across. And the borders of Colombia and Ecuador were hot spots.

"I think imma let y'all have that one. I'll stay here tonight and will just cross in the morning," I told the couple from Minnesota.

"Hey, I understand. Maybe we'll catch ya around," one of the Minnesotans said.

Once we said our farewells, they were off.

As I walked around the confusing bus station, I weighed my options. My money had gotten low from the previous stop, and since it was Sunday, there was no place to exchange money. I would have to spend money for a taxi that would probably rip me off, *and* I would have to stay in a hostel. Because Ecuador used American money, I would have been able to spend money by exchanging it if I crossed the border. However, I knew never to cross the border at night because people would wait at border lines for foreign travelers.

Damn, maybe I should have left with them. At least I wouldn't have been alone, I thought.

After sitting with my thoughts a bit more, I decided, *Fuck it. I'll cross the border tonight.*

Section 3: Direction

Out in the ocean blue or under a starry view, I traveled with no guide.

Trekking up jagged land, running down desert sand, and admiring the valley side.

To be given all this space, how can I stay in one place? But deep down, I know that I'm lost.

More than protection, I could use some direction, but I do wonder if it comes with a cost.

Behind a glaze of morning fog, there's trees in every direction.

My eyes scan across this silk white curtain that has no rip or tear.

I'm neither scared nor worried as I've been as carefree as a plastic bag dancing in a summer's breeze.

It's quiet here, even when standing in the middle of extraverts with beer on their breath.

But I find myself taking more than a second to look up for directions.

How enjoyable is paradise when trying to follow the same pair of footprints on beach sand?

Unsure of what I seek, I recline on bus seats and go wherever I'm driven.

Asking myself: how does one find what they can't see in their mind, but the soul knows it's hidden?

14

Excitement

We arrived in Quito around 1 a.m. Still drowsy from the bus ride, I wasted no time grabbing a cab to head to a hostel. I forced my eyes open as we made our way through the lifeless city. I felt like a drunk passenger being taken home, so my forgetting I'd checked into the hostel did not surprise me when I woke up the next morning.

Groggily, I awoke to a room full of strangers in twin-size beds that looked more like someone's house than a hostel. I noticed polished wooden floors and homestyle furniture as I searched for the bathroom. Scrambled eggs, toast, and mixed fruit caught my eye as I wandered into the kitchen. I had only enough time to eat and look at a few brochures about the Galápagos Islands before I knew I wanted to change hostels. Though the hostel had a warm feeling, I wanted something more lively, especially after having just left what was practically a nursing home.

I booked a few nights at a hostel across the street called Vibes, and when I entered, the name of the hostel instantly met my expectations. Artwork covered the walls of the hostel; a bar, guitar, TV, pool table, foosball table, couches, and bean bag chairs occupied the lobby. Light even spilled into the lobby from two large square cutouts in the ceiling. I did not realize how many rooms the hostel had until the receptionist led me up to the roof where other rooms were available.

It was not long before I started mingling with other travelers. I gravitated toward a group of girls from Ireland and a guy from Australia with whom I spent most of my time in Quito, exploring whatever street we went down. From dining at restaurants to touring the city, it seemed like we went everywhere together. On one occasion at the hostel, we had a few beers and taught each other dances. I showed the girls the salsa I had learned, and they showed me some Irish dancing. I would have shown them "The Nae Nae" dance, but I was horrible at that shit.

One day, we all took a day trip to a hot spring about three hours away. I had never been to a hot spring before. My body wanted to melt like butter from its bliss as I lowered myself into the hot, steamy water. We thought we might have been the only ones in the spring due to the rain clouds forming in the sky, but we eventually spotted one couple.

We all introduced ourselves, learning that the guy hailed from the United Kingdom (U.K.). I was more interested in the girl with him who was from Washington, D.C., mainly because it was my first time seeing another black traveler. Finally seeing someone who looked like me exploring the world, I desired to spark another conversation, one where I felt like she could speak my language. Despite my curiosity, I did not barrage her with questions and decided to enjoy our time instead.

For a long while, we all chatted in the hot spring, relaxing in the hot water even after it began drizzling. As the rain began pouring, we started packing our things to leave.

We ran into a nearby restaurant across the street, dripping with water and laughing as we shook our clothes while the girls tended to their hair. The restaurant looked somewhat upscale as the guests and waiters eyed us closely. We stood collectively wearing damp clothes, towels either in hand or around our shoulders, as we waited for a ride.

After catching a ride to the bus station in a pickup truck and jumping on a bus back to the city, exhaustion was not strong enough to describe how I felt. I welcomed sleep that night until I woke up around 4 a.m. from sudden movements coming from the top bunk of my bed. As I listened to the subtle, sporadic rocks, it did not take me long to put two and two together. *Somebody having sex again*, I thought. I had gotten used to the idea that every so often people were going to have sex in the room. It was just going to happen.

I scanned the room, trying to see if anyone else might have been up, but I noticed something different about this time. There was not much movement, just small grunts from the girl above me. The covers had dampened the small light that came from under them, but it was strong enough to bounce off the ceiling and walls. And just like the light above my head, I realized she was alone, pleasuring herself.

The thought of this shocked me and aroused me as well. The urge of wanting to ask her if she needed any help warmed the pit of my stomach. It even influenced me to touch myself as I looked around to see if anyone could see me this time. It had already been a couple of months since the last time I had sex, so I did not mind being open to the idea. But before I knew it, her soft moans and subtle rocks had stopped. Then her little light followed shortly after. I lay there and pondered what she would have said if I would have asked to join. Would she have been ashamed? Possibly willing? Maybe upset? Regardless, she could not have been too disgusted because of her boldness to masturbate in a room full of strangers.

—

During my last couple of days in Quito, the Irish girls left for the Galápagos Islands, leaving the Australian guy and me behind. We visited one of the biggest attractions and the largest church in the city: The Basilica of San Juan. The concrete structure stretched high above what the locals considered the "old city" of Quito. The church seemed out of place in how miraculous it was. It looked like something from a Disney movie with its carefully carved arches and stone cutouts. Its enormous glass windows reflected various colors of light. Marble floors met our feet as we entered. Even our voices echoed as we toured the immense cathedral. We climbed stairs and ladders to reach the top, which ended with a remarkable view of the city: a landscape of hills covered with buildings all around.

We ended our trip with a visit to the equator, which ran right across the city. While there, I overheard a group of middle schoolers from the U.S. The sight of them baffled me for a few reasons. One, it was still during the school year. Two, we were in the middle of the equator. And three, seeing U.S. school kids when I had been around foreigners and living out of a bag for six weeks blew my mind.

What program is this? What in the hell do your parents do? I thought.

Though they might not have appreciated the experience until later in life, it was amazing to see the kids doing something extraordinary at a young age. Out of eleven students, however, there was not a single black kid in sight, not a single one, nor any other race for that matter. It would be nice for kids of color to be exposed to world travel as well. Back home, traveling to Atlanta or Charlotte made us think we had been somewhere, but there was so much more to see. And I wish there were more opportunities for us to do so.

—

Days for me in Quito were fun, even more so at the hostel than outside. My days consisted of drinking beers, sharing stories, meeting people, playing pool, and going around the hostel shooting each other with silly strings. Amidst all this fun, I knew it would not last forever. One day, the fun and freedom would end.

More importantly, I wanted to learn more about myself. What I liked, what I did not like. What I was more attracted to. And honestly, I did not feel like I was learning anything. Hoping to make sense of it all, I continued jotting down my thoughts in my journal.

I've been gone for six weeks and the biggest progress I've made was getting on the plane. Which is huge, but when it comes to progress spiritually, I don't feel any different. I want to become my own person, my own man, to find my purpose, my passion, my drive, to find some kind of awakening. The things that are important in life. I have a long trip ahead of me. I miss family and friends and I'm sure they miss me as well. I want to travel forever. One because I love it, and two because I don't know what to do when I get home. I have no plans. I guess I'll just work a part-time job and try to think of my own business. I miss music and songwriting. I want to learn how to play an instrument and learn a language. So much I want to do. I just hope God sees fit for me to do it all. So I stay humble and thankful. I'm in search of balance. I search for strength, for willpower, for discipline, for patience. I have such a long way to go; I don't care that I'm using so many I's. I search for peace of mind. I search for perspective. I search and I search and I will keep searching. And I will search for me and I.

Baños was the name of my next destination, which means bathroom in Spanish. Located about four hours south of Quito by bus, it was the place where plenty of thrill-seekers traveled.

Every morning, a white van pulled up to the hostel for anyone seeking adventures like kayaking and zip lining, just to name a few. Each day offered a different activity. And sure enough, on my first morning at the house, I spotted a white van parked out front with the door open. I decided to go investigate as two men prepared the van while awaiting guests.

"Hola, where you guys going this morning?"

The driver looked over his black shades as he turned around. "Canyoning. You coming?"

"Canyoning? Oh okay. Uhhh, sure I'll go." *What the fuck is canyoning?*

I had never heard of canyoning, but my assumption led me to believe we would be walking around canyon-type terrain. *If anything, I should be about to see some cool views*, I thought.

Minutes later, I found myself along with six others being issued wetsuits and helmets.

"Do you guys know how to swim?" one of the men asked.

What the hell is going on?

I had never been an avid fan of getting in the water, so my imagination never even veered into thinking about needing wetsuits and helmets to get in it. Being that we were far out from the hostel now, I could not turn back around. Jitters started creeping into my bones while everyone else appeared relaxed, chatting away. I remained alert as we approached our destination.

We arrived in time to watch another group advance up the moss-covered stones of the canyon. We changed clothes right outside of the van and slipped into our wetsuits as the rain began pouring.

"Listen, I do not know how to swim, bro," I admitted to one guide.

"No problem, man; you will be fine with life jacket."

How deep is this damn water? I pondered, wondering what to expect.

I soon learned what awaited me: jumping off twenty-four-foot cliffs, plunging into pools of water, rappelling down rushing waterfalls, and zip-lining. What began as a frightening experience slowly turned into one of the best experiences. Chilled canyon water flowed from our ankles up to our hips at times, water so clear that you could see the smooth stones and rocks that shifted below the soles of our feet. Fearful of getting sick, I tried my best not to get any water in my mouth, but it was inevitable. And after a while, I stopped caring. I was too busy enjoying the feeling of being like Tomb Raider again, making our way through this watery crack of earth.

On the last waterfall we rappelled down, I knew how I needed to position myself to rappel safely.

"Okay, friend, lean back in a sitting position. Once you get close to the water, let go of the rope and fall straight back," the guide instructed.

"Alright." I leaned back into a sitting position and started making my way down.

"Nice. Stop. Let's get your picture right there," shouted the guide from above.

I posed giving a thumbs-up as the water from the fall splashed so closely that I needed to squint.

After he took the snapshot, I continued making my way back down. Right at about three-fourths of the way, I let go of the rope and fell back into the water. I landed in the water as the force of the fall began pulling me down unexpectedly. *Did I land too close?* I wondered.

And in the course of the fall, my harness slipped loose and before I knew it, my ankles had gotten tangled in the harness. I could not kick my feet freely to avoid being sucked in by the fall. Though I tried my best not to panic, I knew this was not good.

"Hey! My feet are caught! My feet are stuck!" I yelled, but to no avail. The guys standing on the other side could not hear me; the crashing water canceled out any noise I made.

Hoping to keep my head above water, I wiggled my feet as much as I could to loosen the harness. Soon after, the others began realizing something was not right with me being out for so long. I got as close as I could to the wall of rock beside me to alleviate the force of the waterfall. In doing so, the force of the pouring water helped knock the tangled harness loose from my feet. I bobbed my way back to the bank relieved to reach the other canyoners.

"Whew. You okay? What happen?"

"I don't know, man. My harness came off." I looked back at the waterfall again, thanking God it did not turn out as bad as it could have as the orange-colored harness washed up on the bank beside me.

Two days later, a few people at the hostel brought up the idea of bungee jumping, which I damn sure did not have any intention of doing. I had heard about freak accidents that happened with bungee jumping: a malfunction with the harness, someone not fastening the clamps on properly, or something becoming loose or popping. And it would be my luck that the same shit would happen to me. But strangely enough, part of my imagination thought about how dope it would be to do it. Even when I agreed to go, it still seemed like it was not part of the plan. When the group was ready to go, the pit of my stomach churned as I trailed behind them.

As I stood there preparing to take the leap, the fact that this was going to happen became more prevalent like a constant wind that was no longer obstructed by buildings. Just like there was nothing in my way on the platform attached to the bridge we were approaching. Knowing I was preparing to dive off it, the gusts of wind added to my jitters.

I placed my hand on the railing as I leaned over to see what 200 meters looked like. Below roared the rushing waters of Río Pastaza, which competed with the wind for the loudest sound.

Reluctantly, I inched toward the bridge. I told the workers I wanted to jump, but I did not want to. I asked them to secure the harness around me, but I did not want to.

I listened as other travelers cheered each other on as they took turns jumping, ending with elated shouts as the next person prepared to jump. Fully aware that each person who jumped was one less in front of me, I repeatedly heard, "3 . . . 2 . . . 1 . . . Go!"

There was no way I could do this. I had reached a wall. I could not mentally bring myself to see anything past standing on the bridge with my harness on.

"Hey, you alright, mate?" one of the hostel guests asked.

"Yeah, I'm good, bruh. I cannot believe I'm about to do this. This is crazy. Ain't no way, bruh," I replied.

"Aw, you'll be fine, mate. No worries."

But I could not help myself or it. I continued to tell myself, "It's just no way."

This type of bungee differed from traditional bungee jumping. It neither bounced nor stretched; it swung. Instead of jumping straight down, I would have to thrust myself off the platform for the safest momentum to swing. Failure to do so could send your nuts straight to your stomach.

"3 . . . 2 . . . 1 . . . Go!"

For every person who dropped, my stomach dropped with them. My hand caressed my abdomen, trying to soothe the uneasy sensation happening behind it. I was next. Hoisting myself over the railing onto the six-foot platform, my body moved smoothly as though sure of itself, but my mind had broken out into chaos.

Nothing appeared in front of me except an open view of God's work. No boundaries, no barriers, just the world out in open space. People behind me spoke what might have been words of encouragement, but their words went unheard. The wind blew so hard that my shirt flailed and whipped wildly as if it wanted to remove itself from my body. Every few seconds, I looked back at the faces of my supporters with their confident eyes and wide smiles, envious of their lack of worry. I hunched over with my hands on my knees, too weak and too frightened to stand up straight.

The voice of one of the bungee workers broke through the whistling wind. "Mi amigo put the cable in front of you."

I clinched the cable connected to my harness and placed it at the edge of the platform, noticing the drop that lay before me as I did so.

"I can't do this . . . It's just no way."

The wind kept me and my stomach off balance as I wanted to vomit. Why was I doing this? Why was I putting myself through this torture?

"3 . . . 2 . . . 1 . . . Go!"

I attempted to jump for a split second, but my shoes felt like they had been soldered to the platform. It only made things harder as voices stirred over my shoulder again.

"Just run, run and dive, run and dive, man."

"Aye, you got it, mate."

"Oh yeah, you got it, man. You got it!"

All I could think about was, *What if something happened to me? What if something goes wrong? What would my dad do if he found out that his son died in a bungee accident on his birthday? What would my brother say if he found out his brother died a day after his birthday?*

But I did not want to die. I wanted to live. It was what I always wanted, what we all want. And there I was, standing about 650 feet in the air staring at death in the form of disturbed water. It was fear: the same fear that molded me. The same fear we struggle with daily, the fear of not letting go and just letting things be.

For the majority of my upbringing, my decisions had been based on fear. Fear of not being enough and not being accepted. Fear of being unable to please others. Fear of being judged. Fear of feeling like I was voiceless and unable to make my own decisions. But I had this need to go against the grain. That was the reason why I quit my job. It was the reason why I bought a one-way plane ticket. It was the reason why I wanted to jump. Because maybe, just once, I could choose to be brave.

"3 . . . 2 . . . 1 . . . Go!"

As soon as the thought left my mind, a moment of calmness washed over me as I stretched my arms and dove.

For the next five seconds, I felt weightless. I knew I had fallen, but my body could not respond. I did not feel a thing, no worries, no pain, no problems, just space and freedom. When the bungee reached its end, a rush of wind met me mid-swing and broke me out of my dreamlike trance. Instantly, my senses heightened like I had been rejuvenated or born again. I could hear cheering high above me as I swung from one side of the bridge to the next. Eccentric wasn't the word. Shaken with excitement, I felt like I wanted to explode. It felt better than any drug, any drink, any pleasure, and I could not stop smiling. Something I had never dreamed of doing, I had done, and I cherished that moment.

Taking that leap showed me I was braver than I thought, even if only for a moment. Though the journey of life is an ongoing war, I knew that day I had won the battle, at least. It was a gigantic leap for me to step out on faith and to work on myself.

—

Before heading to Montañita, a city on the beach with no more than seven streets, I heard talks about ayahuasca again from a traveler from the U.K. I first caught wind of this brew right before leaving Bogotá, overhearing a conversation at the hostel about how this plant-based psychedelic could change your life. I did not think much of it at the time, except as an opportunity for people to get high on something. But there I was hearing about it again. The traveler told me about an ayahuasca retreat in Iquitos, Peru called Dreamglade.

"There you can stay for several days and participate in ayahuasca ceremonies. They will take care of all of your accommodations," he explained.

"Is it as tough as I've heard people say it is?" I asked.

"They say once you've done it, you're never really the same again. But a place like Dreamglade is one of the best retreats in Peru. I hear nothing but good things."

"Yeah, I may give it a shot."

"Well, if you do it, my only advice would be don't fight it. Just surrender."

Growing more curious, I pondered his words over my last two days in Baños. During that time, I had the pleasure of seeing Ty and Troy, who had just arrived from Montañita. They mentioned how relaxed the city was; the people chilled during the day, partied at night, did drugs between the two, and surfed to pass the time. After my misadventures in Baños, I could use some relaxation on the Beach of Montañita.

—

The sun shined directly over me when I stepped off the bus onto the streets of Montañita. Dry heat and sunshine forced me to squint my eyes as I walked. Mostly everyone walked around in tank tops, swim shorts, and sandals, a few of them wearing hats and shades.

I trudged through the heatwave temperature to the hostel, Chill House, where, to my surprise, I crossed paths with the Australian I had met in Quito. We chatted for a bit, and he told me the girls from Ireland had left just the day before.

The Chill House was exactly that. Chill. An outside hostel where the only inside parts were our rooms. Hammocks were tied to bamboo trees and wooden pillars. Bamboo tables, bench swings, and chair swings comprised the main part of the hostel. Though the setup certainly lived up to its name, I would soon find out that things would not always be so chill for me.

15

Isolation

Outside of hitting the beach, making money entered my mind when I arrived in Montañita. I figured if I could decrease my spending or earn some cash, then I could travel longer. I could not volunteer at the hostel because they already had enough help, so saving money went straight out of the window. As I continued to plot, I spent most of my time enjoying Montañita.

When I was not staring at large iguanas crossing the street, or trying to avoid getting peed on as they laid high on tree branches, I lounged on the beach. It became a place of relief from mosquitos even though it seemed only a few yards away from my hostel.

Like a revolving door, people would go in the water, and people would come out. Some carried their surfboards to ride waves and others went in just to cool off. There might have been more business on the beach than on the street as vendors walked up and down soliciting customers. They sold everything from fresh coconuts to handmade bracelets to pepperoni pizza. Some sold more than food and drinks; one vendor offered me weed and cocaine a few times.

That was the lifestyle of Montañita. People searched for a vibe all day every day. But more than anything, I looked forward to the sunset. Back home, we faced the Atlantic, so we could only see the sunrise from the ocean, but being that Montañita faced the Pacific, I finally had a chance to see the sunset on the water.

Though everyone could have been from anywhere in the world, with different languages and cultural backgrounds, everyone would gather on the beach and watch the sun set. Appreciating the one part of the day that never seemed to get old. Gazing upon the orange circle in the sky. It was like God's grand finale at the end of each day, having His amber ball of fire ease its way down behind the edge of the earth.

—

In between my beach visits, I continued looking for work. I almost landed two jobs as a waiter, but they required me to speak Spanish. One of the guys back at the hostel mentioned that he knew someone who could offer me a job. When I asked about the job, he told me the pay would be crappy but I would get to walk the beach and see chicks all day. After making sure the job did not involve me selling cocaine, I thought about it a bit longer and decided if I was going to walk a hot ass beach all day, I was going to at least sell something I wanted to sell: lemonade.

During my high school days, I used to work at the University of South Carolina football games as a vendor on weekends. I walked up and down the stadium steps surrounded by 80,000 screaming fans with a rack of cups filled with lemonade shouting, "Lemonade! Lemonade! Get ya lemonade!" It was not too bad of a gig; I got in the games for free and was allowed to keep the leftover lemonade.

The more I thought about it, the more it made sense. Besides, no one sold lemonade. I decided I would make and sell my own lemonade on the beach, which would sell without question. It seemed like the perfect plan, that is, until I learned lemons were not a native fruit of Ecuador.

Once I adjusted my plans to reflect my new venture, limeade, I walked down to a small market and bought my supplies: limes, sugar, ice, cups, and a Styrofoam cooler with a strap. After making a few batches to perfect the flavor, I asked some people to taste the limeade to get their thoughts. Once I got their approval, off to the beach I went.

Before I left, I drew a logo on my cooler to create my brand. I drew a picture of a lime with sunglasses and wrote the word "Limonada" under it, which I think I misspelled. I always had a slight interest in starting a small business but struggled to pinpoint a specific area. My limeade business seemed like the perfect opportunity to test the waters.

By the close of my short business day, my earnings roughly equaled up to two meals and a beer. I did not sell nearly as much limeade as I had hoped because the ice melted before I even got settled on the beach. Even though the idea was good, and I had given it a good effort, my selling days were over.

—

Every morning I wrote in my journal, or at least tried to. I often trekked to the beach to write, mainly because it was the best place to catch a breeze and I did not have to worry about slapping mosquitos every five seconds. It was easy to see how someone could spend so much time in Montañita. It made you feel like you had no responsibilities. I wondered if that was how retirement felt.

At night, I would go out to the beach when I needed a break from people. I would think about my life and where it was headed. How fortunate I was to be sitting on the beach sands of Montañita. Although the sand felt just as cool and fine as the sand in Myrtle Beach, and the ocean air coming from the Pacific smelled like that from the Atlantic, I seemed to appreciate it more in Montañita. Running my fingers through the sands, grabbing a soft clump of reality, and letting the cool breeze blow it out of my palm let me know this experience was real. I was actually there.

Sadness would wash over me as I stared out into the dark sea; I wanted to share those moments with my friends and family.

I wished they could experience those things with me. In some weird way, it felt less real without them. Like I could not make the connection between where I was and what I had always known. I had traveled over 2,000 miles away from home and still felt the need to search for an answer without knowing what question to ask. And in the next two days, I would be even farther, crossing over to Peru.

While I enjoyed being in Montañita, I had done all I could do there. Besides, Montañita was expensive compared to other places I had been. With this thought reminding me that I had run out of smaller bills, I decided to walk down the beach one last time to the Western Union a few streets over. I walked in to find only one lady, sitting behind a desk.

"Cambio? Change? Can I get change?" I asked, holding up a hundred-dollar bill.

"No, no, no," the lady objected as she shook her head.

I stood there confused, thinking maybe she did not have enough to break the bill. The lady picked up the phone and continued on as if I had already left, so I did. Though I walked out a bit disappointed, thankfully I had enough money to get to my next destination.

Though I had hoped to see that last bit of sunshine before I left, the clouds had definitely set in both literally and figuratively. Just a few yards from my hostel, two police officers sped toward me on motorcycles, one holding a gun in his hand.

Immediately, I froze in my tracks, and my brain shifted into autopilot. I raised my hands to my shoulders as the officers got off their bikes.

"Pasaporte," they demanded.

I reached for my passport and handed it to the officer who held the gun, confused about why they had stopped me. My eyes followed his gun until he put it away. I looked around as bystanders stared from the street and out of building windows. The owner of my hostel even came outside to scope out the situation.

One of the officers pointed at my pockets and my shoes, wanting to check them. The other one asked me something I did not understand.

"I don't know what you asking," I said, shrugging my shoulders.

"He say, 'Do you have drug?'" someone translated from the window of a nearby hostel.

The officer put two fingers to his lips and said, "Marijuana."

Do I have drugs? Why the hell does he think I have drugs?

"No señor. No marijuana."

The thought of why he believed I had drugs puzzled me. Then the answer hit me like a ton of bricks. *Did the Western Union lady call the police on me? 'Cause a hundred-dollar bill? Can't be. Right? No, it had to be her. She thought I sold drugs?*

When the police finished harassing me, they let me go, and I hurried over to my hostel. My choice to leave Montañita could not have come at a better time. I thought about that all the way to Guayaquil, Ecuador. The suspicion that the lady behind the desk assumed I sold drugs just because I had a large bill got under my skin. Unfortunately, things like that happened all the time back in the States, more so to People of Color, which sometimes ended tragically. All because of the assumption that someone had something or was something solely because of their appearance. It was a gamble being dark-complexioned back home, a lottery where you did not want your number called.

For the next three hours, I sat in the food court awaiting my bus. While there, I caught sight of one food business that rubbed me the wrong way. The business logo featured an image of a monkey with a bone in the shape of a fork in its hair, Menestra Del Negro, which translated to Stew of the Black. Wondering if the logo was supposed to portray a Black person left me in a gray area of thinking. Jokingly, I thought to myself that the food they were serving was not even soul food. *Who in the hell eats beans with*

137

eggs? My brief lightness of the situation gradually faded away, hoping that the locals did not view Black people in that way.

Hours later, I arrived at the Peruvian border. The night rain poured steadily as I stood in line, still sleepy from being woken up to get stamped in. I had gotten comfortable with just packing up and leaving. I wore my four travel bracelets proudly as I began molding myself into a seasoned traveler.

—

Day was breaking when I arrived in Mancora, Peru. Normally, I would walk outside of the bus terminal in search of a taxi, but this was the first time drivers were in search of me. Eight cab drivers greeted me, all trying to persuade me to use their taxi. Their enthusiasm impressed me. I got a kick out of saying where I was going and then hearing a burst of voices trying to talk over the next. They even held up their hands and fingers to display their cost. I noticed one older gentleman in the back, quietly watching all the commotion. *There's my driver*, I thought. Then off we went, scooting through the not yet busy streets in a three-wheeled buggy.

The slight mist in the air made the morning more refreshing. Dogs roamed the roads as we passed by unfinished buildings with tin and thatched rooftops. Handmade fences of sticks and wire guarded fields of grass and dirt. Everything seemed pleasant.

When we arrived, I noticed the hostel sat behind a tall wooden gate with low trees that hung right above the door. A sleepy receptionist welcomed me and gave me a rundown of the services they offered. When he told me they offered laundry services, I quickly handed over my dirty clothes, relieved to know I would have some fresh laundry. He showed me to my room, and I eased my way in, trying not to disturb the other slumbering guests.

Mancora felt just as hot as Montañita, but it was not nearly as lively. I did not have a problem with it, but strangely, I knew I would not be there for long. Not because the beach was not as well kept as the one in Montañita, having washed-up debris alongside the shore, but it just did not have that "stay here" feel. I still entertained the idea of working, but I knew it would not be there.

Though at another hostel, a few friends were in Mancora as well, which made my stay more enjoyable. Regan, who I had met in Quito, Baños, and again while in Montañita, had messaged me to meet up. She had volunteered as a bartender and would be there for a few days. To my surprise, not only did I see Regan, but I also saw the Irish girls I met in Quito, as well as Ty and Troy. Needless to say, I spent more time at their hostel than mine.

While Regan worked the bar one evening, I asked her about the hostel requiring its guests to leave their wallets and phones at the door of the bar before heading back for the night. She told me it was the hostel's way of protecting us from getting robbed. Not long after that conversation, I heard a story from an Irish guy who had gotten robbed of his phone one night. The crazy thing is, he ended up running into the robber the next day and confronting him. What's even crazier is that the robber gave him his phone back. Either the robber was dumb enough to come back to the beach the next day, or maybe there was such a thing as the luck of the Irish.

—

Toward the end of my stay in Mancora, I received some bad news. My grandfather's neighbor, Mr. B, had passed away, yet another loss that hurt me deeply. When I was growing up, Mr. B played basketball with me, treated me with pieces of candy here and there, and always had the funniest laugh. It felt like things were moving so fast back home while things just drifted in South America. I roamed around freely with no place to be, carrying a bag of clothes and a handful of perspectives.

Ty and Troy prepared to head back home after receiving their own bad news. I had met up with Ty and his dad throughout most of my trip. As many people as I had met and had to leave on my trip, knowing I would not run into them again hurt the most.

Before leaving, Ty gifted me a small bag of weed. Even though I did not smoke, oddly, I was grateful for his gesture. It made me think about how life was like this unstoppable object we cling on to that moves in whatever space it is given. And no matter where or how we hold on, our experiences of ups and downs can be opposite at any given time, like the flailing of feathers at the end of a bird's wing even though it heads in one direction.

On the same day, Kendrick Lamar released his album *To Pimp a Butterfly*. As a music lover, nothing felt more relatable at the time than that album. With me being out in the world while family and loved ones faced issues back home, remorse of leaving had already set in. My feelings felt similar to Kendrick's, trying to cope with receiving a taste of this new journey while struggling with being away from the people and things I had always known.

I sat outside by the bar with one of the hostel workers, to whom I gifted the weed, while we played the album on some old computer speakers. The combined sounds of jazz, funk, and hip-hop were like surgical instruments operating to allow the lyrics to come in and heal the soul.

—

Once my friends left, Mancora turned dull. Not only did it become dull, but I also noticed these strange looks from people. Sure, I had walked around with my shirt off sometimes, but I had certainly seen others do the same. Then I thought, as silly as it sounded, *Is this their first time seeing a Black person?* I guess that would have been an uncommon thing to see, because there was no one remotely close to my complexion there. As I walked down the main street, passing local shops, people stared uncomfortably long as I strolled by. However, I figured the next day I would not have to worry about it because I would be in a new city.

It began raining as I loaded my bags into the three-wheeled buggy to head back to the bus station, thankful the rain had cooled the temperature. I found it funny how over a couple of days, the once energetic people I saw when I first arrived now just stared and looked at me.

My next stop would be Huanchaco, Peru. Since my last two stops had been beach locations, I told myself this would be my last one for a while.

16

Displacement

I arrived at my hostel around 9 a.m., curious about what Huanchaco offered. The small, peach-colored building sat between a long strip of concrete and unfinished, cement brick buildings, which looked like a poor version of Miami beach. The beach sand nearly covered the road, as it came up to just where the hostel property lay. Honestly, it looked as though none of the places kept any business. I walked into the half hostel, half restaurant building, instantly knowing I was the only guest.

To my surprise, I glimpsed another backpack on one of the beds when I entered my room. While going through my normal routine of contacting my family and connecting to the Wi-Fi, a girl named Ele walked in and greeted me.

Ele was from Greece, and she had been traveling by herself for some time. We talked for a good while, discussing our travels, her obsession with Costa Rica, and her desire to go back. Being that Ele and I were the only ones at the hostel, we did not bother discussing if we were going to hang out. Together, we roamed the streets, tried ceviche for the first time, and visited a nearby archeological tour site.

Despite being surrounded by beautiful history, I could not concentrate on it. Something else occupied my thoughts. Something that troubled me. Something I noticed while walking down the street with Ele. Something I noticed on the tour. More stares from people. But this time it annoyed me more than it did in Mancora. Some people even smiled, and not in a welcoming way. It threw off my mood entirely. Even people from other small groups of the tour looked over to catch a glimpse. Were those people distracted by my skin color? Did it bother them that much?

There I stood with my skinny limbs extending out of my white t-shirt and cargo shorts, trying to pose as Ele prepared to take my picture. I struggled to focus on the camera and smile while trying not to worry about the spectators. I did not mention anything to Ele about it, knowing she would not understand. The situation made me want to leave on the first day.

On our way back to the hostel, a guy stopped us on the street.

"Hey, you guys need a good restaurant to eat at? Are you all from out of town?" he asked.

Obviously, I thought, though it impressed me how clear his English was.

"Yes. I am from Greece," Ele said.

"I'm from the States," I added.

"Welcome, I'm Hector. I'm Colombian, but I used to live in New York."

Oh, that explains it.

"You guys should come to check out my restaurant when you have some time. It's right here across the street. We serve the best ceviche in town."

"Oh nice. Okay. We'll make sure to do that," I replied.

Hector treated us friendly as we stood chatting, still insisting that we come back and visit his restaurant. He seemed like an honest person. *Maybe this is a good opportunity to talk to a business owner? Coming from the States and having a business in a different country, he has to have some insightful knowledge.* The following day, I decided to go talk to Hector about starting a business.

We sat at the top of his restaurant, looking out into the endless ocean as people sauntered down below. It was easily the tallest building in Huanchaco as it towered over its neighboring buildings, sticking out like a sore thumb. The breeze complimented the evening sunshine as we sat in two wooden chairs, chatting about entrepreneurship.

"How'd you start your business?" I asked. "I feel I want to start something of my own, but I don't know what really."

"To be honest, amigo, in some ways the business made itself. I started out doing an adult club, then I noticed people enjoyed the food. So I focused more on that, plus it was a lot of hassle running an adult club. Before I knew it, people started coming in to exchange money. So, I started to get into exchanging money as well. The biggest thing I learned was to just go with the flow of business. Hell, you might start doing one thing, but end up doing another depending on the needs of the consumer," Hector explained.

I had never thought of it that way before, but it did make sense.

"I feel ya. Not sure where would be good to start, though," I replied.

Hector suggested doing business with him selling "Jordan" shoes in a collaborative effort. Being that no one could get their hands on them there, I could ship Jordans to him, and he could sell them and split the profit.

How he came up with that idea is beyond me, and I was not too thrilled about it. I sat listening to Hector a bit longer then randomly asked a question that I did not expect to come up.

"Hector, do you know if people here have something against black people, or like darker-colored people? I've just been noticing these funny looks from the locals."

After I left the archeological tour, the questionable looks I received still bothered me. Even as I walked to meet Hector, people in groups grinned and alerted others around them as I passed. Why was I noticing this now? Had people *been* looking at me this way? Ernesto and Ruben had not. Gustavo, Romel, and his roommates had not. Even Jefe and his goons had not. I figured Hector had been there long enough to know how locals felt about darker people.

He paused for a moment to think.

"Hmm, no amigo, I don't know why they would do that. Maybe they're just trying to figure you out because you are different and that you are a tourist." He continued, "Back in Colombia, it's people of all kinds of shades. Complexions from my shade to yours."

Though his statement made me think about the dark-complexioned people in San Cipriano, I suspected it had to have been more than just "trying to figure me out." I knew when someone was laughing at you. I had experienced this same laughter in grade school. Growing up, my nose was much flatter than most kids, and I was called "flat face," "ninja turtle," and even "Chris Rock," a reference I never understood. But being mocked because of my dark skin in a country full of people with different shades baffled me.

Shortly after, I thanked Hector for the talk and decided to head back to the hostel.

As I walked on the beach, a patrol car eased up right beside me. I looked over at the officer, who had already rolled down his window.

"Dónde?" the officer asked, asking where I was from.

"Estados Unidos. Cocos Beach Hostel," I responded.

145

"Está bein."

After giving me his approval, he nodded and drove off.

I simply walked down the beach, listening to music while drinking water, and I got questioned. At that moment I thought about a shirt my favorite rapper Andre 3000 wore once that read, "Across cultures, darker people suffer the most. Why?" I asked myself the same question.

When things seemed like they could not have gotten any worse, I got word that one of my good friends back home had been arrested. Disappointment, anger, and hurt were just a few emotions that I experienced. Even though I felt complete by following my dream of traveling, I knew when I returned home, pieces of my life would be gone.

—

Later on, Ele and I went to the beach to watch the sunset. As I watched the majestic display, a few locals watched as well. I could not help but wonder if they would have noticed me if the sunset did not have their attention. Would they have noticed that I reveled in God's amber ball of fire easing behind the edge of the earth as much as them? That I, too, cherished the day's grand finale? The question of whether the remaining places I visited would be this way lingered in my mind. I hoped to God not.

On the morning of my and Ele's last day, we relaxed at the beach as she laid out to get a tan. I listened to Kendrick's *To Pimp A Butterfly* (*TPAB*) album, which in a couple of days had made its way to my top five favorite hip-hop albums of all time.

"Ele, did you make up your mind if you're going back to Costa Rica?" I asked, still wondering about what the locals thought of black people.

"Yeah, I miss it there. It was expensive, but it's so beautiful there. It's where I belong. I used to work there as well. So I messaged my old boss, and he said I could get my job back. So I think I'm going for it. I feel like I belong there."

"Well, I'm glad that worked out for you. That's all you talk about."

"Haha. Where are you heading next?"

"It will be Lima for me. I need a break from the beach." *And hopefully these damn looks.* "Plus, it will be nice to visit a big city since Lima is the capital," I continued.

"Nice. Yeah, that would be a nice change of pace."

It felt good knowing that I would be heading to another city that was not a beach. I could only hope that things would get better along the way.

Later that night, Ele and I said our goodbyes. Then I caught my bus, and she caught her flight. I realized that if I had not met Ele, my time in Huanchaco would have been horrible, and probably shorter. I was glad I had someone there with me.

While traveling to Lima, I listened to more of Kendrick's *TPAB*. I thought about the hundred-dollar bill, the police stops, the monkey logo, the stares, the laughs. I wondered if things would be the same or get worse because they had not gotten better. Though I sat on a night bus peering out of the window, I also knew I was holding onto an unstoppable object that was moving in whatever space it was given. And I was experiencing its ups and downs.

17

Yearning

For the next few hours, I walked, and walked, and walked, engulfed in the heart of Lima and its massive infrastructure and innumerable businesses. *Did I just get dropped back off in the States?* I thought. Had I not known where I was, I could have sworn someone had taken me back to Western civilization. With me now being shadowed by tall buildings and feeling cautious of passing traffic, it felt like I had completely left South America. I was sure this place had a Starbucks around one of its corners.

I searched for the places the receptionist recommended I should visit. The recommendations led me to walk several blocks and board multiple buses, which made me uneasy about getting back.

On my list of stops, the zoo had been one of the last ones before I headed back to the hostel. I knew what to expect, but while there, I found something I did not know I would cherish. A section of the zoo displayed different plants and trees, with one species being the cedar tree. The cedar trees reminded me of the ones back home in my mom's yard; even the smell made me miss home. I reached out and touched one, wondering what my mom was doing. Even if it was for a moment, I appreciated seeing the cedar trees more than anything I had seen the entire day.

By the time I returned from all the walking and bus riding, it seemed like I had just finished a full day of work. Proud of myself for not getting lost while heading back to my side of town, I ended the day by watching the sunset. My hostel was near a park on the edge of a cliff that overlooked the Pacific Ocean. Feeling exhausted, I plopped down on a park bench and peered out into the water.

Before long, cool breezes came off the ocean as the sunlight disappeared. Not only did the sun eventually leave, but it also left me thinking about everything. Family, friends, my trip, how far I had come, my purpose, my homeboy and his arrest, those funny looks, Mr. B, Aunt Mary. *Was this a bad decision? Should I not be here? Things weren't supposed to be like this. Maybe I shouldn't have gone on this trip*, I thought. I did not envision my trip being this way. Eventually, the ocean's breeze turned my warm tears into cool trickles down my face.

I figured my therapist Kendrick would know what to say. I listened to *TPAB* for the eighth time back at the hostel. Songs like "I", "Alright," and "Complexion" became shoulders for me to lean on, guides for a disturbed and lost traveler. Kendrick's lyrics of encouragement and self-love felt as much needed as the shoes I wore. Funny how I found myself in the middle of traveling, still needing an escape. I needed to write. I needed to talk to someone. So I figured I would talk to myself on paper.

For the next two days, I sat on the same bench as before, writing from midday to sunset, leaving only for food. I learned two things while writing. One, what I needed was a mental journey, not a physical one. Even if what I wrote made sense or not, I needed to explore it in that way. And two, I had nothing to do in Lima. There were museums and touristic activities but nothing fulfilling.

As I prepared to finish up some writing, looking forward to another sunset, a guy around my age came to sit on the opposite end of the bench. I preferred some space, but I appreciated him starting a conversation. After my experience with the staring locals for the past couple of days, it gave me a breath of fresh air.

149

"What are you writing?" he asked.

"Mainly about the day. I'm keeping a journal of my trip, but just anything that comes to mind. I write music here as well sometimes. Kinda a hobby of mine," I explained.

"That is good. Right now, I am learning the Hebrew language, and I'm also in theater. I dream to be an actor. I am in school for that."

"Oh, that is excellent. I believe everyone has some type of artist in them, whether it be writing or acting, or drawing. Keep going with that," I encouraged him.

"Yes, thank you. It is my passion." He paused. "Do you have any weed?"

I stared at the stranger for a moment, wondering where that came from.

"No. No, I don't have any weed," I replied.

"Oh, okay, okay, claro."

Shortly after, the conversation ended, and the stranger left just as suddenly as he had appeared.

Could that have been what people saw me as? A drug dealer? Were they associating me with drugs? I thought back to when those two officers stopped me in Ecuador. The idea of them assuming that was who I was confused me. Did they think all black people were drug dealers or something? Though Lima reminded me of home, I quickly realized it was not.

On my last night in Lima, I hung out with a few of the guests, some of whom I had met previously and considered friends. Somewhere between typical travel talk and people's sex chronicles, I realized something. You might not always find yourself in places that treat you how you should be treated, but you can certainly surround yourself with the people who do. Being around good people made everything else irrelevant. They created an oasis in deserts deprived of belonging. And ironically enough, my next destination would be an actual desert.

I decided to travel south of Lima to Huacachina, Peru, after seeing a flyer at the hostel offering sandboarding there. Even though I did not imagine Peru having a desert, the change of scenery sparked my interest.

On the way there, I stopped in the city of Paracas to see the Islas Ballestas, The Ballestas Islands. With two boats full of people and several minutes of crossing water, hoping the morning fog would clear, we found ourselves staring at a mountain of rock. Sea lions covered the rocks at the base and birds around the top. And from the stench, bird shit covered them as well. The Islands looked like they had buckets of white paint splattered on them that had begun to turn yellow over time. Birds with blue feet popped out from the contrasting rust-colored rocks, while the seals lay sprawled out below as our boats circled the rocks. Even penguins propped themselves up against the jagged rock formations.

The peculiar scene looked like a hot mess, and the stench did not help. I pulled out my phone to record the mounds of rock when suddenly bird shit fell on my shoulder from a passing bird. Though upset, I needed to laugh at myself.

Anxious to see the desert, I wasted no time purchasing my ticket to Huacachina once we arrived back on land. With my bus rides in Peru, I had become used to seeing way more dirt than I envisioned. I imagined the country to be lush and green, mainly from images I saw of Machu Picchu. But the thought of going to the desert got me hyped. It made me feel like Santiago in my favorite book, *The Alchemist*. I had only dreamed of seeing vast dunes with curves and contours in perfect symmetry. And now I would finally get to see them for myself.

—

The water reflected the surrounding palm trees and tips of dunes in the center of the oasis. I took some time to explore the city and eventually headed toward the dunes. After all, they did not seem that difficult to maneuver as I began making my way up one. I saw a young boy run wildly down the dune while his mother and

151

smaller brother watched from the top. They both broke out in laughter when the boy plowed face-first into the fine, golden sand.

Becoming short of breath, I began second-guessing myself, thinking I looked like a fool for being naïve enough to think it would be easy. Each step seemed to sink deeper than the next. Once at the top, however, I no longer cared about my heavy breathing. I gazed upon endless waves of golden sand. Though the sun had set behind the dunes, it did not detract from the immeasurable hills of sand that lay before me.

I stayed well into the evening as the sky turned purple, hoping to get a view of the stars. Lights from the buildings and streets below looked enchanting as they glistened off the water in the center of the oasis. Tightly, I sat on the soft sand, chilled from the absence of the sun that had now been replaced with the night's air. I clenched my teeth from the coolness, determined to see if the stars would show. I imagined that I had traveled across the Sahara like "The Alchemist," on a quest to find my purpose or some meaning in it all. Truthfully, I did not have the faintest idea of what I had been searching for. I just wanted to travel and find whatever in me felt empty.

After abandoning the thought of stargazing, I inched back down the dune. When I reached the bottom, I poured the sand out of my shoes and headed to my hostel. I was surprised to run into the Irish girls when I arrived back.

"Yoo, what's up!" I exclaimed. "How are you all? I remember you all talking about coming here. I wondered if I would run into ya again."

"Russell, it's good to see you. We're still going strong. Just arrived here, actually," one of the girls said.

"Yeah, it's always a pleasure. How has your trip been?" another one replied.

I thought about what I had been experiencing. The situation had not improved since I last saw them.

"It's been great!" I said. "Just coming from Lima. Well . . . Paracas. Don't plan on slowing down yet, ha."

The following day, we all agreed to go sandboarding, the only thing to do in Huacachina. The trip included us, along with fifteen more people, and two dune buggies. We shot up and down dunes like roller coasters as we yelled. Some threw their hands up and others held on to the roll cage. We all took turns sliding down the dunes on our boards, our feet fastened to the board with special shoes that weighed like bricks around the ankles. As we alternated between sliding on our feet and on our stomachs, each dune we slid down appeared higher than the next. The once soft, powdery sand began feeling like quick stings on the skin from the speed of our decline. Thinking back, I had not had that much fun since I left Baños and its many adventures. I loved every minute.

Later, we ended up gazing at a sunset over the dunes as far as the eye could see. The sand looked like golden silk as the desert appeared smooth and wrinkled at the same time. I could not put my finger on what this feeling was, but I did not want it to end. I had forgotten the past couple of days that by now had turned into weeks. No, I knew what it was. It was my oasis in the desert.

As we sped back to town in our dune buggies, the hat that I had worn since the beginning of the trip flew off my head and into the desert sands. I looked back as we rode, but it had already been swallowed by the desert's abyss. I do not know why, but it seemed symbolic of some meaning I did not yet understand. All I knew was, the feeling was as strong as if I had left a piece of myself behind.

While that thought sat in the back of my mind, I turned my sights toward one of the biggest reasons why I made this trip, what I had gazed at so many times on my computer screen at work, even more than Angel Falls: Machu Picchu.

18

Frustration

Looking out my window, I gazed at misty mountains as the sun rose. A slight fog lightly covered the lush grass like a blanket. Trickles of water maneuvered through the thick grass like streams of traffic commuting to work, and the sun gleamed off the running water like hundreds of mini headlights. As we passed small cobblestone houses, I wondered if the people inside were just waking up.

After a nineteen-hour bus ride, we arrived in Cusco, and were welcomed by a sea of brown-top buildings, all looking uniform. Cusco was not a sky-scraping city, but it was a busy one. Locals walked around wearing a mixture of street clothes and traditional Peruvian attire. Until then, I had never seen the blend of the two. I spotted women wearing sweater jackets, hats, and dresses, with their colorful woven blankets tied over their shoulders like bags. Some carried items, while others carried babies. The guys wore wool hats with ear flaps on them.

Once I made it to my hostel, like always, I informed my family of my arrival. Speaking to my dad and FaceTiming my mom felt refreshing. I knew it would give them that extra boost of assurance that I was fine, some type of human interaction to let them know their son was actually on the other side of the phone and not some bot stringing together words and phrases through text. And honestly, I needed to hear and see them, too.

I made the most out of my time in Cusco, going on tours to different historic ruins like the Sacred Valley or visiting the market where indigenous women handmade vibrant blankets and clothing. Even after seeing the Ollantaytambo—the ruins of a massive Inca fortress—with its amazing views, nothing excited me more than Machu Picchu.

As I gazed at the Salkantay poster that hung on the wall at the hostel, its snow-capped mountain lured me to sign up. I booked a five-day and four-night tour out on the Salkantay Trail, five days of walking on rigorous terrain to Machu Picchu. No electronics, no social media, no city life. Only nature. I had done nothing that extreme, and I did not know what to expect.

And the timing could not have been any better. As I attempted to enjoy a game of ping-pong in the main area of my hostel, a worker sat staring at me from behind the reception desk. Since my arrival, there had been one hostel worker in particular who felt the need to smirk whenever he looked at me. I had been aware that these looks were still happening, but I pushed them to the back of my mind. But something about his sly grin ate away at my coolness as my grip tightened around the ping-pong paddle. I had always been the type to stay cool and to keep a level head, but this annoyance got the best of me.

"Yo, what the fuck are you looking at? What's so funny?" I said, pointing with my paddle.

Clearly taken aback, the other guests stopped in their tracks and looked in my direction. My opponent at the other end of the table straightened out of his stance, trying to figure out what had just happened.

The hostel worker sat and looked on quietly as I approached him. I realized his English might not have been good, so I spoke to the coworker next to him.

"Could you ask him, 'Is there a problem?' What is he laughing at? What's so damn funny?"

All eyes were on me as I glared at him, waiting for his coworker to translate. She uttered something, and he shook his head. My blood boiled as I forced myself to walk away, throwing my paddle back onto the table, and guests followed me with their eyes as I exited. Frustration coursed its way through my body, resulting from me being upset at what had transpired, as well as my response. I had never reacted to a situation in that way. Why now? I was the peacekeeper. Why was I so easily ready to fight someone who could not even communicate with me?

As I sat in my room tossing these questions around in my mind, I considered an ugly truth. Was it because I felt as if I could get away with it? That being from the States somehow made me superior? That I was better than them and that their rules were not mine? I could not help but think where I grew up had begun rubbing off on me. I even wondered if that was what white people felt like. Taking more time to reflect, I stayed in my room for the rest of the day, anticipating my trek. Five days and four nights away from civilization were much needed.

Around 4:30 a.m., the van pulled up to the hostel already carrying other hikers. Though my surroundings were barely visible from the darkness, I did not need to be told people were dozing back off to sleep from the quietness of the ride. Even myself.

I awoke to the stirring of the van and the voice of the guide once we stopped. Not long after, I found myself sitting in front of a lively bunch of trekkers who came from all over the world, including the U.K., France, Spain, Uruguay, and Belgium. Some traveled alone and others with friends; some arrived with experience and others with none. A middle-aged couple had even brought their young son along. I continued listening as they spoke about their trekking backgrounds. It all sounded interesting, which added to my excitement. They all were from different parts of the world but had the same mission: to conquer the Salkantay Trail to reach Machu Picchu.

156

We began climbing up the side of a damp and slightly muddy hill to begin our starting point. The early morning fog shortened our visibility as we trailed behind each other along the slope of the hill. For the next eight hours, we trekked beaten paths along hillsides, across low streams of water beneath stones and rocks, and in open spaces surrounded by hills and mountains. We stopped eventually for a quick break, of snacks and water we all had packed. I carried crackers, fruits, and bottles of water that I sipped occasionally, not wanting to run out. The sun had finally begun coming out, leaving only the clouds that mystically lingered around the top of a snow-capped mountain before us. Dirt and gravel crunched under our shoes, unsynchronized and varied as we spaced out from one another.

"Yo, what's up, man?" one trekker said once he got in close range.

"Hey, what's up, bro?" I replied.

"I'm good, man. You hanging in there? Where you from?"

"From the States. South Carolina. You?"

"France. I'm Malik. Nice to meet you, man."

"Word. Okay. Russell."

Malik and I continued chatting, which helped pass the time. He had been the most relatable out of everyone I had spoken to up to that point, and the only other person of color. The thought crossed my mind, but I did not mention what I had been experiencing with the unwanted stares. Malik had a lighter complexion, so I doubted if he even had to deal with it. He blended right in.

We continued on our trek as fatigue started weighing in. Before leaving Huanchaco, Ele had given me a bag of coca leaves. Besides being associated with cocaine, the leaves themselves are energy boosters. The Incas even used them when they traveled. Other trekkers carried some as well as we pushed forward, throwing a couple in our mouths and spitting every so often like we had chewing tobacco. I could not tell if the coca leaves worked or not, but we eventually made it to our campsite for the night, an enormous shed covered by a tarp with tables and tents already set up inside.

The temperature had dropped significantly since we had reached the mountains. I wore a light jacket, a scarf around my neck, and some basketball shorts under my pants, which were not enough to keep me warm. Everyone else appeared more prepared for the weather than I was.

It was only the early part of the evening, so after lunch, people began chatting and playing games, and a few others, including myself, went to scour the landscape. I marveled at the surrounding mountain ranges with stones and fall rocks that laid out along its inclined hills leading up to mountains. I could see dandelions and what looked like lavender sprinkled about in some areas, and I even spotted one or two wild horses that grazed along the hills. *Everything is so peaceful and beautiful*, I thought.

This isolation felt therapeutic, like a breakaway from the hurt and confusion I had been feeling. I did not know what to make out of what I had been experiencing. This teetering between ugliness and beauty. *What do I make of this space? What is this?* I wondered. I continued looking out into the mountains until the light faded.

Before heading into our tents, we received sleeping bags; I could not tell whether mine was damp or just cold. As the late hours arrived, so did a drop in temperature. I had convinced myself that my sleeping bag had to be damp from it not warming up at all. I curled up in the fetus position, holding my nuts in one hand and my ass in the other, hoping to find warmth anywhere. Even with all my clothes still on, I woke up throughout the night shivering, anticipating the sunrise.

We did not waste any time starting our day at 5 a.m. for a breakfast of soup and cheese, as well as conversation. One trekker from the U.K. mentioned an older man was selling trekking sticks. I decided to try one upon agreeing with him that the hills could be harsh on your knees. After purchasing the stick from the old man,

I felt better about being able to take the pressure off my knees. Besides, I still had three more days ahead of me.

I tested out my trekking stick as we traveled to Salkantay Mountain. Confidence rushed through my body as Salkantay Mountain peered over the hills in the distance. Thick clouds rimmed the top of the mountain, masking its complete beauty.

There I was trekking in the Peruvian Andes with people from different parts of the world. The feeling of being out in the open, focusing only on putting one foot in front of the other, felt like all I ever needed to do. All I had was my book bag, my scarf, my hat, and my trekking stick, but it seemed like I had so much more. We moved like one organism across Mother Nature's contours, admiring the landscape that shaped our background.

With coca leaves in our mouths, we began to zig and zag our way up the hill of rocks and stone. I realized buying the stick had been a wise choice as my feet slipped and rolled on loose rock. Our pace had been ambitious as we eventually passed another group that had begun before us. But the further up we traveled, the more our people started falling behind.

When we reached about 4,400 meters up, the altitude started affecting me. My body felt entirely drained. I wished for the earth to level out soon, but the ground continued upward. Even the once energizing coca leaves could no longer assist me. Physically depleted, I began stopping more frequently to catch my breath.

I moved as if my body had flipped a switch to go on autopilot. I could no longer focus on the scenery of mountains and valleys, only on reaching the top. Frustration made itself apparent as my self-motivating pep talks were not getting through to my body.

"C'mon, man . . . shit. You made it this far . . . keep going . . . keep going."

When the sun reached its peak, I was able to take the time to stop and catch a moment of relief, even though the weather on the Salkantay Trail made it a challenge to remove my jacket and scarf. Upon spotting the 4,600 mark up ahead, I wanted to drop down and sit right where I stood, simply from the thought of making it to the top.

As I struggled to make my way to the top, Malik came to joke and chat with me to keep me moving and keep my mind off of exhaustion. I could only say two or three words at a time before I had to catch my breath. Never in my life had I been as tired as I was at that moment. I would stop walking and look at the top, walk again, stop, and look at the top. Before long, I just kept my head down and continued moving forward. I could hear voices at the top of the hill as I panted while dragging my feet and stick.

Why is it that when we work so hard at something we want to give up the most when it is almost over? I had struggled with this habit for some time. Never being able to just finish. The thought of it made me more upset with myself. I did not want to look up any longer. My lungs wanted to burst out of my chest, trying to suck in more air than they could. With a dry mouth and legs that felt like lead, I continued. I did not even want to think because it seemed like it added to the exhaustion.

When I made it to the top, I dropped my bag and my stick and put my hands on my knees. It took me a moment to lift my head to see my accomplishment. I could hear that we had made it, but I had yet to see it as my eyes stayed glued to the rocks on the ground. And when I did see it, Salkantay Mountain was right in front of me. At 6,200 meters into the air, it towered over me as I gazed in amazement, only to drop my head again from my weakness and its unbelievable beauty.

One by one, people started coming to the top, repeating the same motions as me. I sat down on a rock, reached into my bag, and pulled out a bottle of water and the first snack I could get my hands on. I ripped open a pack of crackers and proceeded to stuff my face, enjoying a small reward for reaching a greater one. I expected the weather to be much cooler once we reached the snow-covered mountain, but we all began peeling off our coats and jackets instead. Our smiles illuminated our relieved faces as we took photos with the conquered Salkantay Mountain at our backs. I made it!

From that morning until we reached our campsite, we trekked for a total of ten hours. And even after that strenuous trek, I still had to look forward to another uncomfortable sleep. Bundled again in my tent wearing all the clothes from earlier, I tried to keep warm in another damp sleeping bag. I even put my feet inside my book bag for as much warmth and dryness as possible. Though the night was harsh, I still felt accomplished.

To distract my mind from the coldness, I listened to Erykah Badu's album *Baduizm*. I played the song "On and On" and kept it on repeat. Not only did that sum up my day, but it also summed up my trip. I had no idea when I would head back home. I just knew I wanted to keep going on and on. Even while being curled up in some damp sleeping bag, I believed being out there served me more purpose than any work I had done for the past year and a half. It seemed as if I now had *real* substance.

—

There was not one cloud in the sky when we continued our trek the next day. We walked smooth roads and my earbuds filled my ears with music, a complete change of pace from the first two days. The challenging part of the trek was over, and now we were walking on pavement. I kept to myself for most of the day, looking out to continuous landscapes and mountain ranges as we maneuvered curvy roads.

I had not spoken to the guide much because I did not know where he stood regarding my complexion. Yet, he had not given me any reason to think he would treat me differently, and he seemed like a more open person. So I decided to see what was the deal with the staring, being that he was a local himself.

"Do people here look at me differently because of my skin?" I asked.

"Um, no, no," he replied. "You know, maybe they think you are a funny guy?"

161

A funny guy? I had not been cracking any jokes, though. The thought of being looked at as amusement or entertainment like some clown bothered me. Maybe my guide was right. Maybe they did think of me as funny because that was how being there felt, like being on display. I left it alone, however, and kept my feet moving until our next stop.

Along the way, I observed some areas where landslides occurred, leaving marks on hills like a name engraved on a tree. Little did I know, that day would turn into one of the worst days I had experienced, something that would leave its mark on me.

When we reached our third campsite, we checked out a nearby hot spring to relax and have fun. After three days of trekking, we believed we all deserved a day at a hot spring. Plus, none of us had showered for that long. As my group and I walked into the entrance of the hot springs, I instantly caught the eyes of other visitors. Men and women alike glanced over to get a look at the dark man. I tried my best not to pay attention to it, but when you are the only one of your kind in a crowd who does not see many of you, you are bound to get noticed.

Once I changed into my swimming shorts, a sensation of vulnerability washed over me. I walked out of the stalls, scrawny and hairy-chested, holding my clothes and shoes. I focused as much of my attention as I could on my group and not on the insecurities I carried as well. While in the water, I tried my best to enjoy myself, but the negative energy that hovered over me had been too overwhelming. People in other groups looked over their shoulders and made comments amongst themselves, which ended with them looking back at me. My group was oblivious to what was going on around us, and I could not blame them. You do not suspect anything when you are unaware of it. How I wished I had been as oblivious to the thought as them. Even though I was with my fellow travelers, I felt like a black swan in a pool with ducks. I felt isolated and excluded from the moment, looking at the bigger picture as if holding the picture frame instead of being in the shot.

I was hesitant to say anything because I believed they would not understand or relate, or they would say I was overreacting. Eventually, I decided to mention it to Malik, uncertain of his response.

"Malik, man, I think the people here have a problem with my skin color. I've been getting these weird looks, bro, and I know I'm not tripping," I said.

"Hey, man, you are good, man, you know. You may just be overthinking, man. You are fine. C'mon enjoy yourself some. Don't worry about it," Malik advised.

Though giving my best efforts to continue making the best of the situation, I finally had enough. Without saying anything, I jumped out of the pool and headed to a sitting area on the other side of the springs, behind a wall where troughs of water continuously poured. This area had the least amount of visibility, completely out of the line of sight. And I used the heavy pouring water for a shield as it rushed down, thundering on my head and back.

For the first time in my life, I felt so humiliated that I wanted to hide. Never in a million years would I have ever thought I would get to a point where I would feel that low about myself. Yet, being hidden felt relieving as I let the water rain down on my ungroomed hair. I could have stayed there for the rest of our time and would have been fine. I wanted to stay there. To avoid looking up and catching any wandering eyes, I kept my head down and watched my skinny black toes twitch and move over the wet stone.

After a while, the group came over to check on me. Though I was slow to get up and follow them, I entered the pool yet again while also explaining my brief disappearance.

"I've just noticed during my trip how many strange looks I've been gettin,' and honestly, I think it's 'cause of my skin color. I've tried not to pay attention to it, but it's hard when I'm aware that it's there," I ranted.

"It's okay, Russell; sometimes people don't understand," someone said.

"Yeah, all perspectives, ya know," said another.

163

I sighed. "I just think it's crazy. South America has people of all kinds of shades. I'm the one that doesn't understand. I know I'm not exaggerating."

And sure enough, once they started paying attention, even they noticed the stares. Some of them even started feeling slightly uncomfortable, as Malik himself began to grow angry.

"Aye, man, fuck them . . . you know. Fuck them," he spat. "We still have a good time, man."

While preparing to leave, I walked past an older couple out in the pool, looking at me and smiling.

"Hey, do you want me to ask them why they look this way? I can translate for you if you want," said Tommy, one of my other group members.

Frustrated, I made a beeline for the couple to ask them myself. Not knowing what to say, I asked, "¿Dónde eres?"

Even though asking where they were from had nothing to do with the situation, I believed I needed to express something. Hoping somehow they would get the message. The mid-fifties couple looked at each other and then back at me without saying anything. I signaled Tommy to come over and asked them what was so funny. He posed his question and translated their answer.

"They say they never saw many dark people before and they thought you were handsome. The husband says they were sorry and don't mean any harm."

As soon as Tommy relayed the message to me, I did not believe it. Even Tommy did not seem too convinced. I could not believe a couple their age, an age where you should have the maturity and sense enough to know the world has all kinds of people, acted like children. As much fútbol was watched there, I knew they had seen a black person on TV. It seemed as though the people who laughed at me lived in some bubble, disconnected from and out of tune with the outside world. As if they were all that existed. While I struggled to make sense of everything, I appreciated Tommy standing up for me. Yet still, I left with no answers.

On the way back to the hostel, I thought about the hot spring incident, and for the rest of the night. I thought about just how hurt I felt. How down I had gotten. I felt so pitiful that I barely spoke for the rest of the night, even as we drank beer by a campfire. Sadly, my damp sleeping bag was the only thing I had to look forward to that night.

I would have never imagined that I would experience something like this while traveling to other countries and seeing the world, things that some people long for and dream about. I thought anywhere else but the States would treat a person of color better. But apparently, some places could make us feel worse.

19

Gratitude

The following day, we left for Aguas Calientes, a town located right below Machu Picchu. I kept to myself most of the day, with thoughts of the hot spring still replaying in my mind. I wondered if the heckling would get worse the further south I ventured. It rained off and on as we navigated through humid weather, perfect for the mosquitos that sucked blood hard enough that one could see red specks on their skin.

With the realization that our adventure was near its end, the once upbeat looks on our faces had now faded away. We went from trekking to walking. No longer did I use my trekking stick to climb uneven hills; I twirled and spun it to pass time as we walked. Despite our hiking becoming mundane, we all looked forward to reaching the town. We had not slept in a bed in four days, and now we could finally have that luxury.

"Okay, muchachos, once we reach the town, we have a big feast for you later in the night. We will be there soon," our guide announced.

My mouth watered at the thought of having something more than soup and coca tea, my diet for the past couple of days.

Once we got close enough, the guide pointed up at the top of a mountain and said, "Up there is Machu Picchu."

"Aww, man, there it is, you guys!"

"Where? Which one?"

"It's that one, yeah?"

Finally, we made it. Excitement rushed through us as we wanted to hike it at that moment, but we knew our eagerness would have to wait until the next day.

Our mood went from excited to disappointed once we arrived, shocked by how touristic the town looked with its merchandising of Machu Picchu. Plastic statues of Incas and stone walls were on display, replicating the ones we would see the next day. No one said a word but our expressions indicated we expected something more, something more sacred.

When we made it to our hostel and entered our rooms, none of us cared about our unmet expectations. I saw my bed and thought about that damp-ass sleeping bag I had to sleep in for three nights in the cold. Knowing I would have a warm bed and a hot meal, I did not know which one I anticipated more. A bittersweet feeling came over me as I thought about how the next day would be our last day, the day we would see what we had all worked so hard for.

Our morning began at 4 a.m., and we eventually found ourselves with other groups at the entrance in the drizzling rain, waiting for the gate to be lifted like runners at a starting line. Once the gates were open, the pool of people merged into a stream as we made our way to the steps of Machu Picchu.

Most of the climbers began turning on mini flashlights and phone lights to help them see in the limited light. Having to lift our knees higher than normal steps, we took step after step over slabs of stone. Roots protruded out of the ground as just another obstacle as we zigged and zagged our way to the top. Eventually, our string of flashlights slowly began separating and pulling away from one another. As fatigue started setting in, I started to feel like I did three days prior.

After a while, I could only hear my heavy breathing and my boots clunking against each stone step. I could not believe these steps would lead me to Machu Picchu, the same images I had once ogled at on my work computer screen. And in just a few moments, I would be standing there at one of the seven wonders of the world.

I caught up with one of my group members from Belgium. We stuck together the rest of the way, hoping to catch the sunrise at the top. Being that dawn had begun illuminating our surroundings, we no longer used our flashlights.

At the top, we stepped out into a parking lot where people not so thrilled to take the steps were already waiting. Out of all the groups, our group made it to the top first, eager to enter the ruins.

When the gates finally opened, we walked into an untouched marvel of mystic ruins that had been all ours for a moment. From the layers of mist and fog, the ruins looked as though they hid secrets. The solid block and stone walls amazed us as we made out the skeleton of what was once an ancient city.

For the next seven hours, we explored the ruins in awe, wandering like schoolchildren on a playground. I touched the near-perfect cut stones in disbelief of how even and smooth they were, wondering how people who did not have close to the amount of technology we have now could create something so precise that still stands today.

Humbled and grateful for this miraculous wonder, we sat at the top of the viewpoints where you could look down into Machu Picchu. You could see other tourists walking around from a distance like ants moving through an ant farm. *I can't believe I'm here. This isn't on a glass screen any longer. I'm here*, I thought. I could not believe that I had imagined seeing Machu Picchu and it materialized with just a few decisions. Who knew I would have to endure so many experiences just to savor this moment?

"The guide said in the next fifteen to twenty years they could be shutting down to the public," the girl from Belgium mentioned.

"Really? How come?" I asked.

"Each year from the number of people, it is sinking or something like that." She continued, "Tourists are taking a toll on the site."

I had always found it interesting that when people's curiosity took over, something so beautiful and sacred could end up ruined and abused. Even when the intention was never to cause harm. With these thoughts in my mind, back down the stairs we went, loosely dropping our weight on every step down, exhausted from spending the entire day there.

Shortly after we arrived back in town, we all started returning home one by one. I wished Malik and everyone a safe trip, and before I knew it, I had boarded a train and caught a van back to Cusco.

When I returned to my hostel, it almost felt like home when I arrived. A familiar place. Same room, same roommates, same bed. It felt good to be back. None of us had taken a shower in five days, so getting back under hot running water felt indescribable. The feeling of fresh clothes touching my body and finally being able to brush my teeth was nothing short of blissful. Because my clippers broke unexplainably, I began using razors for shaving. Each time, I would manage to leave behind one or two rough patches under my neck.

It seemed like the end of some adventure movie as I stood in front of the bathroom mirror reflecting on the trip. The trek itself, meeting the other trekkers, the hot springs situation, finally seeing Machu Picchu. As a whole, I could only think of comparing it to a diamond with blemishes, not perfect but still precious. Still appreciated.

—

I needed to waste time until my flight to the ayahuasca retreat in a couple of weeks, so I continued south to Puno, Peru, before heading to Arequipa for the flight. While leaving from Cusco to Puno, I started feeling as sick as a dog. During my first three days there, my stomach turned nauseous but not as horrible as it was in Venezuela. I lay in bed with chills and fever not even wanting to get up to eat, partially because I did not have an appetite. Even the sight of food upset me.

As I recovered, I got a chance to know my roommate quite well, who suggested I might have had altitude sickness. She was from Norway but of Peruvian descent. Throughout my travels, I had met quite a few travelers with different stories. Some had left their jobs, like me, some had taken a break from school, and others traveled full-time. But my roommate traveled for a different reason. She traveled to meet her biological parents.

We talked for hours as dusk began to fall, unconcerned about the room losing its light. She would be visiting her biological parents the following day, and it made me nervous for her. I could hear the emotion in her voice as she took deep breaths every other sentence, thinking about the day ahead. I had told myself that this trip would give me plenty of perspectives, but for someone traveling to meet their real parents for the first time, their trip would be life-changing.

Unfortunately, I never got a chance to ask my roommate how that meeting went. She left before I could ask, but I hoped everything went beautifully.

Section 4: Patience

There's yellow eyes fixed and masked behind tall blades of grass, but you're still unable to see,

Someone who embraces the time and keeps composure while trailing behind. There's no one more patient than me.

Though my heart can sense my yearn, as my gut rolls and turns, even a fisherman will agree,

With his steady hand above water as he waits along the lake's border. There's no one more patient than me.

Carrying this virtuous gift, I'm being tested to and fro.

A pupil forced to wear whatever image my teacher sees through theirs.

They say time heals all, but I seem to find myself idling, wounded from assumptions.

I want to tap my restless fingers to the rhythm of my bouncing leg.

But instead I wait while listening to music.

People have admired my patience like a flower's bloom, but are unaware of the fear that it's rooted in.

As still as a photo, dressed in a kimono, a sensei can sit under a tree,

In a zen-like state, and begin to meditate, but there's no one more patient than me.

20

Curiosity

Once the altitude sickness loosened its grip, I signed up for the Lake Titicaca tour, where you could live with a family for a day. I was unsure if it would be a good or bad idea, given what I had experienced from locals. They were about to get quite the surprise, however.

Lake Titicaca is the largest lake in South America and lies on the Peruvian and Bolivian borders. I remembered hearing something about the lake back in elementary school, but I spent most of my time giggling at the "Titi" part.

Despite my stomach still feeling uneasy, it felt good to be out and adventurous again. Rain clouds hovered above as we loaded onto the boat, but they did not ruin our tour. We stopped to visit some indigenous people who lived on the lake as the guide explained their culture and lifestyle and that they made everything with totora reeds—plants commonly found along the edges of Lake Titicaca—from the houses to their boats to the island itself. The women knitted sweaters, and the children sang songs for us as we sat, on totora reeds, and watched.

We then left to meet up with our family for a day. I wondered how they would receive me being black, how they would treat me, and if they would look at me differently than the other travelers. After a forty-five-minute trip, we arrived at the island where a line of women awaited us, all of them dressed in white sweaters, deep blue dresses, and long black hoods that hung down to their lower backs. They stood patiently waiting, some with their hands behind their backs, as we unloaded from the boat. While families usually housed at least two or three guests, I ended up getting a family to myself.

After meeting our hosts, we followed them to their homes, observing the island as we strolled rock and stone roads. We walked along the hillside, looking down at the small homes and sectioned-off plots of land, which I assumed were used for farming. Lines of stacked stones bordered the sectioned-off land, as well as the roads we traveled.

My "mom" for the day, Maria Cari, was an older, quiet, dark-haired woman in her late sixties, who stood about shoulder height. I followed her home, where she introduced me to her husband, Simon Cari, my "dad" for the day. They had no children and no formal education. They spoke Quechua—an indigenous language—but could speak some Spanish, so we communicated as best we could.

Mr. Cari worked most of the day farming and tending to cattle, and Mrs. Cari spent her time knitting and crafting. While showing me the items she handmade, she gifted me a knitted hat made from Alpaca wool. Mrs. Cari then showed me to my room, which held a bed, a pot, a desk, a coat hook, a trash can, and a light. The clay walls and wooden floors made me feel as if I had traveled back in time.

The lifestyle there was easygoing and modest. The environment did not seem stressful or busy. People worked just to have the necessities. On the island, there were no cars or transportation. Everyone walked. There was no modern technology or even machinery. Everyone worked by hand and adopted a vegetarian life. Outside of maybe some cheese, they mainly ate rice, vegetables, and soup. And that is exactly what we ate for supper.

Only housing a stove, a sink, a few cupboards, and a table with two small wooden benches, the eating quarters were stationed in a separate clay compartment. The room itself probably could hold only four, maybe five, people at the most.

I sat there in my black jacket with my scruffy face, still wearing my earflap hat, sitting across from Mr. Cari. My stomach still felt weird as I motioned to them, rubbing my stomach and shaking my head.

"Stomach. Stomach hurt. Feel bad," I said.

They looked at each other and spoke words I could not understand. Mrs. Cari then poured some hot water into a cup, walked outside, broke off a twig with small leaves, placed it in the cup, and swirled it around a few times. She handed it to me, and, cautiously, I drank it. I sipped on the mint-tasting drink and instantly felt its effects as it soothed my stomach.

"Es muña. Muña," she said.

I learned that Mrs. Cari made the tea from muña leaves, which are beneficial for altitude sickness and digestion. Noticing it gave me relief, she went back out and brought in some more muña leaves for me to keep.

We ate soup and potatoes as the Caris carried on a conversation just like older American couples. Mrs. Cari talked away while Mr. Cari made a few grunts here and there, which entertained me. After supper, they sang in Quechua as Mr. Cari played his guitar and Mrs. Cari danced, encouraging me to get up and dance with her.

All the groups and their families gathered for a big dance later that night. Mrs. Cari gave me the traditional poncho that the men wore to the dance. The heavy blue poncho draped down past my knees as we walked to the dance. Mrs. Cari's small flashlight pierced through the pitch-black darkness, giving a path of light to our steps. With it being that dark, the display of the stars shined brightly as I tried to watch them as well as my steps. For the first time, I could make out the Milky Way. As a child, the pictures I had seen of it always mesmerized me. Now, I could stare at this marvel as it stretched across the sky like a tear in space.

Following our walk, Mrs. Cari and I entered a building to find the families and their guests dressed up as well. The guys wore their ponchos and earflap hats, and the girls wore beautiful handmade hoods and dresses. We danced traditional dances and even held hands and danced in one rotating circle while the band played, enjoying ourselves for about an hour and a half before we headed in for the night.

As we all retired for the evening, Mrs. Cari gave me a small flashlight to use throughout the night. Though the weather was freezing cold, the thick blanket that I lay under could have warmed up a freezer. The blanket was so heavy that it pressed my feet down, preventing them from resting comfortably in their natural position. Unsure of what the blanket was made of, I was convinced that it could single-handedly defeat winter.

The next morning, we ate breakfast, and I had one last serving of muña tea before the groups gathered to leave the island. Mrs. Cari walked me back down to the boats, where we met up with the other groups, while Mr. Cari went off to start his workday.

I wondered how the people there were so much friendlier than those in the city. Why was it that in the city, where people were exposed to more, they appeared more ignorant than the ones secluded from the outside world? I assumed it would be the other way around, but it was not. They treated me just as they would have anyone else. They treated me with kindness, and I wished I had experienced more of it. Though the thought puzzled me, I just enjoyed the boat ride across Lake Titicaca back to Puno, listening to UGK.

—

As I waited downstairs in the hostel lobby the following afternoon to leave for Arequipa, I saw another guy preparing to leave as well. Another black guy. Until that point, there had not been another black male that I had seen even remotely close to my complexion. He looked a hell of a lot more well-groomed than I was, like he had just stepped out of the barber's chair. When we saw each other, we both knew we had to speak to each other.

"Yo,' what's going on, man?" I asked.

"Hey, man, what's up?" he responded.

"You're heading out, or is this your first day in Puno?"

"About to head out; there isn't much here, really."

"Yeah, I was debating whether to stay here or go to Arequipa."

"You definitely should go to Arequipa, bro, trust," he emphasized. "Once you've done Lake Titicaca, that's it. It's a helluva lot better in Arequipa. I've already been."

"Ha, say no more. Plus, my stomach has been crazy these past couple of days," I added.

"Then, yes, you're doing the right thing, ha," he joked.

Talking to someone who looked like me felt therapeutic. Someone experiencing the world in the same skin I was in. Someone relatable who could speak my language.

After our exchange, we both took a cab to the bus station, where we waited for our buses. I watched as people stared at us as we moved through the station, and I wondered if he noticed the same. Though I desperately wanted to ask if he noticed those looks, I decided not to ask, mainly because I did not want him to start paying attention and possibly add negativity to his trip. Maybe, through his eyes, he enjoyed himself and never gave it any thought; I did not want to take that from him. I understood that sometimes withholding information is the best option. Just like good seeds, bad ones could be planted as well. Therefore, we said our farewells and went our separate ways.

21

Confusion

For the next two weeks, I settled in the city of Arequipa, longer than any other place I had been. My expectation wavered between whether this extended stay would be good for me, or a living nightmare. I had not stayed in one place longer than seven days, and now to spend two weeks in an area where I might have these "lookers" would be a challenge.

Once out and about, after dealing with my stomach again, I realized that what the black guy had told me back in Puno was right. There was more to do in Arequipa. I visited a couple of historical places like Santa Catalina Monastery, where during the 16th century young women would go to become nuns and could not return home, and one of the city museums that housed the mummy of Juanita, a little girl who was sacrificed to the Inca Gods in the 15th century. I even signed up for Spanish and cooking classes, both of which I was trash at.

It did not take the entire two weeks for me to conclude that these looks would continue as I tried making the best out of my time in the city. While out one day, I had a striking revelation that maybe the stares resulted from my uncut hair. After all, it was not like my hair had stopped growing once I made the trip, which possibly explained why no one looked at me suspiciously at the beginning of my journey. I looked well kept then. This thought relieved me. I had not had a proper haircut or shave in over three months, and that was enough to make me laugh at myself when I looked in the mirror. Maybe it was all the hair that looked funny to them. It made sense as I realized all the men were clean-shaven: no facial hair, no mustache, no beard, no nothing.

Yet, other travelers I met looked just as rough as me and did not receive those stares. Reminding myself of the hot springs and police encounters, my optimism disappeared as quickly as it came. I realized that there could be no other reason for their stares but my skin color. *Did I need to experience this?* I wondered. *If so, why?*

When I would go out to shop or to get something to eat, I remained focused on the task and was not concerned about the people around me. Amidst my efforts to be incognito, I found a small alley with restaurants and other stores that received little traffic. That alley had become a haven for me to go eat. I considered it my place of peace in a space of judgment and stares. My moment of intermission before going back on stage and into the spotlight.

Walking back to my hostel one day, I stopped by a market to pick up some fruit. I stepped into a gigantic warehouse that had vendors and tables loaded with fresh goods in every direction, with people making their way down and across rows of various spices, vegetables, and exotic fruits. While scanning the many items, something caught my attention hanging above one stand further down. I moved closer to get a better look. The random object appeared to be a doll-like figure of a black child with black hair, black skin, and even dark-colored clothes. I did not see any sign nearby explaining the reason for it being there, so I glanced around to see if anyone noticed me looking. Ironically, I did not catch stares this time. My stomach felt like a belly of fire as I walked away.

—

Being that I had not had a consistent schedule since I left the States, I figured attending classes and having homework would be like being reacquainted with an old friend. And honestly, I believed having something consistent would be nice. I even wondered how my teacher would receive me. If she was a reflection of anything I had experienced so far, then it was going to be a long couple of days.

And, as I should have guessed, my teacher wore that same awkward look I had witnessed many times before when I introduced myself on my first day of class.

"Hola, I'm Russell." I reached out my hand to shake hers, but her slow reaction indicated she was still trying to process her new student.

"Good morning, I am Lindsey," she said, finally extending her hand.

Lindsey might have been four or five years older than me and looked extremely studious. I could tell she had been teaching for a while. With me being the only student in class, it felt more like a tutoring session as we began.

My cooking class was scheduled right after Spanish class. Though the teacher could not speak English, she seemed far more welcoming. The head of the school, who seemed thrilled to have me, translated the information the teacher provided as we navigated the small kitchen.

Every day, I walked eight blocks up and four blocks over for class, which took about thirty minutes. I did not mind the long walk because I had always loved walking. But just as consistent as my new schedule were the lookers that came with it. To help tune everything out, I wore earbuds, hoping music would flood out thoughts about the spectators. But it helped only so much. Even students looked out of their class windows, pointing and giggling along with their classmates. I got so furious that one day after class, I stormed back to the hostel and questioned the receptionist about it.

"Excuse me, can you tell me, do the people not like my complexion?" I asked, desperately in need of an answer.

Being Peruvian herself, the receptionist looked at me calmly and spoke, "Depending on the family, yes."

"Why? Why is that?" I questioned.

"I am not certain. Some just feel like it is not beautiful."

Those words broke whatever spell that might have given me doubt about whether my skin was the issue. She had been the first person to tell me the truth about what the people saw in my complexion. It lifted a veil that helped me see things more clearly, like the fact that the homeless people I saw were all darker complexions. That all the models in advertisements and posters were lighter-complexioned people. Models that did not even represent the image of the people in the city. I noticed some individuals would put this noticeably pale coat on their skin like sunscreen. Were they intentionally trying to make their skin lighter? As silly as the question seemed, I still wondered.

—

As time passed, my Spanish teacher must have thought the dark, fuzzy man was not so bad as she began opening up.

"I am meeting up with a few friends later. You are welcome to join us," Lindsey said at the end of class one day.

"Oh, I appreciate that. Umm, that's cool, I may join you all," I replied.

"You can find me on Facebook, and I will send you the information there."

"Sure, okay. Thanks."

As I headed back to my hostel, I thought about the kind gesture. The more I pondered about it, the more I felt things would not go the way I hoped they would. I had not forgotten what I had already experienced. While I talked myself into thinking maybe this opportunity could change someone's perspective, I preferred not to chance it and end up being looked at as something on display for her friends to mock. Even though Lindsey sent the location, I did not show.

Lindsey came to class the next morning extremely tired. She had been participating in protests related to nearby mining that affected the people. She did not mention anything about me not showing up. Instead, she asked if I would like to come out and support the protests. The thought lingered in my mind that maybe things might have been okay had I shown up, so I agreed to go.

The class was just about over as I prepared for my final exam the next day. While studying, I met a guy from Chile named Paolo. He saw me studying and decided to help me out. However, he figured he would help me out by talking to me in Spanish. Even when I clearly demonstrated I did not know what the hell he was talking about, he continued.

"Um, the best way to learn is with song and translated words. If you learn song, it will be easier to learn the words," he explained.

"So listening to words in the song will help me learn the words?" I asked.

"Yes, that's how I learn English. Please give it a try."

After awkwardly listening to a few love songs with English subtitles, I realized the exercise helped build my confidence, even though none of the words had anything to do with the exam.

I walked into the classroom the next morning, confident and assured. But what happened next is all too familiar in grade schools across the globe. All the homework, all the studying, and all the Spanish love songs did not see this coming. The test Lindsey gave me was seventy-five percent of the shit we did not review. I had not even seen most of it. To spare the details, I did not pass. But luckily, it did not count against me.

Taking a break from celebrating my final exam by playing pool at the hostel, I decided to go down to the plaza to check out the protest Lindsey had told me about. While standing there among all those people, I thought to myself, *Why would I want to help these people protest? These are the same people that stare and laugh at me walking down the street because of my complexion. No matter if I did help,*

181

they would still treat me the same. Hell, walking here I caught a few eyes. I did not see any point in supporting people who looked at me like something entertaining to watch. After a moment of contemplating, I headed back to the hostel.

In my last couple of days in Arequipa, I signed up for a three-day Colca Canyon tour I had heard about. I figured another trek would be a pleasant distraction from those mocking looks. With it being 2015, I just did not understand how a person's skin color was an issue, especially in a place where the entire race includes an array of colors. I could not help but think about my own culture and how we toyed around with the idea of "team light skin" and "team dark skin." Wondering if I would ever truly escape from it, I figured that maybe this was something I would never understand.

22

Anticipation

The day before I began my classes, I FaceTimed my mom. We engaged in our normal conversations until she broke some unexpected news.

"Well, I go in to see the doctor in two days," she spoke softly.

"Oh, okay. Going in for ya usual checkup?" I asked, sensing that it was more than a regular checkup yet hoping I was wrong.

"Not exactly. It will be just a small heart procedure. Been having a little tough time breathing and a slight pain in my chest, so they're going to check my heart."

"Heart procedure? You've been having problems with your heart, Ma?"

"Well, yeah. Just a little pain, though. They'll be injecting dye into me to see the blood flow. The doctor said a portion of my heart is enlarged."

Knowing something had been off when we started the conversation, I asked, "How come you didn't say nothin'?"

"I didn't want you to be worried about the ol' lady, ha. I'll be fine," she said, trying to reassure me.

My mother has always been like that, trying not to get anyone worried about her health issues. My grandparents, too. But she was right. I was worried. I did not want anything to happen to my mother. And being over 3000 miles away from her, finding out she had heart problems and being unable to do anything or even be there, felt horrible.

I did not mention the onlookers or what I had been experiencing to my mother. I mainly wanted to stay up-to-date with her health leading up to her procedure. Thinking it might ease my mother's nerves in some way, I told a couple of my closest friends to check on her from time to time while I was gone.

The next time my mother and I FaceTimed, she gave me a walkthrough of the house. It had been so long since I had seen it. Everything was still the same; even my room was still preserved exactly how I had left it.

It felt good to look at home again, even through the phone. We continued the walkthrough for a few more minutes until my mom asked me a question.

"Do you think I'm a good mother?" she asked.

Though the question was random, it was one I had heard before.

"Yes, Mom, you are a good mother," I replied, shaking my head.

I never liked hearing my mother say that. It made me feel like she lacked confidence and was seeking approval. But I believe I hated hearing it so much because it sounded like me. Insecurities had followed me for the longest, and certain moments from my trip had done nothing but make them more evident.

A harsher reality was that I believed I was the one who should have been asking her if I was a good son. I knew my mother, and I, were stronger than this.

"You keep asking if you're a good mom, and I keep telling you you are, ma," I continued.

She replied, "I know, but I just want to make sure you know."

I knew this recent health scare weighed on her; I could hear the worry in her voice.

Moments like those make you realize what is important: your loved ones. As we ended our call, my mother and I told each other to take care, and we assured each other that everything would be fine. I knew it would be. In that moment, we had to be strong for each other, even if we were thousands of miles away.

Three days later, I received an update from my mother, saying her procedure went well. I was beyond relieved. I knew everything would go well, and it felt good to hear some great news. It was like a beam of light piercing gray skies. For the time being, the doctor had instructed my mother not to lift anything over five pounds or to drive a motor vehicle. Despite my mom being unable to drive, her spirits had been up, which definitely lifted mine.

—

They say when you go back home after backpacking things are different, usually because you have a different perspective on life. The only thing I hoped for was that I knew my purpose when I returned home. Something I could remain focused on.

During that time, I thought about what I was going to do when I got back. I wanted to work on my business and stay in an apartment. I even considered starting a production company. I just wanted to be successful in whatever I did. But most of all, I wanted to be happy. I knew having a business of my own would be tough to start, maybe even tougher to maintain. But I believed I had something to offer the world. I wanted to inspire people. If I could inspire someone, then I could change a person's perspective. That would probably be the greatest reward I could ever receive.

With my ayahuasca trip being days away, I hoped it would help me think clearly. Give me a chance to talk with God and see

His vision. But only time would tell. Until then, I could do nothing but wait and prepare to trek through Colca Canyon.

Section 5: Rebirth

The space is confined for a period of time, but the caterpillar knows it's needed.

To reach his potential, a breakdown is essential, he must take off the old and leave it.

It will all be worth it, although not perfect, because in his own skin he feels resistance.

But he endures the process, because he yearns for progress, for he is destined to redefine his existence.

Water runs over my face and traces my brows as my eyes tighten.

Once down to my ankles, before slipping between the cracks of my toes I imagine yesterday's unhealthy thoughts and habits being washed away in my morning shower.

Though only for a few minutes, this closed space gives me a moment to separate from the world, cleansing my body as well as my perspective.

Hoping what's inside will crystalize enough, its shine will break through my calloused behaviors.

Imperfections and flaws can be seen dripping from my palm that branches off into crooked fingers.

And even still I know behind the barriers of my hands and flesh my genius exists, swirling around like a genie in a lamp.

Though he may be immersed, the water will burst, beginning the merger of new life and dreams.

Barring his new gift, he starts to lift, for the butterfly has earned his wings.

23

Confirmation

Three months after embarking on this journey, homesickness began setting in. I had been away from home for 100 days, and not being around friends and family began affecting me, along with not having the luxuries of home. I missed having my car, playing video games, eating at Chick-fil-A and Krispy Kreme, sleeping in my bed, watching cartoons in English, and going to the gym—all things I would do on any random day. After being stagnant for almost two weeks, my surroundings began to depress me. My trek through Colca Canyon could not have come at a better time.

The three-day journey began in a van with four others at 3 a.m. I stayed awake as we headed to our destination. Once we stopped for breakfast, I met my group, who were older and had traveled from Paris, as we sat and ate. I remained mindful of not eating pork to prepare for my ayahuasca retreat.

Outside of its canyons, Colca Canyon is known for its massive condors. I watched these gigantic birds soar in the skies as their wingspan stretched out farther than the height of an average human. But even more breathtaking than the birds were the canyons themselves. Though right in front of me, in some strange way, they seemed unreachable. I could smell the fresh air, feel the sunshine, and see the condors soaring, but the canyon itself seemed to be behind glass. Something that could not be touched, only admired.

"Everyone, we have a four-hour walk," our guide announced as we began our trek.

After trekking the Salkantay Trail, this will be a piece of cake, I thought. As the sun beamed in our faces, we gradually progressed down the canyon as I listened to Big K.R.I.T, Frank Ocean, and Coldplay in my earbuds. We occasionally spotted other groups, but most of the time, it seemed like we had the canyons to ourselves.

Throughout the hike, the lower part of my blue jeans started collecting dust, while my white t-shirt began gathering sweat. The sun felt good on my skin as I enjoyed the peacefulness of the canyon before reaching our destination. Once there, we settled down in an area of living quarters consisting of clay buildings and thatched roofs. I had an entire room to myself with six beds in it; I did not mind all the space.

We ate vegetable soup for lunch and sat around learning more about each other. Some were preparing to start new jobs, while others were on vacation from their jobs. I was the only person who had quit their job.

Slowly but surely, I began transforming into the traveler I had once met. The one who the beginners or vacationers looked at as experienced. Questions started evolving from "What do you do?" to "How are you doing it?" It was only a couple of months prior when I had begun my trip and did not have a clue about what I was doing. Now, people who were on vacation looked at me like I was some wise nomad, though I certainly did not feel like one; and they wanted to know more.

After dinner, none of us were ready to retire for the night, so I pulled out the playing cards I had packed for cases like these. I showed the group one of the most popular card games of all time. One of the most played games at any barbeque, picnic, family gathering, or any other Black social function. The most infamous game that would surely start an argument, even among partners.

189

Arguably one of the most notorious friend-ending games next to UNO. I taught four Frenchmen how to play Spades. Not only did they love the game, but they also became exceptionally good at it fast. We played, laughed, and listened to music for the rest of the night.

I enjoyed moments like these. They added sugar to the lemons that my trip handed me at times. I loved that my joy could be found in playing a simple game of cards and was not based on what the past couple of days looked like. I could only hope that such moments were ones I would always remember.

—

The next morning we began our trek around 7 a.m., observing small towns as we passed stone churches, schools, and farmers with their donkeys. We could also see towns in the distance, looking like specks of white dots clustered together. It reminded me of being in an old Western film as we maneuvered around the canyon edges. Paths of weeds and high brush lightly swept our pants in some parts. Both budding and fully-bloomed dandelions flickered in the canyon's breeze, taking the tension from the sun off our skin. Even the gravel under our shoes crunched and crackled until we made it to our place of rest, an oasis in the middle of a canyon.

Ultimately, the oasis turned into a small community of shacks. Below the oasis flowed a river that we could hear as it moved through the canyon. I spotted red, yellow, and orange flowers planted in front of shacks as hammocks hung from trees. The community even had a pool nearby.

We settled in, ate lunch, and played some more Spades. After a while, the group decided to go swimming, but I spent my time listening to music. I grabbed a wooden chair from inside my room and sat it right outside in the open space.

The sun had fallen behind the canyon as I sat reveling in my surroundings. Songs from Adele played softly in my earbuds while the grandness of her voice matched that of the surrounding canyons. I gazed high above at the towering canyons, admiring how the land dipped and fell, how it protruded and rose. Though I could not see the river below, I could decipher how it flowed from the spaces and canyon formation up ahead. Sitting there, I did what I do best: I got lost in thought. I thought about life and what I would do when I returned home. Ironically, the contours of the canyon reflected those of my thoughts. I didn't have a sure and straight direction of what life would look like. It remained uncertain.

Even though time appeared to stop, the night continued as we talked and a chill filled the air. In mid-conversation, I overheard the guide mentioning something that interrupted my train of thought.

"Wait, did you say it's scorpions in this canyon?" I asked, waiting for clarification.

He replied, "Yes, that is right. It is common to see."

"Yeah, I heard something about that, but I haven't seen any," said one of the group members.

I haven't either, so, hopefully, it will stay that way, I thought.

"Neither have I, thank goodness," said Ms. Kate, a guest I had met while at the camp.

Ms. Kate was in her early sixties and had traveled alone from Detroit. Though we were from two different races and generations and lived nearly 600 miles apart, talking to her made me feel closer to home.

"That's amazing you've made this trip, Ms. Kate. Especially alone," I said.

"Well, it's always been a dream of mine to travel. I realize I'm not getting any younger, so I decided to enjoy life and go for it," she replied. "Back home, I did nothing but work my time away. I was just sick of it. I did it long enough, so I gave it up. Plus, I'm no longer married and all my kids are grown and out of the house. So why not?"

191

"That almost sounds like me, Ms. Kate, well . . . without the kids and married part. Now, I'm just trying to figure out what imma do when I get back."

"Good thing you got smart early. You still have your whole life ahead of you, so don't feel bad. Even at my age, I don't have a clue as well. The most important thing is just to enjoy it while you can. Trust me, when you get older, that doesn't mean you'll have it figured out. Because even we still find ourselves searching for answers at times."

I sat there listening to Ms. Kate, admiring her for stepping out on faith, especially at her age. Listening to this living proof that it was never too late to follow where your heart moved you. We talked all evening until the group parted ways for the night.

When sleeping in shacks or outdoorsy buildings, I had learned to check my room before heading to bed. From time to time, I spotted a few bugs, like spiders here or there. Though I hardly killed them, I mainly wanted to be aware of my surroundings. That night, I did my inspection as usual, examining all corners of the room and by the door. Everything checked out until I checked under the bed.

"Oh . . . shit."

My quick one-minute bed check turned into a ten-minute stare at a scorpion. The motionless brown scorpion was the size of my palm as I stared at it, hoping my eyes were playing tricks on me.

Until that point, I had never seen an actual scorpion outside of television. Countless questions filled my mind as I looked on. *How in the hell am I going to sleep knowing a scorpion is under my bed? How do I kill this? Do scorpions climb? Is it poisonous? Are there more? Why isn't it moving? Is it sleeping? Will I sleep?* I knew nothing about scorpions. All I knew was, if I attempted to kill it and did not succeed, then I would have an aggravated scorpion ready to strike. I stood there hunched over with my hands on my knees, without a plan, and frustrated.

I grabbed the chair I had earlier and hoisted myself up to ease into the bed. Once in bed, I lay completely still so that I would not alarm my unexpected guest. Within a matter of minutes, I went from trying to sleep to being on night watch.

Periodically, I would take the light on my phone and peek under the bed to make sure the critter remained still. As soon as I got comfortable enough to finally rest my eyes, I checked one last time. A chill ran down my spine as my cell phone light swept the floor.

The scorpion had vanished.

Without touching the ground, I eased back onto the wooden chair to flick the light on. I looked around in a panic as my eyes scanned the room. I exhaled a sigh of relief when I spotted the creature slipping back outside through the door crack. Grateful that my shift was over, I flipped the switch and fell asleep, a bit more at ease.

—

Gathering my things as we prepared to trek back up the canyon, I thought it would be a perfect time to see the stars. I stepped out into the night's chill as it nipped at my neck. My group had already been pointing up at the constellations while I went over to wake up Ms. Kate, per her request.

After Ms. Kate's wake-up call, I walked over to where the group huddled and gazed at the vast white specs in endless space. Even the Milky Way stood out, just as obviously, if not moreso, than before at Lake Titicaca.

"You guys can see the Constellations perfect now. And look, there's Scorpius," one group member pointed out.

I found the sight of Scorpius amusing since I had seen a scorpion the previous night. Though I did not quite understand what it meant, I interpreted it as a good sign. Maybe a sign of how the unknown can be beautiful? Like me going from being frightened of not knowing much about scorpions to seeing a scorpion made of stars, which is not highly visible in the Northern Hemisphere. I could only see it from this part of the world.

Four months ago, I had come to South America afraid, not knowing what to expect. Besides a few hiccups, it had been a beautiful trip. Either way, I believed it was all happening for a reason.

After stargazing, we had a light breakfast and started our trek back up the canyon. My group and I, along with a handful of others, began the night trek. Once at the top, we witnessed an impeccable view as trekkers emerged from the canyon. Distant fields and snow-capped mountains made the scenery even more beautiful. Sunflowers and withered corn stalks decorated either side as we walked along the dirt path. As we headed to town to eat, we trekked through the lush grass and golden fields that were just as beautiful as the canyons we had left. Upon reaching the town, fatigue had finally taken its toll on us, as the only thing we wanted was to return to our hostels.

Later that evening, we arrived back in Arequipa and agreed to meet up for dinner. I took everyone to my favorite alley spot, and we ate and drank on the rooftop of one of the nearby restaurants. We laughed and talked about our time and how they enjoyed playing Spades. I thought about Ms. Kate and how I had appreciated our conversation. I did not think to ask where she would be heading next, but I knew where I was going.

For my last two days in Arequipa, I relaxed and studied more about ayahuasca, which means "Spirit Vine" or "Death Vine." Most people who participated in ayahuasca rituals viewed it as medicine and not a drug. I searched the retreat's website, reading every word on every page, to form my own opinion.

I read about the staff and their shaman, along with testimonies from previous retreaters from all over the world, and how the experience changed lives. I felt anxious and hopeful, a range of emotions that left me pondering my thoughts for the rest of the day.

The morning I traveled to Iquitos seemed bittersweet. I had grown attached to Arequipa, even with all of its unpleasant looks and stares. I stayed there for a little over two weeks, longer than any other place I had previously visited. However, preparing to see fresh places excited me. I never wanted to feel stagnant. After messaging my mother to let her know I would be without Wi-Fi for a few days, I embarked on a new adventure.

It took three plane rides to get to Iquitos, the middle of the Amazon. Somewhere along the way, I began experiencing a nauseous stomach . . . again. When I was not thinking about how bad I felt physically, I thought more about the retreat and how I began feeling better about it spiritually. As crazy as it sounds, it seemed like I was getting ready to meet God. He had watched over me and protected me this far, and I knew He would continue to watch over me.

24

Discovery

When I touched down in Iquitos, so did the thick humidity in the air. It felt so heavy that it seemed as if I carried more weight with my bags. Instantly, I could distinguish the difference between Iquitos and other places. Not because most of its residents lived in stilt homes on the river, or that the only way to Iquitos was by plane or boat. Nor was it the fact that these places did not look touristic. It appeared as if there was a sense of camaraderie among the people. People worked together in the street markets, carrying crates of fruits, cutting up fish, or selling fresh vegetables and homemade brews under tarps that stretched in either direction.

Once my driver dropped me off, I entered my stale temperature hostel, so stale that the fans seemed to do nothing but circulate the staleness. I noticed a few mosquitos even occupied the hostel, which added another level of discomfort. None of that mattered as my heart suddenly sunk deep inside my stomach. While trying to record a video of the new location, I accidentally deleted all my pictures and videos. I wanted to record my last video of "the old me" before taking the ayahuasca, but I somehow deleted everything. I guess there was no better way to demonstrate starting a new journey than to delete all of my media. For me, the accidental slip up symbolized a clean slate, starting over for my "new self" to be.

While walking the streets, I spotted a group of girls playing fútbol in an open field down below. Watching them play made me realize how much a person needs contentment. As the children played, other kids and parents watched on from their makeshift homes made with tin roofs and wood. Planks of wood crossed over the water from home to home as the wetlands of the Amazon comprised their backyards. Massive areas of grass preceded larger areas of water. Compared to society back home, people would have perceived this community as poor. But in actuality, they had everything they needed: a house, clothes, family, work. The essentials.

I pondered this thought while thinking about the retreat the next day. Because I did not know what to expect, which was a good thing from what I had heard, I would be participating with no expectations and an open mind. I knew this experience would be life-changing for me, especially the idea that I might speak to God. Whether that would be metaphorically or spiritually, I needed that reconnection, one I had been missing for so long. The retreat presented an opportunity to learn my purpose. To release any worries and troubles. To face unknown fears. To see a reflection of myself. I wanted to meet me for the first time.

Seeking some relief from what seemed like waiting in limbo, I rose from the couch to stretch as I anticipated my ride. And just like my itinerary mentioned, an off-road truck pulled up outside of the hostel. As I approached the truck with my belongings, a slender, baldheaded man got out to greet me.

"Aye, you must be Russell," said the man, heading to the bed of his truck.

"Yeah, I am." Surprisingly, he seemed normal, even though I had little to compare him to. I had never met anyone who actively did psychedelics.

"Pleasure to meet you. I'm Stacy. I'm the owner of the retreat. We can put your stuff here in the back. Unfortunately, we might have to make some room back there for you, too. The others are already loaded up in the truck."

"Uhh, oh okay. That's cool."

I climbed into the back of the semi-covered cargo bed, with the luggage of the other guests inside.

With the truck rocking and bouncing its way to the retreat, I found it challenging to find comfort on the shifting bags. Before long, I determined the paved streets had turned to dirt roads, even with my vision skewed from the truck's tarp draping over me. Though we might have been an hour away from town, we had driven ourselves completely out of civilization. I sat there on the pile of bags unsure of what to expect, but I was not worried. In fact, I felt as light as I could be, letting the moment carry me just like the truck carrying our luggage, and my concerns that I had now tossed along with them.

After a thirty-minute drive, we arrived at a retreat that resembled one big hut connected to a line of other hut-like structures. Structures with thatched roofs and screens all around. The staff called the large hut the "Maloka," the place where we would spend the most time, particularly for our ayahuasca ceremonies. Small mattresses made with sheets and pillows rimmed the edge of the Maloka.

I, along with five others, left my shoes outside before walking in, allowing my feet to meet the polished wooden floor. We had no internet, but some electricity for the kitchen area. Outside of that, we were unplugged from society.

Attentively, I toured the place, gazing out into the lily-padded lake in front of the huts surrounded by trees. We had been driven to the middle of nowhere, but I did not mind being secluded. The seclusion gave me peace as I heard birds calling and insects zipping by.

For lunch, we ate only fruits and vegetables: beets, avocado, carrots, bananas, cantaloupe, and cucumbers, just to name a few. We later took plant baths, which involved nothing more than dosing buckets of water mixed with plants on ourselves. It served as a spiritual cleansing right before the ceremony.

As the nighttime approached, we all gathered in the Maloka. We each sat on our thin mattresses in a circle with only one lit candle in the center providing light as sounds from the lightless Amazon permeated the screens.

We were told Stella, our shaman, had practiced administering the ayahuasca medicine for many years. Stella was a short lady in her late forties with thin, black hair. She did not wear any crazy witch doctor attire with bones, bird feathers, or some exaggerated jewelry. Instead, she wore a ceremonial blouse and dress with intricate designs and multi-colored patterns.

As Stacy began giving his introduction, we gathered around him before taking the ayahuasca, as if preparing to hear a scary story around a campfire. Everyone except for me had taken a psychedelic drug like LSD, which gave them a leg up on what to expect from the ayahuasca. Though I had never sought out LSD, I wished then that I had some idea of what was about to happen. I scanned everyone's faces to see if they were at all bothered. Nothing.

Stacy talked to us for about ten minutes, giving us words of wisdom and encouragement.

"Every person's experience is unique. Don't resist it, don't fight it, welcome it. And if you ever feel like you are overwhelmed, I like to tell participants to be like a solid rock, in a flowing river. No matter what is going on, stay firm, focused, and relaxed. Breathe."

"And in case ya do panic, it may not feel like it, but remember, the madness doesn't last forever," Drew, one of the few staff members, added.

I listened, trying to soak up every word and every piece of advice I could. The sensation behind my stomach felt like that of someone standing in line preparing to ride a rollercoaster.

Maybe I'm a little in over my head, I thought. *Ayahuasca has been known to take participants on a trip that has been said to change lives. And for many, that trip has never been easy. What things will I face? How difficult will it be for me? Would there be something brought up about me that I never thought to think of? Is this really something that I would want to see?*

As my mind continued wandering, the single candle continued flickering as we began. Stacy brought out a twenty-four-ounce plastic bottle filled to the top with ayahuasca, seeping thick, brown liquid from under the cap. One by one, he called us up by name to receive our dose.

"Russell," he said in his British accent as I approached, my stomach queasy from nervousness. Stacy poured the dark fluid into a double shot glass. I took the glass and drank it without breathing, knowing the taste would be horrible. The drink tasted worse than any cough medicine I had ever had. I had drunk a glass of marijuana, thick marijuana that I had to swallow several times for it to go down. A look of disgust covered my face and everyone else's, like we were trying to see who could close their eyes the tightest. After ingesting the Spirit Vine, we returned to our spots, and Drew blew out the candle.

Pitch blackness. I could only sense the sounds of the insects around. I sat straight up, waiting for something to happen while Stella began singing ritual songs. For the ayahuasca to take effect, we would need to "purge," or vomit, for which they had set plastic bowls near our beds. I was unsure of the chemical reaction that occurred in the body, but I knew we needed to vomit for the ayahuasca to work, either that way or by defecating. Such a place was close by if needed. And for the past couple of days, my stomach had still been upset, so I hoped it would not be the latter.

As my eyes started adjusting to the darkness, I could make out the dark figures of everyone else. After a few moments, Stacy and Drew began walking around and checking on everyone. Though I could hear someone purging, I was not sure who.

I had heard stories of people not feeling anything at all, which would have been the ultimate disappointment for me. I continued sitting there waiting as I heard another purge coming from the left of me. Soon after, Stacy came over to check on me.

"Here, Russell, try drinking some water to help you purge. It will loosen the ayahuasca."

The thick substance made it difficult to purge, even challenging to dry heave. When I drank the water, I threw up slightly but still experienced no effects. Stella continued singing, almost eerily, and then Stacy gave me another shot of ayahuasca. I followed the shot with water and looked down into the round bowl that sat in my lap, purging immediately. Right before the room began spinning, I moved the bowl to the side of me and lay down on the mattress.

From that moment on, I could only remember going from 0 to 100. I lost control. I felt like a puppet, and the ayahuasca was the puppet master, using my limbs as it pleased. My arms wailed, my legs kicked, and I experienced shortness of breath as I panicked. Drew and Stacy rushed over to my aid, but there was no use. I was fully aware of what was happening, but I was no longer controlling my body. Something had taken over, and all I could do was submit to it.

It seemed like I had entered hell, forced to escape my thoughts. Repeating each thought in an endless cycle. My emotions began pouring out from the war inside my mind as I resisted being restrained. Trying to escape this feeling, I knocked over the bowl of vomit as I grabbed, scratched, and even attempted to bite Drew and Stacy.

"I can't break through! I can't break through!" I yelled, in tears from not being able to overcome this sensation.

The ritual songs Stella sang, which were supposed to help guide us, had now turned twisted and haunting. It led me down a trail that had become a dark one, almost mocking my struggle. I was being thrown around in my mind, unable to focus and unable to get a grip on what was happening. At one moment, I felt all alone, figuratively and literally, believing they had cleared everyone out of the Maloka.

I began constructing an abstract picture in my mind, giving my best efforts to make sense of what I was seeing. Maybe God? God was not some person with a white beard, nor some blinding light. God was a system. A system of continuous and repetitive motion. Everything was intricate and precise, like one grand cluster of cogs twisting and turning, falling in place smoothly every time. However, where I was, there was no time. It did not exist. As far as I was concerned, I was seeing the beginning and end. The concept of time had escaped me. God had me repeating things and patterns in my mind, over and over again, seemingly until I got it right.

The guests who were in the ceremony had turned their attention to me, giving me support to make it through.

"Come on, Russ."

"You got this, Russ."

Then the encouraging voices I once heard had now gone off-pitch, some voices deep and others high. I began hearing voices in my head, but strangely, it was like they were working together.

"What are you doing?"

"He needs to see this."

"Impossible."

I did everything in my power to calm down, hearing Stacy say, "Be the rock, Russell. Be the rock."

As I opened my eyes, hoping to find the escape I yearned for, I saw Stacy and Drew as dark figures with thin blue auras around them and horns on their head like Darth Maul from *Star Wars*. Then, abruptly, a feeling of peace and calmness like the eye of the storm had come over me. It seemed like I was floating as light as a feather while my surreal description of Stacy and Drew faded away. Experiencing this unfamiliar sensation of being detached from my body, I wondered where this peace was the whole time.

"He stopped breathing," Stacy stated.

Stacy's words sounded like a foreign language when they flowed through my ears. Once I realized I was not breathing, I took one enormous gasp of air, catapulting me back into the thick of the storm as I kicked and swung.

Once, I thought I had shit on myself, and I did not care if I did. I just wanted to get out of whatever this was. I just wanted relief.

"He has a lot of strength in him." I heard Stacy say.

Even with me feeling stranded out in a sea of calamity, those words were like honey to a bitter mouth. I had always seen myself as weak and inadequate, which made me question if that was why I kept repeating, "I can't break through." I never quite got over the hurdle and gave up too easily during challenges. I often doubted myself and my abilities, believing I could never advance to the next step.

Slowly, the effects of the ayahuasca began wearing off, well enough that they thought I had gathered myself enough to be assisted to the bathroom. Thankfully, I did not shit on myself.

Drew helped carry me to the bathroom, like helping a drunk person get into the passenger seat of a car. I sat there on the toilet, gradually sobering up. The more the effects wore off, the happier I became. I was unsure if it was because of the effects of the N, N-Dimethyltryptamine (DMT) or because I was happy it was over.

While sitting there, I realized how much doubt I had in myself, how much control I wanted, and how much I overthought. Everything unfolded right in front of me, as if I were reading it out of a book. All my issues came to light as I sat in a dark wooden stall. I felt like I was born again. Little did I know, the entire ordeal had lasted about four hours. I was proud of myself for making it through.

Physically drained from exerting all my energy, Drew helped me back to the Maloka. Once I returned, I lay down, emotionally exhausted, muscles tense from banging my arms and legs on the floor. I lay there thinking that it probably looked like an exorcism to everyone else.

One by one, we were called up to sit in front of the shaman before the ceremony ended. While walking to sit Indian style in front of Stella, I could only shake my head at the euphoric feeling I had. As Stella blew sage smoke in my face, I thought about my family and how much I loved them. I thought about my friends and how much I missed them. I thought about how the ayahuasca showed me a reflection of myself and my thoughts. How I stressed about not being sure of what I wanted to do in life. How much I worried about what others thought and my fear of failure. In my barrage of questioning, I realized something. I realized that nothing truly mattered. Nothing mattered at all. If I decided to do music, fine. If not, fine. If I wanted to travel halfway across the world, fine. It did not matter what anyone thought. It did not matter what anyone did. No one had the answers about how life should be. Who cared anyway? I realized we were here, and that was good enough for me. I also realized God was not a person but a reflection of ourselves.

Stella blew some more smoke and dashed what smelled like lemon oil on me. Hurriedly, I wanted to document what I had experienced, but I could not find my pen. It did not matter, though. I had peace.

Every morning when the group arose, everyone shared what they experienced the night before. Some claimed they saw different shapes and colors, while others just felt peace and had visions. I described my experience to the group the best way I could, but my inability to find the words left them better off just using their imagination.

With many participants choosing to stop after having an experience like mine, Stacy asked me if I would like to continue with the remaining ceremonies. Feeling certain about my decision, I agreed to continue. Hearing Stacy say that he respected me for my decision made me feel proud for having the courage to continue.

That day consisted of the sounds of Stacy's helpers hammering on wooden frames while constructing another hut. Saws shredding through wood echoed through the thick Amazon, at times overshadowing the noise of birds that chirped. Dean and I sat at the dock, watching our group members delight in the lake as he smoked, taking puffs of tobacco.

Out of everyone, Dean and I probably became the closest of friends. He told me about life back home in Liverpool, England, and how he had an amazing talent for solving Rubik's Cubes. No matter how I twisted, turned, and rotated the cube, I was without success; but, Dean figured it out in just seconds. Smoke spread from the rolled-up tobacco that hung from his lips as he tilted his head, looking down, figuring out each pattern.

I sat there enjoying my time with these strangers. With no cell phone and no technology, I felt completely unplugged from everything, and I liked it. During that time, I reflected on the three things I had learned about myself on the previous night: my overthinking, wanting control, and having self-doubt. The more I thought about it, the less I could argue at the realization that it was true.

We gathered back in the Maloka to prepare for the next ceremony as soon as the sun had set, repeating the same routine as the night before. One lit candle, Stacy's speech, our dose of ayahuasca, Drew blowing out the candle, and then Stella's singing. Nothing happened at first as I followed my dose with a drink of water, but then I slowly began slipping into its effects.

I focused on my composure and deep breathing, as everything felt beautiful this time around. I felt in sync and in tune with everything around me. The songs Stella sang that once seemed to mock me had now been in harmony. Her a capella singing laid over the melodies of the chirping insects and Amazon ambiance. Sometimes I felt like I would lose it, but I simply took deeper breaths as I lay tingling, feeling light as a feather.

After a while, I had the urge to defecate, so I asked Drew to help me to the bathroom. While in the bathroom, I thought about back home and how everything was before I left. I thought about all the people I knew, the unhealthy relationship I was in, and the unproductive routines I had. As I pondered on that thought, I needed to purge. We were told that whenever you purge on a thought that is not good for you, it was the ayahuasca helping you release it. It helped me realize I needed to love and respect myself more than I had.

Following my purge, Drew helped me back to the hut as the effects of the ayahuasca began wearing off. I was grateful for the peaceful experience my second time around.

The humidity in the air forced me to remove my shirt, and I no longer cared about showing my scrawny, hairy chest. There, no one judged one another. We all knew everyone came to the retreat to work on themselves and to face their insecurities, all in search of self-love. And there I sat in the middle of the Amazon with a group of individuals who I might have completely ignored on any regular day. I no longer gave any thought to the outside world. In some ways, being disconnected from everything reconnected me to the essence of what life is: to be present.

On the last day of the ceremony, sadness washed over all of us, knowing the next day we would be departing. Leading up to the ceremony, I read a book called *The War on Art* by Steven Pressfield, which discussed the three essential components of creating great art: resistance, being professional, and realizing the existence of a higher power. The book inspired me to enter my last ceremony with an intent: to get inspired with creativity and ideas.

As soon as the sun disappeared from the sky, the last ceremony began. After a while, frustration settled in, as I had a difficult time purging, which lasted even longer than the first night. Then, suddenly, the urge to defecate hit me. I rushed to the bathroom, and as soon as I "purged from the bottom" and finally threw up, I began experiencing the effects of the ayahuasca. When I walked out of the bathroom, Drew was standing outside waiting for me, supporting me as he had done ever since I arrived.

Once I returned to the hut and lay down, the effects heightened, but I experienced a feeling of peace. I began seeing the colors green and yellow. Then the colors began taking shape. Though everything was so random, any and everything I thought of seemed to make sense. Yet, nothing inspired me. I did not get annoyed, however. I waited patiently and let the answer come to me like spring flowers attracting bees.

Before long, a string of ideas started forming. Ironically, as silly as some of them sounded, they all led me back to the conclusion of my first night: "Who cares?" ... "Nothing matters" ... "Do what makes you feel good." At that moment, I felt nothing but love and peace, or maybe the DMT. I realized it was not creativity I needed. It was education. Self-education. It did not matter what I did. I just needed the tools and information to do so. Then and there, all the ceremonies seemed to connect.

The first night was my cleansing; the second night was the ayahuasca showing me it was nothing to fear. And last, the third night showed me exactly what I had come for. Despite the hut being pitch black, I reached over to my backpack to pull out a pen and paper, jotting down thoughts and ideas like a madman, freely writing words elongated and wildly disregarding the margins and lines.

As Stella sang her songs, I thought about the first night and how afraid I was. Going through my cleansing experience made me realize it was only trying to help me. My first night was so challenging because it wanted me to learn anything and everything. That's why it seemed like I was in some endless loop, caught in some insolvable pattern. That's why there was so much repetition. We learn by repeating.

I lay there in bliss, not wanting to leave this realm of tranquility. With every exhale, pin-like tingles filled my body as I lay undisturbed. I felt like I could answer anything if I asked myself enough questions. I did not want it to end. Even with the effects wearing off, I continued chasing the euphoric feeling, like rushing to stop a door from closing. But when it ended, it could not have ended any better. I had always fallen asleep before the ceremony ended, but now I stayed awake. I found out that after each ceremony, everyone went outside and relaxed on the dock. The stars shined, and the full moon lit up our faces as we discussed each other's experiences.

While preparing to head back to town the following day, I snapped pictures and toured the retreat one last time. I dreaded facing the reality of leaving, and so I dragged along through the afternoon, hoping the time would do the same.

When it was finally time to leave, we piled back into the truck again. I returned to my spot with all the luggage in the canopy-covered flatbed. As we departed, Drew, along with others who stayed, waved us goodbye as I waved back from under the canopy, bursting into tears. I cried because I knew I would miss the serenity of everything. I cried because no one judged me there and I could be unarmored around strangers who now knew me more than anyone else. I cried because I felt renewed. Because the experience gave me the answers I needed. Because I knew I would miss Dreamglade. After wiping away my tears, I put on my earbuds and played Big Krit's song "Saturdays = Celebration." The day had been a celebration for me indeed. I looked at things differently now. Strangely, it seemed like my world had become different now.

The once dirty road I watched gradually turned into pavement as cabs and mopeds zipped by. I could see drivers gazing at the back of the truck, where my skinny legs rested on the tailgate. They looked and smiled, so I gave them the peace sign and a wave. And wouldn't you know? They threw up the peace sign and waved back. No longer did it seem like they were making fun of me or looking at me like some strange being. But as a human. *Maybe the world is whatever I make it out to be?* I wondered. I could only hope that it lasted.

Being back at the hostel felt bittersweet. Even the same mugginess welcomed me at the door. I finally reconnected with my family via Wi-Fi and returned to social media, stepping back into the matrix. The once minimum noise that soothed the spirit had now been just a memory. A memory that I could only reflect on as sounds from the street noise and notification alerts now surrounded me.

I met up with a few members from the retreat a couple of hours later. For our remaining time in Iquitos, we explored the area. We ventured toward the docks, where we passed through the busy street market. From baskets of fruits and vegetables to spices and herbs, even tobacco and homemade ayahuasca, all were for sale.

Moving too quickly to hang around and enjoy the market, we zigged and zagged through the crowds of people heading toward the docks to ride one of the boats. I heard one lady yell "Negro!"—meaning Black. She waved and blew me a kiss, so I waved and blew one back. Where did this complete shift come from? Was it because I decided to look at my situation differently now? A week ago, strangers had mocked me for my complexion. Now, the locals welcomed me. Maybe I began seeing the beauty that existed because I had opened my eyes more. I had learned to notice the love that was there as opposed to the love that was not.

While on the boat tour, we spotted families and their shacks, separated by spaces of water. Canoes were tied up, roped around short pieces of wood, floating gently outside people's homes. You could see where water levels had risen over time by the lines of erosion that had formed around the shacks.

I rode in the boat, feeling light as a feather. Admiring my surroundings with the warm air and humming motor. Appreciative of my time in Iquitos and at Dreamglade. Grateful for what I had learned and all the amazing souls I had met.

Upon returning from our outing, we grabbed some food before going our separate ways. Though we were done with the retreat, I could not determine if I had stepped back into reality or left it. I had tapped into some source I knew was there, and I only hoped it would continue to last. What I did know was, for the moment, I was happy. I had found a joy that almost hurt to know I had gone so long without. In all, I would never forget the time I shared with these people, and I would miss them dearly.

25

Reflection

Flying 30,000 feet over the Peruvian Amazon, I felt like I had left a part of me behind in Iquitos. I had spent close to two months in Peru, and now I turned my sights toward La Paz, Bolivia, which made me excited and anxious. I carried with me new ideas, a new creative spark, and a new outlook on life.

My positivity came to a brief halt when I missed my flight, resulting in me having to spend the night in Lima. I returned to the same hostel as before in the district of Miraflores and its beautiful cliffside view. The people continued their park activities even with the sun already even with the blue ocean line. I sat on the bench thinking about the retreat and what all I had learned, with one or two funny looks already testing me.

Though disappointed I would have to spend the night in Lima, the vast ocean brought ease to my mind. I remained focused on embarking on my new journey to La Paz. Trying to save a few dollars, I decided to travel by bus, not realizing it would be a thirty-hour bus ride. Had I caught my flight, I could have made the trip in six hours. But my regret gradually faded as the hours went by, reacquainting me with places I had already visited.

Each city we rode through brought back memories as I reminisced about the people I met and the things I did. We traveled through the city of Paracas, where we sailed out to see the rock formations covered with sea lions and exotic birds. We zipped by the desert dunes of Ica, where my hat was probably buried deep in the sand by now. We also made our way through Arequipa, where I could still see volcanoes in the distance poking at the blue sky. I even thought about the trip to Colca Canyon and my Spanish lessons I could not remember now.

As we approached the Bolivia border, I made one more pass through Puno and Lake Titicaca, where I stayed with Mr. Simon and Mrs. Maria. I thought about how I had seen the Milky Way for the first time and how immense the lake was. So many memories to cherish.

I spent my thirty-hour trip writing, listening to music, and taking naps here and there. At times, I could not help but smile to myself, even as a little boy cried for what seemed like the entire trip. I thought about how a twenty-five-year-old Black male had grabbed the bull by the horns and had the world as his oyster. This brought me joy. I smiled because I had taken my life into my own hands, even if only for a few months.

"Bienvenidos A Bolivia" read the rusted sign as we walked under it. Once we arrived at the border, we exited the bus and crossed the bridge for immigration papers. Bolivia had been the first country where I needed a visa to enter. Luckily, the government allowed travelers to get one as soon as they entered the country.

Brick buildings lined up across from each other, old and lacking attention. Portions of buildings that had been painted now faded from the weather. I walked up to a table in the middle of the street where a lady sat waiting to write down my identification on paper. As I observed the locals who walked the street among the buildings, I noticed they looked beaten, beaten by hard labor. I sensed that everyone earned their own. Unlike in other places, I did not receive any funny looks. The people were much darker compared to the other countries I had visited. They seemed unconcerned about me and where I was from, which I did not mind at all. Once cleared, we loaded back onto the bus and continued on our way.

Because night had fallen when we reached La Paz, I did not expect to see as many lights as I did. I could not see the buildings, but I could recognize the multitude of lights that peppered the valley landscape that was La Paz. Traffic surprised me the same as I rode in the back of a taxi in search of my hostel, which turned out to be a party hostel.

I walked into the two-story hostel with people lounging around and the thumping of music coming from the floor above. After a thirty-hour bus ride, I began to second guess if coming to a party hostel had been a good idea.

La Paz reminded me of Bogotá with its gray skies and its inescapable chilliness. Its slanted streets could easily give one shortness of breath. Outside of hanging around the hostel and meeting old and new people, I did not do anything too adventurous. I made up for the boredom by cycling down what is considered the most dangerous road in South America called "Death Road," my sole purpose in visiting La Paz.

The road was mainly used for cycling, now that there was an alternative and safer route for drivers, but occasionally one or two vehicles dared enough to challenge their nerves. Over the edge of the cliff lay a 2,000-foot drop without any guard rails or protection from falling. With parts of the road being eroded from harsh weather and landslides, the name Death Road was fitting. During the early to mid-90s, the road averaged around 200 to 300 deaths each year. Its sharp curves and unpredictable elements, ranging from clouds of dust to blankets of fog, caused limited visibility and close to thirty vehicles a year to plummet.

As twisted as it seemed to make a thrill-seeking tour of something that had caused people to lose their lives, people still signed up, including me. My trip had begun with me flirting in dangerous territory, venturing out into the unknown, so why not?

I figured it would at least be a cool story to tell. Plus, we would get free t-shirts at the end.

Twenty-one of us lined up side by side as we exited the van awaiting instructions. We each wore a pair of thick pants and a zipper jacket with gloves that left no skin visible. In large, red stitching, the word "Altitude" stretched diagonally across the chest of the yellow and dark blue uniform. We wore elbow pads and knee pads that covered the shins under our suits and helmets that shielded everything but our eyes on our heads. Even with all that protection, nothing would save our asses if we fell off the side of the cliff.

At the beginning of the course, we zipped down what looked like newly paved roads. We sped down smooth asphalt, having only a car or two passing by every so often. Gusts of air beat our torsos, causing resistance as some of us leaned in with our helmets down. The rotating clicking sounds of turning chains fought with a burst of wind that filled my ears as we rode around curves. Feeling fresh morning air while blazing down a mountain on a lifeless highway made it seem as though we owned the road, but this was merely a warm-up until we reached Death Road itself.

Next, we arrived at an offroad path of loose rocks and wet dirt. As we made our way around, we could see the infamous road up ahead, hugging closely to the mountain's stone wall. As we approached, immense fog lingered over the edge of the cliff, virtually impenetrable. It was almost impossible to perceive with our eyes how far up we were.

In addition to the sketchy road with no guard railings and a lack of visibility, we had to watch out for falling rocks, which I admit was slightly wild. However, I did not quite understand why we were trailed by an ambulance. If we were to fall, and have any imaginable chance of survival, I would have preferred the emergency medical technicians (EMTs) to be stationed at the bottom. But just like the protective gear, I appreciated the thought.

After about three hours of zipping down dirt and mud, steering clear of surprisingly one or two construction truck-type vehicles, riding under waterfalls, and bending around curves, we survived Death Road. Without question, I could see how one mishap could end tragically for any motorist, given the conditions. But our precautions did not put a damper on our exhilarating ride.

With how stressed out I had been with overthinking, especially about what other people thought about me, I needed the break. I needed the thrill. I needed a chance to enjoy myself and not think for once.

—

Though my stay in La Paz was short, I struck up a conversation with two guys from Scandinavia before leaving. The question they posed left me stuck.

"What is your tribe?" one asked.

"My tribe?" I repeated.

"Yes, your tribe," said the other.

I stood there not sure if they were being jackasses or just naively asking the question.

"You are African American, but what is your heritage? Where are you from? Your tribe," the first guy continued.

"Yeah, not sure," I replied.

For some time, their question stuck in my mind like a nail in wood. I had never considered learning about my heritage. Why did it take two Scandinavian guys asking me about my roots for me to be curious enough to learn about them? Why did I think about this now? I could not think of one time when I had been curious about my roots in the past. To know where I came from. To have some identity and to know from where my ancestry truly emerged instead of from a slave ship. Because I was never encouraged to find out that information, I figured my family had not thought about it either.

I left La Paz that evening to catch a night bus on the way to Sucre, Bolivia, still collecting bracelets as I went, relieved that I had only a twelve-hour bus ride. Bus terminals had become a regular thing to me now. I had grown comfortable with parading around the terminal, hauling my bags in search of a company heading where I needed to go. And this time I needed to go to Uyuni, Bolivia, to the Salt Flats.

Imagine yourself standing in the center of a flat, crusted surface of white salt that stretched out for miles in every direction. The images I had seen before appeared dreamlike, like one photo where rain caused the ground to look like you were standing on one giant mirror. This place truly seemed unworldly. But first I needed to get past a twelve-hour trip with no bathroom breaks.

Even so, I always looked forward to night buses. Next to showers, they were my ideal places to think. I did not have to think about moving or driving. The bus did that for me while I peered out the windows, lost in thought. And I thought plenty. I thought about what I wanted to do when I got back, the places I had been, and all the people I had seen. I thought about Dreamglade and how it helped me. I missed the environment, the camaraderie, and the love. It gave me an idea and a vision. I just needed to do my part now.

I stepped off the bus in Sucre around 7:30 a.m., meeting cold weather, clear skies, and tour agency representatives trying to round up as many tourists as possible. They knew tourists came to Uyuni for one reason: to see the Salt Flats.

Altogether, six of us signed up for the trip, which included more than exploring the Salt Flats. We visited other places like the Train Cemetery, where train cars and engines sat abandoned for nearly the past 100 years. We also visited Dakar Bolivia, where they held races every year for the Dakar Rally out in the middle of nowhere.

From where we were, I could tell we were knocking at the Salt Flats' front door. After loading back into our SUV, we continued as the ground began morphing into the salted surface I had seen in photos. We had to use those thick, off-road tires for tough terrain to ride on that kind of surface. And even after making

215

a stop, we noticed a chunk of tire the size of a baseball had begun peeling off. But fortunately, based on the driver's reaction, it was not a big deal.

Soon after, it was evident that the spacious area had now transformed into the Salt Flats. Open space of nothing but hard white salt and blue sky. The surroundings were surreal, as if we had stepped onto a blank canvas that God left untouched. Hexagon-shaped patterns of crusted salt covered the entire salt flats like we had walked into a sketch of an enormous honeycomb. The remarkable thing about the Salt Flats was not only the landscape but also the unique photos it offered. The flats gave the illusion that objects were larger or smaller than they appeared. From the photos we snapped, I had been chased by dinosaurs, stood on a pack of lifesaver candies, sat on a roll of toilet tissue, and sailed in a broken peanut shell.

Though we roamed the Salt Flats for about thirty minutes, it did not seem nearly as long as it should have been. Upon leaving, we drove for about two more hours until we reached our shelter for the night, a hostel made of salt. From the walls to the tables to the seats, everything was made of salt. The guide even mentioned that we could lick the walls if we wanted, but I was not that much of a skeptic.

Once settled in, we drank a few beers and shared stories like I had done many other nights before. Though the location, the people, and the stories changed, the feeling was always the same: good company and camaraderie with total strangers. It filled me and nourished my soul every time.

We continued the tour the following day, which involved seeing lagoons and spotting foxes and rabbits. Distant hills with ice-capped volcanoes stood out in every direction, making everything around them look like bumps of dirt. Flat, dry land stretched out as far as we could ride in our SUV. Around midday, the temperature still had us wrapped up in light coats and scarves, but not a single cloud appeared in the sky.

As beautiful as the day was, I would later uncover some information that would help me understand this dark cloud that seemed to linger throughout my travels. Though the ayahuasca helped me release the concern I felt about the strange looks I had received, it still lingered in the back of my mind. Curious to know more about their perspective, I overheard some of my group members having an interesting conversation over dinner.

"Yeah, so, my good friend went traveling around Peru a while and was invited to dinner at a teacher's house in Lima. He told me that when he got there, there was a photo of Adolf Hitler on his wall. He never asked why it was there, but thought it was just the strangest thing," disclosed one of the group members.

"Hmm, yeah, that is odd. He had to have known what that man has done, yeah?" the other one replied.

Could some people in South America have been influenced by Hitler's ideologies about Blacks? Though this realization only left me wanting to know more, it lifted some of the pressure off my conscience to help make sense of it all.

At 4:45 a.m., we prepared for our departure at the end of our tour. The cold had crept its way around my bones as I took some time to gaze up at the stars. No matter the circumstance, the Milky Way always reminded me why it was always worth it to admire it whenever I could.

As we drove to our last stop, I noticed the cold had made its way into the car, with frost forming on the windows inside. We all sat bundled in our clothes, sitting tightly to keep warm as daylight broke. Crazy enough, our last stop was at the hot springs. Though some of my group members were bold enough to hop in as steam rose from the spring, I stayed in the car. My common sense was much stronger than my will to take the risk.

After the rest of the group had their fun, we continued on to the border, where the group waited as one of my group members, Isabelle, and I stood in line to cross the Chilean border. We were the only two who would cross into Chile, while the rest would head back to Uyuni. We stood in a line of other border hoppers in the nipping cold for about thirty minutes.

Eyes watering from the brisk wind, I stood there with my hands in my pockets, my arms positioned firmly by my sides. My scarf covered my nose and mouth, while my wool alpaca hat warmed my head. I stood at the border thinking my time in Bolivia had passed quickly, but I had accomplished everything I wanted to do in a little over a week.

Isabelle and I said our goodbyes to the group and snapped our last round of pictures as we boarded the bus. Isabelle was a German girl who had been traveling alone for a couple of weeks. Since we had already been around each other for a few days, we knew we would probably stick together at our next stop.

Though the trip was only thirty minutes, Isabelle and I sat there almost falling asleep from the warm heat of the bus. I glanced at my bracelets that loosely slid up and down my wrist, thinking it seemed like I had been traveling forever. But I was more than some traveler; I was a backpacker. Moving when I wanted to move. Going where I wanted to go. And it felt good.

26

Shift

Upon our arrival at the Chilean check-in early in the afternoon, Isabella and I recognized two other girls from the Salt Flats tour. We invited Jesse and Ella, who were from the U.K., to join us, as we all were in search of a hostel. We four—Jesse, Ella, Isabella, and I—stuck together and rode the bus to San Pedro, Chile, to the Atacama Desert, the driest place on earth.

When we arrived in San Pedro, it seemed as if someone had dropped us off in some western cowboy town. Visually, it may have been the coolest town I had ever visited, with its red dirt streets and clay buildings. We walked around in the dry heat until we found a good hostel called Hostal Matty.

After settling into the hostel and taking a much-needed shower, we set out to roam the town. One thing I noticed throughout South America was how many stray dogs there were, but no country showed affection to dogs the way Chile did. And it showed through the dogs themselves. They walked down the street among the people as though they had just as much right to do so as everyone else. Dogs would walk up to you and allow you to pet them in exchange for food. Some would lie down right outside of shops and even walk in them, and no one would bat an eye. And sometimes, they would walk next to you just to be a temporary companion.

Jesse, Ella, Isabella, and I walked past small restaurants, tour agencies, gift shops—and bike rental shops, which seemed to be every other store. I did not notice any bizarre looks until I sat down in a restaurant for lunch, receiving uncomfortable stares from someone across from us and a few laughs as I tried to order my food in Spanish.

Without thinking, I leaned over in their direction and asked, "Donde?" I thought to myself that maybe they were visiting from Peru.

They paused briefly, and then one of the men replied, "Chile".

Fuck. Chile got them, too.

"Do you know who that is?" Jess asked me.

I shook my head. "Nah, I don't."

The girls burst out laughing, which made me laugh. Plus, it made me feel as though the other family thought we were laughing at them. It felt satisfying. I mentioned nothing to the girls about it, but it seemed like I had been trying to escape this judgmental mentality ever since I entered Peru. I could not help but wonder how much further this thinking spanned.

With those thoughts already on my mind, things did not improve when I arrived back at the hostel to find out my Uncle H. J. had passed away. He was the third person who had passed away since I left. I felt terrible for my grandmother, knowing she had lost one sister and now one brother. And yet, there I was, thousands of miles away, enjoying life while my loved ones were back home grieving.

Once again, I believed arriving back home would be like puzzle pieces missing from a bigger picture, multiple stories left unfinished. Was I wrong for leaving? At times, I felt guilty for doing so. But did that mean I should not experience life and take advantage of it while I could? Was there a cost of living? Even a cost for feeling enjoyment? At that moment, I decided I would return home in two months. That would put me at six months. Half a year. Yes, six months felt like the right time to head back.

While sitting with the girls at dinner, the fact that I had finally determined a time frame seemed surreal. The words tossed around in my mind just as they were: words. *Am I ready?* I thought.

—

San Pedro could easily be in my top five favorite places that I visited. Everything including the clear skies, the landscapes, and even more so the tours. The girls and I took the Valley de la Luna and Death Valley tour, where we witnessed the Atacama Desert at its best. Flowing water from hundreds of years ago created nothing but dunes and red stone landscapes. Rock formations and jagged rocks formed with minerals of hardened salt over the years looked like snowflakes dashed all around. The red desert was so striking that it seemed like we were walking on Mars. We ran down the sides of dunes, wailing our arms with bursts of laughs while holding our shoes in our hands. The warm sand covered our feet with each step, zig-zagging in a descending line. There was not a speck of cloud in the blue, unblemished sky.

To top the day off, we climbed up a mound of red rocks to the top of a viewpoint to watch the sunset. From the top, it looked like we were staring down into a crater. Salt comprised most of the base below with small clumps of rocks, and beyond the crater sat mountains and volcanoes along with blue skies. Isabelle and Ella went off to take pictures a few feet ahead, while Jesse and I sat and talked on the Mars rock-like surface. It was one of the more meaningful conversations I had in South America, chatting with Jesse with the sun beaming off her black Ray-Ban shades.

"Whatever I do, I just want it to have purpose, ya know? Something with meaning," she said.

"Same," I replied. "I think everyone wants that, really. But I love the fact that when we are out in the world traveling, how many times we run into like-minded individuals. It's like a community that can relate to one another. A family, really."

"Right, it just goes to show how much more we all are alike than different. And though everything I own now is in a backpack, I feel a sense of power being out here."

"Yes, I feel the same. Unfortunately, it has to come to an end one day."

Moments like these seemed to sum up what backpacking was all about. To have rough rocks of the earth as seats with the sun kissing your face as it sets. To be in a foreign location knowing all you have is what you have at that moment as you share that moment with someone from another part of the world.

Shortly after, shadows from the other side filled the crater, creeping up slowly toward us as the sun set.

"Okay, everyone, turn around so you can see why the sunsets here are so special," announced our tour guide.

We looked around and beheld a rainbow of colors reflecting off the mountains and sky. Various hues of purple, pink, and orange created one of the most memorable sights for me, the best representation of watching the day die out.

Back at the hostel, I wondered what my boys back home would say if I told them I stayed in a room with three young European girls and did not have sex with at least one of them. I could not quite escape the things I had learned from my peers growing up. Needing to feed that male ego of "I'm fucking x amount of girls from x amount of places if given the chance." Part of my mind saw this as a dream come true, a fantasy. Four free, traveling souls away from home open to having some foursome because we were carefree backpackers who would not see each other anymore, anyway. But nope, I lay across the bed with three girls in night clothes like we were having a slumber party, chatting about eating chocolate-filled croissants for breakfast and touring Diablo Canyon on bikes.

And for the next six hours, I could feel every minute on the narrow leather seats with no shocks. We did not know what to expect, but we could count on the weather to be perfectly sunny as always. We rode over dirt pathways, and even a stream of water that soaked our shoes, to reach the canyons. Outside of the harsh ride on our bikes, you could not ask for a more beautiful day. We navigated our way alongside large rocks on twisting and winding dirt paths like ants moving between cracks of cement. At some points, spaces were so narrow that one could stretch both arms out and touch the rock on each side. The clumps of bulging rocks were like walls that made us feel isolated from the world.

We later ended the night with a stargazing tour. Pitch blackness surrounded us from the view of my window seat as we, and twenty-one other guests, made our way to some secluded area that was more like a house than an observatory. The stars shined brighter than they had in Colca Canyon and Uyuni. Several high-tech telescopes formed a circle, pointing at Jupiter and Saturn, as well as different zodiac signs and constellations. We saw the Milky Way, Orion's belt, and the Jewelry Box, just to name a few.

—

Knowing we all would have to separate, my last two days in San Pedro were bittersweet. We stopped around town, treating ourselves to ice cream and more chocolate croissants and sending postcards to our families.

Having never sent a postcard before, I picked up two of them from a local shop for my grandparents and my mom: one of Death Valley and one of Valley De La Luna. I thought they would get a kick out of them, being that we mainly communicated via email and Facebook. And I thought by sending them something tangible, they would cherish it more and find some comfort in seeing my actual handwriting. I wanted to send them something I had physically touched to make us feel closer together.

On my departure day, I knew I would miss the girls. They enjoyed listening to my accent, and I enjoyed laughing at their attempts to imitate a southern accent. We clicked and vibed so well together, but I knew I had to move on.

I walked to the bus station to admire the weather one last time. Though I loved it, I would have loved to restore the moisture it had snatched from my skin. Most of the time, my lips would dry quickly, and my skin was ashy as hell, despite drinking water and lotioning my body.

As the bus pulled out of the station, I put on my earbuds and gazed out of my window, taking in another striking view of Death Valley one last time. And oddly enough, I did not know why, but it seemed like my trip was over. It was like I did not want to leave. Of course, being a backpacker, one could travel anywhere whenever they wanted. But it seemed like I had reached a point where I traveled just to be traveling now.

While I still wanted to go to Brazil, I did not have anything spectacular to look forward to like Angel Falls, Machu Picchu, or the Salt Flats. I had seen pretty much all that I wanted to see. And maybe it had something to do with the weather changing as well. The further south I went, the more I noticed how much cooler the days and nights had become. No longer the warm, summer-fun feel. The fun had gone. Even though I continued traveling, it seemed like my journey had ended. Yet, there I rode on a bus, heading further south, on my way to La Serena, Chile, leaving Mars and coming back to Earth. Reality.

Section 6: Appreciation

Gazing at golden rays over a gorgeous evening's haze, for any pain this sight could soothe.

As the sun begins to tire, I contemplate and admire, for to the night the light will lose.

How could this be? Knowing something so convincingly, yet it's hard to describe.

How things can happen so quick, that one can easily forget, just how good it feels to be alive.

My appreciation exceeds that of aged wine soaking in wooden oak barrels.

Without the need of moving legs and notes, my heart dances to the same sheet of music as the moment.

Like the radiance from a fireplace delicately touching the skin, it gives me a warm feeling.

And it's as satisfying as a deep breath.

Aren't these encounters and experiences from my memories' vineyard just as sweet and rich as ripe grapes?

A wave of unexpected gratefulness softens my eyes and relaxes my shoulders,

Causing me not to want anything except to sit a little while longer.

Even days thought shattered, every moment mattered, including the ones rough and jaded.

But I realized that, once I took a step back, that's how you fully appreciate a mosaic.

27

Desire

The streetlights still burned as I sat at the bus stop upon my arrival in La Serena. The sun struggled to rise just as I struggled to move. For no reason at all, I sat there waiting, watching taxis pick up other travelers. I had not one hurry bone in my body, as I sat reflecting on how it seemed like my trip was over.

Glancing around, I began feeling like every city became the same now. Was it because I believed there was nothing else to look forward to? Maybe I did not like these cities as much as the more rural areas. Or maybe my backpacking tank was empty, and I was not excited about traveling anymore.

With just enough money, I booked a room for a night. While checking into my new hostel, I noticed a framed picture of the hostel I had just left in San Pedro. I assumed some connection existed between them, which made me feel slightly better, since I enjoyed it so much.

While out roaming the streets, I could not remember the reason I came to La Serena. The beach, maybe? The town did not have too much to offer, from what I could tell. I began looking ahead to prepare myself to enter Argentina whenever I made it there. U.S. citizens paid a fee to get into Argentina, so I gathered all the information I needed on the hostel computer. Feeling unenthused about my stay, I contemplated if I should leave the following day. And when the next day came, I received my answer.

After breakfast, I went out to buy a charger because I began noticing how worn mine had become. I walked past a local who was either homeless or not well kept based on his dingy clothes and dusty look. Walking past me, he looked to the other side of the street and shouted out, "Aye doctor, un negro!" Maybe he did not think I knew what he had said, but I looked across the street where two doctors stood smirking and looking away. To imagine that if something happened to me and I had to depend on doctors who judged me because of my skin color troubled me. With these thoughts in mind, I purchased the charger and rushed back to the hostel, packing up my things to hop on the first bus heading to Santiago.

No matter where I went, I could not escape the judgment I continuously tried to avoid. Maybe that added to the feeling of my trip being over. The further I traveled, the more scrutiny I received. Why did they look at me like some clown? Were people of a darker color being portrayed as a joke in other parts of the world as well? Even in a country where people of all shades lived? I had hoped things would be better in the next city, or the city after that. Each stop had now become a gamble, knowing that my chances were unfavorable. The experience had become mundane and, because there were few travelers who looked like me, no one could relate.

I found enjoyment in gazing out the window at the landscapes we passed on my bus rides. The different curvatures of the land always seemed to relate to me. Its strange hills and peculiar mountains were all different everywhere I traveled. The land seemed more understanding than humans at times; sometimes it changed and shifted, and no place was the same. No matter how unique something looked, it was just as much the land here as it was there. I only wished everyone would see it that way.

It took us about six hours to arrive in Santiago, the capital of Chile. They had one of the largest bus terminals I had seen with different floors to drop off passengers. The number of people coming and going could easily trigger one's anxiety.

Without wasting much time, I picked up a few snacks and maneuvered through the crowds of people and out the door to flag down a taxi. Traffic had been so congested that many of the drivers turned aggressive and hostile. So much so that my taxi driver and another driver nearly got into an altercation, resulting in the other driver pulling out a steel pipe and smacking my driver's front bumper with it. If I had not been in the car, then they might have had a scuffle. I figured if the people there cared more about kicking each other's asses, then I should not have a problem.

Things got off to a rough start on my first morning in Santiago, however. Sitting alone at breakfast, I read my emails, receiving one from my grandmother telling me another one of our neighbors, Mr. Rock, had passed away. This loss increased the count to four people who had passed away since I had been gone. I literally could not believe that I had lost four people over four months: two family members and two family friends. Gone.

My day dragged along, putting a damper on the excitement of being in a new city. Still, I searched for something to do. Flyers at the front desk of the hostel advertised city tours downtown, and I decided to take a tour, hoping it would take my mind off things.

Between being informed about the rich indigenous culture through murals painted throughout the city and modern attractions where half-dressed women served you coffee, I could not help but notice the number of dogs that roamed the city. Even the tour guide mentioned the city's love for them. Locals would feed the dogs and even clothe them, from neckerchiefs to shirts. The locals fed the dogs so well that the dogs had gotten fat, one stretching out the hoodie he wore.

The great thing about being in Santiago was that I already knew someone there, Paolo, who I had met in Arequipa. He had helped me study for my Spanish exam. Paolo was one of the very few people, like Ernesto and Ruben in Venezuela, who I could say had me in their best interest.

Paolo insisted that he take me on his version of a city tour. He showed me parts of the city that were not so touristic, like the local markets. Paolo's English was not the best, yet we had a delightful conversation. He discussed the history there and how the people were divided, just like Democrats and Republicans back home. He also introduced me to a popular dessert made of dried peaches, cinnamon, wheat, and honey. I questioned the dessert at first, looking at the pile of husk wheat seeds bunched at the bottom of the syrupy liquid. Though delicious, it had so much sugar packed in it that I could feel diabetes entering my body.

Because I trusted his opinion, I felt comfortable asking Paolo if there was anything against Black people there, or if he had heard any ill comments at all.

"Hey, let me ask you somethin.' Do you know if some of the people don't like Black people, or people my color?"

He looked a bit confused for a moment. "No, there are not things like that. I have not heard bad things."

Even with hearing those words from him, I still remembered all the things I had encountered, and I was certain it would be something that would always bother me.

—

Santiago had to have been one of the busiest cities I had visited where I was the most adventurous on my own. I even took subways out of the city to check out a bike and wine tour, hosted at a popular vineyard on the eastern outskirts of Santiago. After twenty subway stops and a taxi ride, I finally made it to the endless rows of autumn-colored grapevines with mountain ranges out in the distance. Upon strolling around outside of the ranch-type distillery, mixing my search for people with a curiosity about where I was, I met a small group of five waiting outside. Two guests were from North Carolina, and it thrilled us to know we were neighbors.

We rode along dirt roads through the fields of vines, eating the grapes we plucked, stashing them in our small baskets in front of our handlebars. Drooping leaves hung over us as we passed large Mayten trees on a road filled with golden leaves. Our green bikes with chrome mudguards crunched leaves under the tires as we cruised in the morning coolness.

While touring different areas of grapes that represented the wine, we tasted a few samples. We went down to a couple of cellars where gigantic barrels of wine that nearly reached the ceiling aged over time. Some parts looked like dungeons in darker areas with bricked walls and barred gates, with smaller barrels lined up down a long hallway. At the end of the tour, I concluded that red wine was trash, and I liked white wine better. However, I still preferred beer over everything.

When I finally returned to the hostel after my long day, someone had apparently stolen my extra pair of shoes and my night slippers. Who in the hell steals night slippers? How desperate does a person have to be to steal used night slippers? No longer could I take showers and step into my night slippers. I had to get out of the shower and step into the boots I had worn throughout the day.

Though I was not as hurt as when someone had stolen $400 from me in Popayan, Colombia, I tried to take my mind off the shoe theft by going on the early morning city tour the next day. We stopped at other historical landmarks and ended at the General Cemetery of Santiago. The size of the cemetery was equivalent to one hundred and seventeen soccer fields, with endless statues, mausoleums, memorials, and headstones in every direction we looked.

We walked down the street between cemented homes with street signs on the corners that made the cemetery look more like a neighborhood. We passed vertical wall-like compartments that housed the dead as well, graves stacked on top of one another like twenty-foot decaying apartment buildings. Engraved names labeled the chipped cement while dying flowers sat on the seals of the graves. Some of the dead, mostly families, even shared compartments, having two and three lists of names on one compartment.

While there, we stopped by the gravesite of "Romualdito," who the people in Santiago considered an "Animita" or a guardian angel. Animitas were people whose lives ended tragically. They believed these guardian angels helped the living by doing favors or granting the blessings they asked for. If the favor happened, then it was tradition to put a plaque, flowers, or candles at the location of where the guardian angel lost their life or at their gravesite. Romualdito was the most famous of them all, having a shrine of plaques, candles, and letters at his grave, thanking him for doing "favors" for people.

Vases of flowers lined across and above his grave with messages of thanks on marble plaques, letters folded and slid between every available space with a small Chilean flag hanging below. From all the appreciation shown, it made the grave itself barely visible. It amazed me that people still paid respect to someone who spent their life as a regular citizen and whose life was taken nearly eighty years ago. That they appreciated his kind heart and his service to people so much that they were still thankful and showed respect for him. That was one hell of a way to be remembered. I could only hope to be fortunate enough to make an impact like that.

During my last few days in Santiago, I decided to make the tedious walk up to the viewpoint on top of a hill, where I concluded that nearly every large city in South America had a giant statue of Jesus Christ with his arms stretched out. Though tired, joy rushed over me once I arrived at the foot of the hill. It reminded me of trekking again. After forty-five minutes of hiking, I ogled at the aging sun as it lit the city below. Light smog hovered over Santiago, dividing where the city met the outlining hills. Locals and tourists took pictures and admired the scenery during the last bit of daylight of the day. Dogs, too.

—

Valparaiso rests on the coast of Chile, looking over a bay with descending streets and artistic buildings. It may have taken me a little over an hour from Santiago to arrive there one afternoon. To save money, I decided to walk to my hostel because it was roughly nearby. Walking about ten blocks along streets lined with stores and bars marked with graffiti, I spotted the hostel ahead on the corner of a forked street. The hostel did not seem to have much life as I checked into an empty five-bed room.

Five months had passed since I began my trip. I thought about how much I had done and how many people I had encountered in that time. I was not that neatly groomed, well-trimmed guy in the pictures from back then anymore. Because my hair had grown out, I now had to stuff my hair under my hat. My mustache had grown over my lip, and below my beard was stubble from my botched attempts at shaving. All the hair seemed to compensate for the weight I had lost. Yet there I was, two wrists loaded with bracelets and a few shoes less.

Like all cities, the best way to get acquainted with one was to search for a city tour. Heading there, I passed corners of stray dogs—spotting at least one with a t-shirt on—and turned on cobbled roads where colorful paintings were displayed on walls and buildings of shops. A local also stopped me, who, from the looks of it, lived on the street with a few others.

"Donde?" he asked.

For some reason, I decided to tell him I came from Jamaica.

"Ahhhhhhhh," he bellowed.

Oddly, the man reached out and hugged me, showing his missing teeth as he laughed. It threw me off so much that I could not focus on what he said. I hurried and continued my walk as the man began singing Bob Marley's lyrics, "No woman, no cry."

The next day, the city held its National Cultural Day, making all the museums and other activities free to the public. Back in Santiago, Paolo recommended visiting the Pablo Neruda Museum, which worked out perfectly now that I did not have to pay.

Located at the top of Valparaiso, the museum was once the home of Pablo Neruda, a poet and former senator of the Republic

232

of Chile. The museum looked peculiar with its many windows and odd-shaped floors, going from straight and angled to round closer to the front. Even though the house did not appear level from the outside, the weirdness and creativity of the museum did not actualize until I entered the building. It looked like I had stepped into *Pee-wee's Playhouse,* with eccentric furniture and objects as decorations. The house seemed more like that of some crazed inventor with unfinished and unreleased patents all around, including antiques, telescopes, and giant spinning globes.

Though not allowed to take photos, we received permission to take snapshots of the primary reason visitors came to the museum: the view. The multiple vast windows made a nearly panoramic view of the city below. The house sat in the center of each direction, undoubtedly the best view in the city. Witnessing everything from the docks, to the beautiful bay, to the many buildings reaching from the left to the right of Valparaiso, the view alone satisfied my trip there.

After visiting the museum, I gathered my things from the hostel and headed to the bus station. Paolo told me Valparaiso was good for a day trip, so I figured there would be no need to stay any longer. However, had I known how long I would have to wait on my bus, I would not have checked out so early. I sat in the same spot at the bus terminal for the next seven hours, spending most of my time drawing graffiti.

I caught the attention of the travelers sitting closest to me until they left, and a pair of new eyes took their place. A boy and a girl, both about seven, sat looking, drawn in by the colors I drew with my crayons. I sketched the word "Valparaiso, Chile" in yellow graffiti-type letters with the Chilean flag behind it. Quietly, they gazed at my paper of yellows and reds with touches of purples and pinks.

Subconsciously, I thought maybe if they could see me drawing, then they would see I enjoyed colors and art just as much as they did. I hoped it would plant some seed in their minds to look beyond skin color. No matter the circumstances, the thought of being looked at differently because of my skin color always disturbed me. No matter how many times I tried to accept it, I could never fully let it go. I figured it might have been too late for the adults, but I could at least show the children there was no difference between a person with dark skin and a person with light skin. Even if it was just showing them that I liked to color, too.

28

Movement

I reached Puerto Varas, Chile, early the next morning. The fresh smell of rain and morning dew lingered in the air as I continued my streak of walking to my hostel. Puerto Varas sat right on the edge of Lake Llanquihue, the second largest lake in Chile.

Restaurants, homes, and shops rimmed the lake as I followed the sidewalk around it. A couple of tuna boats idled in the massive lake with birds hovering above. *It's an ideal place for the writer*, I thought. The lake was not in a big city with heavy traffic but in a small, quiet town by the water with lush grass and alluring, gray skies. Even the German influenced buildings were a nice touch. German flags hung on walls and on some buildings, which intrigued my curiosity, since one could easily imagine they were touring some rural countryside in Europe.

I strolled past one of the local restaurants where I saw a waitress grab the attention of a cook and point at me from the side door. It seemed as if I would never get out of this shit. From what I had experienced as being Black throughout my trip, along with the piece of information I had received about the Peruvian teacher with Hitler's picture on his wall, I thought maybe the influence here covered the full spectrum of Germany, both good and bad.

When I entered my hostel, the receptionist looked welcoming and surprised all at once. Before long, it seemed like one of those interactions where people appear a little too helpful. I remember having a conversation with my friends about this, agreeing we had experienced this mostly when we were the only Black person in a room and a group of white people tried to make us feel comfortable. And it was painfully obvious. She explained things extra carefully, making sure that there were no missed details about anything.

The thing is, the receptionist was not a local but an American. I could tell she had been there for a while. Though unsure if I was the first American she had seen in a while, I was surely the first Black one.

—

I strolled downstairs the following morning to begin the nature reserve tour that the overly helpful receptionist had told me about. Three others waited as I arrived. As we loaded into the van, the weather looked as though it would rain at any minute.

On the way there, we passed by the aftermath of a volcanic eruption that had occurred a month prior. Ash accumulated along the sides of the road, looking like mounds of soil as we passed. When one of my group members inquired about the activity of the volcano, our tour guide mentioned that it could be months before another eruption occurred, which helped ease my mind.

Light rain fell as we walked between vegetated rock walls and moss-covered boulders in the natural reserve. While there, I received an opportunity to learn a little about our small group. One couple had been traveling for some time and planned to visit Torres Del Paine in Patagonia next, a place I had recently put on my radar to visit. The last group member, Nicholas, worked for Trip Advisor, so he traveled often for business yet enjoyed himself as well. He had a metal rod in one leg that I noticed from how stiffly he moved it. Though the result of a medical condition, it did not stop him from getting around. He pressed through just like the rest of us, bending under and maneuvering around falling, moss-covered logs.

We continued on our way, observing waterfalls and seven-hundred-year-old trees that one could not wrap their arms around. Outside of breaking a sweat, our ponchos kept us dry for the rest of our time until we returned to town.

—

Later that night, we all went out for food. While talking to Nicholas, I learned that people mistook him for being the music artist Pitbull, just shorter and thinner. With his bald head and thin mustache, I guess it could have been possible. He told me about a story of him getting pulled over by police that ended with them taking a group picture. It even got him out of a ticket.

Once we were done, the couple retired to the hostel, and Nicholas and I checked out a local club. Though I was not thrilled about going, I tagged along so that he would not be alone. I learned that night that if you ever want to know who someone is, give them drinks. What began as a forty-five-minute visit just to "check it out," turned into a three-hour wait for Nicholas.

With a glass of beer, I sat at a table watching Nicholas try mingling and dancing with every girl who passed him. One thing I can say is, he did not let his leg stop him from having fun. But it was getting late, and I was annoyed. I even wondered if he was telling the women that he *was* Pitbull.

As I kept to myself for most of the time, a Chilean couple who sat in front of me looked back every so often to glance at me. *Here we go again*, I thought.

After a while, they both looked back at me as the guy asked, "Donde?"

To get a reaction from them, I said Germany, to which they turned around even more shocked. They tried asking me more, but I could not understand them. Even if I wanted to reply, I would have just kept them guessing, much like my curiosity about the German flags I noticed hanging on the wall of the club.

The time was close to 3 a.m. now, and Nicholas was still not ready to leave, so I just left him. Backpackers always tried to stick together when they traveled anywhere, but I had had enough of the shit. Walking out of the door, a drunk local caught my attention and said something ending in "Negro," which made his friends laugh. I snapped my head back around as he blew me a kiss to taunt me. For a split second, if there was ever a time I did not care about my consequences, it was then. My blood boiled as I took a few steps toward him with my fist clenched. But the last thing I needed was to have my family worried because I had gotten my ass thrown in jail, and possibly stomped out, in a foreign country.

I wanted to gather all the frustration I had from all the racial encounters and throw that shit in one punch. Instead, I walked away and took the long way back to the hostel. Though I know it was the smart thing to do, I felt weak whenever I tried to be the bigger man. The walk away always felt the same, whether it was at home or in Chile. Ironically, there was not much else to do in Puerto Varas, except to leave.

—

Cold weather and rain awaited me after a nearly seven-hour trip to San Carlos de Bariloche. As I crossed over to Argentina, I could still make out the ice-capped mountains that sat right across from the lake. *Probably a sight to see in the summer*, I thought. I came there hoping to book a tour to Torres del Paine National Park only to have a hostel receptionist inform me that I could not. Further south I would have to go. Further into the cold.

That night I could not sleep. Lying in my heated room, I woke up a few minutes past four o'clock, unable to fall back asleep. Had I gotten tired of traveling? Ever since leaving San Pedro, I questioned if I was still enjoying myself, like my trip was already over. Did my high of traveling leave me? Was that possible? No longer thrilled about being anywhere anymore, the cold weather started reflecting what I felt as I continued down to El Calafate, Argentina.

The landscape began changing from snow-capped mountains to layers of snow blanketing flatlands. Bursts of sunshine found their way through cracks of dense clouds every chance they could, gleaming off pearl-colored clouds below as we rode around the curve of a cliff, making me feel as if we had detoured through heaven. Images like these showed me that I could still see beauty in my trip despite how I felt.

Once I arrived at El Calafate, it took no time for the crisp wind to cut through my thin clothes, chilling my bones as I walked down the street. The clothes I had were unfit for this weather. Store windows displayed winter jackets and what looked like ski attire as I searched for my hostel. I began questioning if it was even worth coming down that far. My answer could have been found in the very few number of backpackers that I saw.

The once overflowing crowds in hostels I once knew now dwindled to a handful of people, if any. My new hostel, which looked more like a summer camp, looked lifeless and deserted. Its cabin-style buildings and spread-out table benches looked like people had not occupied them since warmer weather. Once again, I found myself at yet another hostel alone.

I came to El Calafate solely to find a tour agency offering tours to Torres del Paine, a national park in the southern region of Chile and Argentina. Its unique ice-covered mountains I saw in pictures looked sharp enough to poke holes in the sky. The perfect skies that complemented the landscape in the photos had now taken a turn as I stood outside of my hostel gazing up at gray skies. After visiting multiple agencies, all of them said they were done for the season—except for one that was willing to make the trip. However, the earliest they could leave would be in two days, meaning I would have to spend two extra days in cold, irritating weather. Though I wanted to make the trip, I was not prepared for it. I could barely take the cold in the city. Who knew how harsh it would be out in nature? Not willing to take the risk, I decided to leave the next morning.

The weather made my eyes water as I walked to the bus station in the morning darkness. After the thirty-two-hour bus ride

I took from Lima, Peru, to La Paz, Bolivia, I said I would never take another bus ride that long again. But soon I would eat my own words. I boarded a bus to embark on a forty-two-hour bus ride to Buenos Aires, Argentina. Forty-two-hours. Nearly two days on a bus. After a quick stop in Rio Gallegos from El Calafate, I embarked on my trip back north, with a front-row seat at that.

I sat right in front of the window on the top deck of the bus. For the next forty hours, I sat in front of an open road, doing what I could to pass the time. I wrote my thoughts on paper, wrote music, listened to music, and even started a conversation, my first full conversation with a stranger in Spanish. Even with the bits and pieces of words I remembered, it had been enough to pass some time. I shared where I was from, where I had traveled, where I was going, how long I had been gone, what the weather and traffic were like back home. I appreciated the fact that someone tried to learn more about me instead of making assumptions.

To fill up the rest of my time, I practically listened to all of the music on my iPod twice over and wrote myself to exhaustion. But for a good portion of my trip, I only heard the humming of the bus while gazing out the window, staring at nothing but flatlands and open space on a road that stretched to the end of human sight. And it was the same from sunup to sundown, stopping at other stations here and there to load and unload passengers. If you were to ask anyone else to take a forty-hour bus ride, it would sound like the worst thing ever. Yet, there seemed to be a sense of excitement for me.

I always looked forward to traveling to another city. It was something I had noticed early on, even when I got on the plane to leave the States. Though places and people could be opposites, I always looked forward to the trip getting there, even more than the actual city itself. You could see the landscapes change along with the time of day. You could observe the different variations of climate and weather. There was always something new and unpredictable to witness.

A person could look at life the same way. We set goals and destinations for ourselves in life for things we want to accomplish and where we want to be at a certain age. But it is not until we have gained those things that we realize that what we valued all along was the journey in getting there.

Maybe that was what I needed to see all along. I never thought I would be at a point where I would grow tired of seeing different places. Maybe I took this trip, not because I was looking for something, but because I just wanted to look.

Most people would never receive a chance to do something like this in their lifetime, yet I was still unsatisfied. I chased something that was intangible. I chased something that no one place could offer. When it was all said and done, each person, place, and thing had been one more piece to a bigger picture. A picture I would value and appreciate the beauty of the most when I looked back and put it all together.

I was thousands of miles away from home, sitting next to my book bag in front of a large window of a double-decker bus. I had lost weight, or the little weight I did have, and I had started getting low on money. My hair looked like Donnie on *The Wild Thornberrys*, my facial hair untrimmed. I had slept in hostels for months, had money and clothes stolen from me, taken cold showers, and gotten sick. I had encountered prejudices, been laughed at and with, and been missed. I had been in the desert, in the mountains, in canyons, and in the Amazon, and I had almost seen glaciers. I had ridden boats, planes, cars, buses, subways, a horse, and a crop-duster. I had hitch-hiked and walked. I had traveled in packs and traveled alone. No one place could have given me all those things.

At that moment, I realized happiness does not come from any particular place. True happiness comes simply from moving. And now, I began moving back up to Buenos Aires. In five weeks, I would be moving back home.

29

Resolve

With Buenos Aires having a population of more than fifteen million people, it was surprising that there seemed to be more than enough buildings to house them all. Putting my freshly stretched arms and legs to use, I stepped off the bus and began searching for Wi-Fi. I got a taxi with the money I had and told the driver to take me to the nearest hostel.

As midnight approached, most hostels either were booked or had stopped taking guests. The driver went to talk to the receptionists, but each time they turned us down. Having searched several hostels, we drove farther than I could afford to once we finally found one. I gave the driver all the pesos I had but felt bad for not having enough for all of his effort. Though expensive, I just wanted a shower and a good night's sleep. I would worry about finding a cheaper hostel in the morning.

The next day, I found the Rock Hostel about fifteen minutes away in walking distance. A female receptionist who wore black eyeliner and a black leather jacket greeted me as I entered the hostel's dark-painted walls. I observed lyrics painted across the wall from Pink Floyd and The Beatles and noticed someone had painted the stairways like piano keys and the front desk like a giant stereo. Aside from loving its creative design, I found it the first time since Santiago that I had met a decent amount of travelers in a hostel. Being around travelers again felt as warm as the weather I began traveling back to. It lifted my spirits tremendously. Once settled in my new hostel, I explored the city and visited the Brazilian embassy to begin the application process for my visa.

While standing among other tourists, awaiting a city tour, I heard my name being called, ultimately running into a few travelers I had met early on. I always found it fascinating to run into the people I had met while traveling. People could go years without running into old classmates around town, but meeting someone again in a different city in a different country always amazed me.

The tour lasted about two hours but was not as interesting as the others I had experienced. Our guide discussed politics and history, of course, and the influence of Italian design on the buildings. I noticed that the building structures appeared more Europeanized the further I traveled south. Even the people looked more European, not only in skin tone but also in facial structure. Once the tour ended, we all agreed to meet up later and check out an event called Mundo Lingo, a social event for backpackers and people from around the world to meet.

Now late into the evening, the temperature had dropped significantly prior to our arrival at the event. Music spilled out into the street before we could make it inside. As we entered, we received stickers to write where we were from and what languages we could speak. I noticed the words U.K., Canada, Germany, and Australia marked across most stickers, with English being the primary language. Nearly everyone held a beer or drink in their hand, so I followed suit right along with everyone else.

Some of the travelers took an interest in my ayahuasca experience. I always got a kick out of people's reactions when they heard I had tried it. Deciding if they wanted to experience the effects of the spirit vine, they sat around me asking questions like I was a monk or wise wizard who had seen outside of the physical realm.

Amid my rubbing shoulders, I got pulled to the side for an interview outside.

"You want me to do an interview?" I asked, though, clearly, I knew she was talking to me.

"Yeah, we're just asking random guests a few questions for our video. You know, things like where you're from. How long have you been traveling? Simple," she replied.

Though I was not one for interviews, I went along with it. I supposed she solicited my participation to broaden the color spectrum of the people they interviewed, something to look good for the footage.

"What do you think about Mundo Lingo?"

"Where all have you been?"

"How's your experience been so far?"

Halfway between not wanting to do it and giving half-ass answers, I muddled my way through it. I replied, "It's cool . . . you can meet a lot of people . . . Venezuela, Colombia, Peru, Ecuador, Chile, Bolivia . . . It's been amazing . . . something I won't forget."

After I finished the interview, I struck up a conversation with a big guy named Hank from the U.K. He reminded me of Hagrid from *Harry Potter* but with less hair. Hank taught at a school and mentioned how he preferred staying outside to avoid all the music taking away from an actual conversation. Hank sported messy hair with black-rimmed glasses, blue slacks, and a gray sports coat as if he had just finished giving a lecture. He looked to be in his early to mid-thirties, standing off by himself waiting for a conversation like a bug zapper waiting for flies.

Though I had never met Hank before that day, I could sense his authenticity as he sought meaningful conversation at the event. He listened carefully and thought before he spoke, giving opinions and advice. So much so, that I felt comfortable telling him about my experience: being a person of color and the locals' perception of me. Primarily the prejudiced ones.

"Instead of looking at the negative, have you taken time to see the positives? Think about it. Some are around people all day who don't have their best interest and will never know it. Instead of feeling bad about how some look at you, look at them as people you can weed out. It will be easier for you to find someone who is sincere and willing to help you. You have an advantage," he replied, so eloquently.

Before Hank spoke those words to me, I had never looked at it that way. And he was right. I did have an advantage. After our talk, I returned to the old saying of looking at the glass half full instead of half empty.

—

While I made time to enjoy myself, I still had to handle some business: completing my visa and paperwork to enter Brazil. After nearly being late for my appointment with the embassy—telling myself I could get five more minutes of sleep—I somehow still made it. The celebration of my timeliness had been short-lived when I learned I still did not have all the requirements to obtain my visa for Brazil. Along with proving my identity, I needed proof of where I would stay and when I would arrive in and leave Brazil.

When would I be leaving? I did not know how long I would be staying exactly. A round-trip plane ticket would have been enough, but the price would have been a bit more than I wanted to pay. Luckily for me, I was not the first backpacker to run into this issue. An issue that the black-leather-jacket-wearing chick at the front desk, Soledad, could solve.

After I explained my dilemma, she told me about a bus agency called South Pass.

"With the South Pass, they take you several places with a flat fee whenever you are ready. A lot of travelers like this."

That would allow me to make more stops, as well as make it across the border. Plus, it would be cheaper than flying there. However, I had one more issue.

"The woman I spoke with told me that I needed proof of entering, as well as exiting Brazil. And to be honest, I don't know when I wanna leave."

"Don't worry. That I will take care of. We going to get it done like a real nigga," she said, rubbing her hands together with a grin. Her saying that unexpectedly made me chuckle.

"Are you sure this will work?" I asked, apprehensively.

"I've done this plenty, trust me. Come back later and we will put this together."

Later that evening, we walked upstairs to her office and past a studio room where a local band began practicing. Watching the band practice as Soledad cooked up a fake ticket using Photoshop reminded me of how much I missed recording music. Hearing the quietness of the room right before you record. The comfortable feeling of studio headphones secured around your ears. The anxiousness you feel right before delivering the words that took you days, weeks, and months to write in audio form. Creating visual stories for listeners that feel as magical as performing alchemy. Letting people listen to how your mind works and how it wanders. Letting them listen to what the uniqueness of your soul sounds like. The only place in the world where the quietness of voices can be heard like those of giants.

When Soledad finished the ticket, everything looked legit, matching up perfectly. I just hoped it looked legit to the embassy on the following day.

The whole way there, it did not dawn on me what legal action the embassy would take if they found out the ticket was fraudulent. The further I got, the more paranoid I became, walking through the door and up the many floors to be met with more doors and people standing in line. As the line dwindled, so did my confidence as I approached the lady behind the plexiglass. I handed over my plane ticket papers, anxiously waiting as she began pecking on her keyboard. After a few moments, she confirmed everything checked out, but I would need to come back on Monday because of some system issues. However, they would need to hold on to my passport until then. Though hesitant, I ended up leaving it, thinking how strange it was that they would need to keep my passport.

For the rest of the day, my conscience weighed heavily on me. I thought it was a sign that I should not go to Brazil. If I went, then I would have had to wait through the weekend without my passport, and I would have had to dish out more money to stay for another two days. And what if she did see it was a fraudulent paper? With all of that on my mind, I followed my gut instinct and returned to the embassy to retrieve my passport. I made it just in time, not knowing they were near closing.

I noticed a different lady working the window, but a sigh of relief did not hit me until I walked out of the building with my passport in hand. I believed I had made the right choice and decided to leave Buenos Aires the next day.

My last day was a busy one. Twelve hours straight to be exact. The day of my departure began at 10:30 a.m. on a city tour. Out of the fifteen people in our group, a middle-aged Black guy stood out to me the most for obvious reasons. With me being the only other Black person, it did not take long for us to strike up a conversation.

Archie, who was British, lived in Atlanta but came to Buenos Aires on vacation. He worked remotely, managing a team of software engineers. I told him my story, and, like the others, it blew him away as we continued discussing it along the tour.

While on the city tour, I paid close attention to the beauty of the buildings. The architectural structures were so diverse from their various European influences that each building looked drastically different from the next. I understood why Buenos Aires was called the "Architecture Wonderland"; the buildings appeared to be cut out from all over the world and pasted around the city.

At the end of the tour, Archie, Johnathan (another guy we met on the tour), and I continued exploring the city, which led us to a few suggested spots. We walked the streets, sharing stories about our trips, some a bit more shameful than others. We found ourselves in a bar, where we had a couple of beers and even shot some pool. The night turned interesting when we found out that Archie not only owned his own business but also was a millionaire. After Archie walked away, Johnathan and I looked at each other as if to say, "Did we just hear that correctly?" Needless to say, drinks were on Archie for the rest of the night.

Even though I was sure Buenos Aires had tons more to offer, I knew I had had enough of the big city, including the questionable bite marks on my arms that might have been from bed bugs. Truth is, I realized that I liked more of the outdoorsy, subtle cities compared to larger ones. Therefore, I left Buenos Aires behind and embarked on a fifteen-hour trip to Mendoza.

30

Bliss

Bus rides had now turned into the same old songs, just like the music I kept in rotation on my iPod. Though routines were the same, the roads always led to something different, and I looked forward to it. The bus rides also gave me time to think. I thought about my trip ending, and I was glad about it. The traveling had become tiresome, and I missed my family and friends. I thought about how life would be once I returned home. I wondered what had changed. I considered if I was ready to go back, ready to start anew. And to be honest, I was unsure.

Just around midnight, the bus pulled up to the Mendoza bus station. It gave me relief knowing I had not arrived in another big city. Though my hostel had been just a few blocks away, I took a taxi there to be safe. The hostel sat behind barred gates as they buzzed me in to enter. The night's cold stopped at the door as my chill subdued to the warmth of the fireplace, whose flames danced as I entered.

The place itself felt homey, with wooden floors and soft-colored walls. A drowsy-eyed receptionist checked me into the quiet hostel and showed me to my room. Backpackers were already fast asleep as I unpacked quietly. After sending a quick message to my mom about my safe arrival, I lay down.

Though the windows were closed, I could faintly hear talking outside in the courtyard. From the accent, it sounded like some girl from the States talking to a guy. I would have thought nothing of the conversation until I heard the girl say "nigger." I went from dozing off to sleep to plain eavesdropping until the two walked back inside. Shortly after, the room door opened, and a girl climbed up to bed, the same girl from outside. Of course, she would be my roommate.

Normally, I began every morning with breakfast and writing in my journal about the previous day. But for the next couple of days, I did not write much. And that was a good thing. Not having enough time to write let me know I had been too busy enjoying my time there.

—

If autumn were a place, then it would be Mendoza: a nice-sized city with turning leaves and trees of browns and yellows. Warm, breezy days followed by cool, quiet nights. The city itself had a warm essence to it. From what I had heard, the climate was perfect for winemaking, what Mendoza was best known for. I even stumbled across an agency advertisement that offered wine tasting while skydiving. The idea entertained me, but it seemed a bit too much.

Though the question of when I would head back home always sat at the forefront of my mind, buying the ticket hit home for me. It was not something I could prolong forever. As I navigated through web pages to find reasonable tickets, I experienced mixed feelings of excitement, joy, and sadness. I hit a snag debating if I should go from Peru to Colombia and then back to the States or from Bolivia to Colombia, and then back to the States. I could take a chance going back into Bolivia, where I read once you exit you cannot enter until sometime later, and I had run out of U.S. Dollars. Or I could just go around Bolivia, back to Chile and Peru, but that would mean spending more money. One guy suggested I could get my visa in Santa Cruz, Bolivia, which puzzled me because I would need to *have* a visa to get to Bolivia. I did not want to get stuck at the border, so I weighed my options and decided to revisit them the following day.

As a perk, the hostel offered dinners to guests, comprising free wine and meat. A dinner of literal meat. Just meat. While sitting there, eating with greasy lips and sipping wine to wash it down, I met a few of the other backpackers in the hostel. The food just kept coming as we talked and ate, and the wine flowed right along with it. The wine was so plentiful that it almost seemed disposable. We received wine for dinner and for just being at the hostel. We also received wine bottles from multiple store owners as we explored Mendoza.

Eight of us from the hostel took the city bus and rode to a local bike store that offered taste testing. I do not think any of us cared too much; we just wanted the free drinks. While pouring and drinking wine, we sat around on stools, using wooden barrels as tables. We tasted at least five different bottles and left with four more on our rented bikes. The effects of the wine had taken their toll on us before midday, as it warmed us up from the slight chill. We visited two more wineries to continue taste testing, which at that point seemed like a montage of glasses being thrown back and refilled.

We took a break to have lunch out in the golden grass fields outside of one winery. Though we were all tipsy, I was certain I was experiencing another one of those moments where I cherished the camaraderie surrounding this group of strangers. We plopped down on the grass in a circle, still sipping wine and taking pictures. As the day turned into the evening, the sun left behind its last bit of warmth, with light breezes still blowing. We sat there not wanting to leave, but eventually, we had to. But not before getting four more free bottles of wine.

Even after arriving back at the hostel for more free wine, I lay in bed, head still spinning, but elated about how gorgeous and fun the day had been. And spillage from the day's festivities carried over to the next one at a picnic in the park. Sandwiches, chips, and cheap wine were laid out on a blanket in front of us, with unraveled bags of loaves of bread, a layer of half-cut avocados, open containers of deli meat, and an open jar of mayonnaise. We used napkins as plates and shared the same knife, spilling drops of wine from our cups that made red blots on our blanket.

We sat in an open area listening to music from a small speaker that one of our group members carried around. The temperature felt perfect: the girls carried light sweaters for the gentle wind that swept by every so often. But for some of us, the wine kept us warm. For several hours, we talked the time away, laughing, drinking, reclining, and relaxing like there was no other group of young adults who could do it better.

As we sat around in a broken circle, I realized the past day or two had been some of the best days I had experienced. This lovely feeling filled some part of me that trekking in Colca Canyon and riding dune buggies in Huacachina had not done. It felt like something that could never get old, the enjoyment of another's company.

But what had begun as one of my better days took a sharp turn as I read about one of the most heinous events ever to happen in South Carolina. A white supremacist killed nine African Americans in Emanuel AME Church in Charleston. With it being so close to home, the news of this tragedy shocked me. It made headlines everywhere I looked online. Even backpackers from the hostel asked me about the shooting, knowing I was from South Carolina.

Tensions were already high from the prevalence of social injustice and police brutality in recent events. One incident was as recent as two months prior. A white police officer shot and killed Walter Scott, an African American male, in Charleston as well.

Though thousands of miles away, the tragedy still impacted me because it was right in my backyard. I checked on my family and friends who either were from or lived in Charleston, thankful that everyone was fine. It was a harsh reality of what I would be returning to in the following weeks. While people had mocked me and laughed at me, at least I did not have to worry about someone—even the ones paid to protect us—trying to kill me because of my skin color.

I had heard about events in Florida, with Travon Martin; Missouri, with Michael Brown; New York, with Eric Garner; and countless others. And now, with Walter Scott and the Emanuel Church shooting, it seemed as if this evil was closing in on me. It even made me think of my friend who had gotten locked up a few months earlier.

—

The next day, I awoke with the previous day's thoughts still on my mind, along with still needing to book a flight home. Shifting my focus to moving forward, I prepared to leave for my next stop, Salta, Argentina.

Before booking the flights, I contemplated going to Iguazu Falls, which rested on the border of Argentina and Brazil. I had given up on the idea of going to Brazil because of limited funds and entry restrictions. While I thought I would at least attempt to see some of it, I decided I had traveled enough and would make my way back up the continent. Besides, it gave me a reason to come back someday.

I decided I would not go through Bolivia but back through Chile and Peru so that I would not have to worry about getting another visa. One backpacker told me about an airline called Viva Air, which offered cheap flights in and out of Colombia. The realization that I was leaving had been difficult to process as I browsed the web page, clicking on drop-down menus and selecting dates. For the past several months, I had been traveling from one place to the next, and now for that to end seemed unreal. After purchasing the first ticket, I bought another one from Cartagena, Colombia, to Charlotte, North Carolina, which made a transit stop to New York before reaching Charlotte.

Once done, it felt like I had finally ripped off a Band-Aid that hurt more than the wound itself. Though somber, I felt content. Knowing this would be my last destination before heading back home, I looked at the word Cartagena, staring at it like the end of a chapter, not only to my trip but also to a chapter in my life. A story called "Remember that time when . . . ." The word Cartagena sounded beautiful to me, and it was the city where I would submit to my journey and ultimately throw in the towel.

Before long, I began making my way to the bus station, and from all my attention being elsewhere, the time had slipped up on me. I rushed to the bus station, halfway saying thanks to all the new friends I had made, but somehow I still ended up missing the bus. I booked another ticket for the next morning and headed back to the hostel. Just when I thought I could at least go back there, they had already booked up that fast. Even my old pals tried to convince the receptionists to fit me in somewhere, but they couldn't. I had to laugh at myself. It was one of the few days where I was not tipsy in Mendoza, and now I needed a drink. However, this time I received a chance to bid my friends a proper farewell as I walked off into the chill night.

I just needed a room for the night, and the recommended hostel would work perfectly, because the entire hostel seemed vacant. But I did not complain about its emptiness. I had a room to myself with a warm heater that blew directly over me. Though I still would not have minded a drink, the warm heater ended my night comfortably.

31

Consciousness

The streets of Salta were quiet as I searched for my hostel in the late afternoon. Just like Mendoza, it did not appear to be a busy city. Maybe less than busy. Mundane even. I had traveled to Salta because I wanted to ride on the Train to the Clouds and to see The Hill of Seven Colors. Minerals that had formed and constructed layers over time gave the hills a rainbow color, something my Spanish teacher recommended I see after taking her class.

After a few minutes of walking, I found my hostel, Hostel in Salta, and two other guests entered at the same time. Every so often, I would be lucky enough to check in to a hostel that offered maps showing where key locations like markets and money exchanges were located. After settling in, I knew that most restaurants were closed on Sundays just about everywhere, so I visited a food market instead. I picked up the basics to make a sandwich: bread, cheese, mayonnaise, and deli meat. While watching Brazil play Venezuela in the Copa América soccer championship, I ate my sandwich, striking conversation with the two guests from earlier, Ella and Charlie. Ella agreed to accompany me to the Hills of Seven Colors the next morning, while Charlie decided to pass on the invitation.

The bus left at seven in the morning, beginning what would turn into a full day of traveling and making stops. Unexpectedly, we stopped at the Train to the Clouds—one of several railroad bridges along its tracks that ran from Salta to Antofagasta, Chile, as well as one of the highest railroads in the world. We stared up into the high rusted bridge that stretched between the hills in our group of about twelve people.

As we continued to our next stop, I learned more about Ella. She was a couple of years younger than me and also did not know what she wanted to do in life. Ella had been the first one to admit that, and I could relate. A weight lifted off my shoulders, knowing I was not the only one. I had encountered enough people that seemed like they had it all planned out, but hearing her say that made me feel like I was not alone.

We stopped at several more places, one being the Hill of Seven Colors, which we could see from the town we visited below the clay hills. The excitement did not last once I realized we could only view it from the city and not go to it.

My anticipation had been building for Jujuy, Argentina's version of the salt flats, though not as vast. While standing out there, the thought hit me that in a few weeks, I would be returning home. And I did not feel any different from when I first started. My once highness from traveling had now just become a numbing feeling to me. I was unsure if that meant I had finally gotten what I came for, or if I had grown tired of traveling. Either way, I still felt like the same person I was when I was working behind a desk toward the end of 2014. I thought I would feel enlightened or wiser or finally have the answers or find out my calling or something. Anything.

As I replayed the past six months in my mind, I thought about the family members and neighbors I had lost while away. I thought about the lives lost in the Emanuel AME church shooting and knew I would be returning home to that tension. I knew I did not regret my trip. The places I had been, the people I had met, the stories I had shared, and being a part of it all. All worth every second. But did I get what I had come for? And if I had, why did I still feel this way?

—

I spent the next two days trying to settle my stomach. It was mostly my mistake from eating unrefrigerated mayonnaise I had stashed away under my bed. I tried being smart by keeping it with me instead of putting it in the refrigerator, hoping no one would tamper with it. Trying to be clever ended with me having the shits.

Charlie told me a story about when he traveled in Southeast Asia and he ate something that had him shitting in, on, and around the toilet. The walls, too. We laughed hard, thankful that my case in Venezuela was not nearly that bad. Charlie could be funny at times, but he was serious about one thing: eating raw meat.

"You eat meat raw meat, bro? Is that how you always eat it?" I asked.

"Nah, not all the time, mate, but it doesn't hurt every once in a while," he answered as I watched him unwrap the pack of raw meat.

"My dad told me that when it comes to meat, you don't need to cook anything. All you need to do is cut the horns, wipe the ass, and you're good to go," he continued.

"Oh, hell nah, bro," I laughed.

And crazy enough, I even tried a piece of the raw meat, thinking my stomach could not feel much worse than it did. The unflavored, chewy piece of meat softened between my teeth as I braced for it to go down. I waited like someone had pulled the pin out of a grenade, anticipating my ass to be blown off later on. But to my surprise, I was completely fine.

During one of our lunch gatherings, two women from Holland spoke about their culture and how others scrutinized them for their holiday character, "Black Pete." It was a character who gave out candy while dressed up in blackface with curly hair and a clown-like outfit. Though unsure of what ignited the conversation, by default, I represented all Black people across the world. So I had to say something. And I ended up saying the dumbest shit ever.

"I understand that in other cultures, people just see things differently. Every place has its traditions, and who is anybody to change that because they don't like it. I mean, Black is just like any other color. It's a color."

I spoke those words knowing how prejudiced blackface was, and how it mocked Black people. It might have been one of the few times I could have shared my perspective with people who might not see how this "tradition" could hurt people, and I blew it. I just sat there listening, not even speaking up on a topic that was indirectly about me.

Ironically, I let the idea of tradition outweigh the idea of progression, the very thing I set out to do. Progression is necessary for growth. If left to tradition, then people could have treated me much differently back home. The Holland girls did not see any harm in tradition, nor did they see it as prejudice.

Even after all I had experienced on my trip as an African American, the one time I could finally speak up to a group of people who spoke English, I dropped the ball. As shameful as it sounds, deep down, I believed I was unqualified to comment. I struggled to speak up about issues that pertained to me, and the thought of having to speak up and represent all People of Color made me feel as if I would not have done it any justice. Almost like my voice would not have mattered. I sat there listening to the conversation like a dog with its tail tucked between its legs.

I did not let their culture affect how I treated them, however. We hung out most of the following day, roaming the town. One girl, in particular, seemed to gravitate toward me, so much so that I might have gotten too comfortable. As we walked back to the hostel that night, I asked her something that surely would have pissed my ancestors off.

"Hey, this might be a little strange to ask. And don't get weirded out or anything but . . . do you mind . . . or like . . . would it be cool if we shared a bed tonight? Like laid down together?" I said.

When the words left my lips, I asked myself, *Why in the hell did I just ask that?*

It had been nearly six months since I had been with a woman sexually, let alone even feeling a woman's touch. I had seen this happen in hostel rooms all the time. Boy and girl bundled up in some bunk bed. And if they were lucky, they did not have to climb up to the top bunk in the middle of the night. Girls had told me how guys would feed them these corny lines about how they missed home and how they had just gotten some sad news before asking if it was okay for them to spoon. And the shit worked.

"I just wanted to ask to see what you thought," I added.

"Oh, oh, it's cool. I get it. Wow, I think that's sweet. I actually wouldn't mind, but I do have a boyfriend. That would weigh on my conscience," she replied.

"Oh! Nah . . . yeah, I get it. I understand that. I just thought I'll ask to see," I said, not sure how to take the rejection.

As we continued our conversation, the rest of our trip back did not feel as awkward as I thought it would be. Somehow she even found me and added me as a friend on social media the morning she left.

I took the rest of my time in Salta to speak with my family. It felt good hearing their voices as they asked questions about when I would be back. Yet, I always gave them an unclear answer.

When I spoke to my grandfather, the only thing on his mind was me getting back to a job when I returned. Even with me being exposed to a new world and having new experiences of my own, where I came from and what I had always known—an environment that sometimes felt stifling and controlling—still overshadowed it. My grandfather always had a way of persuading you to do things his way, even though his intentions were good and meant to be helpful.

My grandfather is an unbending rod, forged from experiences of his own. To him, his way was the way, no matter how different my upbringing or lifestyle compared to his. For the past few months, I had thought of myself as more of a man, stepping out on faith but unable to gain any leverage in the eyes of the ones who mattered most. Had I been running after all? Running from the sensation of not feeling like a man? Where and when it mattered the most . . . back home?

—

I tried to take advantage of my last day in Salta, joining up with Daniel, a traveler from the States. We planned to hike up to San Bernardo Cerro Turistico, which was a little more than an hour away.

We were told that the hike up San Bernardo consisted of one thousand steps. Though when we finished hiking, we realized it was closer to eight hundred. I enjoyed hiking again. We took frequent breaks, looking over Salta from different viewpoints, each one higher than the next. We spotted restaurants, man-made waterfalls, and cable cars to help others get to the top. But there was one thing that made hiking up the hills of cities all the same. Each time I climbed a hill and reached the top made me realize how small I was. And how someone as small as me could still cover so much ground. How someone so small could make their way out of a maze of clustered blocks and lines that looked smothering and suffocating.

Though I had already begun my trip back up the continent, it had officially started now. I had heard the trip from Salta to San Pedro was one of the most beautiful scenic trips one could make in South America. And that would be nothing short of the truth.

32

Repetition

Landscapes of valleys with endless curves of roads stretching across the bellies of dry hills caught my eye as we traveled along. The midday sun warmed my face as it shined through the bus window. I watched the dips and bends and slopes and slants of the earth's crust lie under perfect blue skies. Once again, I found myself appreciating the ride, not concerned about when I would reach my destination. Everything seemed so golden, from the sun to the glare of the land. Everything was so serene.

We stopped momentarily when crossing the border as they checked for immigration cards. Once finished, I stood along with the rest of the other travelers back at the bus. I stood out on the smooth asphalt and looked down the straight road, scanning both directions. The sun felt good, the light breeze felt good, and I felt good. I had packed my hair under my navy blue Huacachina hat, with some sticking out like Arnold from *Hey Arnold*. My trekking boots had torn slightly, worn from the miles, rocks, mud, terrain, streets, steps, water, heat, and air, and not having any other pair of shoes to wear. Proof that I was not dreaming, nearly half a year of evidence rested right below my ankles.

When I arrived back in San Pedro, Chile, everything was still so fresh and so familiar. The clear skies were still there, just as

I had left them, like the volcanoes that stood like guardians in the distance. The same lazy stray dogs lay in the red dirt streets next to the same clay-like buildings I remembered from before. I needed neither a map nor direction; I knew where I needed to go.

Arriving back in Chile was like reuniting with an old friend, the place where I last felt that traveling spirit before heading further south into the cold. Being there made me miss the girls. I thought about how Jess, Elle, Isabelle, and I went on the stargazing tour and toured the Valley de la Luna. I remembered the postcards I sent my grandparents and mom, which they had just received the previous week.

Hoping to recapture some of the magic, I tried to revisit the same hostel, Hostel Matty, but they were booked. I found a hostel closer to the bus station, which had one of the best landscapes, a scenic view of volcanoes.

This time, I shared a room with guys from France, one being a tall, slender Black guy. With them still being neatly shaved and groomed, I could tell they were early on in their trip. Part of me wanted to warn my Black roommate about what I had experienced. Another part of me wanted to know if he had noticed anything unusual. He appeared unbothered as I woke up the next morning and noticed a girl lying in bed with him. I woke up to the hostel cat lying next to me. Jokingly, I wondered if he had used that "I'm a traveler and I'm lonely" line.

Though I still had not perfected my technique, I took the time to shave. The splashes of water felt refreshing on my face once I finished. As I looked in the mirror, the hat full of stuffed hair seemed silly, so I took the hat off and let my hair free. And it felt good. I would be leaving for Arica, Chile, later that night, which was near the Chilean and Peruvian border.

For the rest of the day, I did not think about anything except working on myself and being as productive as I could be once I got home. I wanted things to be different. I wanted to get better at everything. I wanted to accomplish so much and to take advantage of what I had learned, not have my trip be in vain.

To pass the time, I sat and watched the skyline of red volcanoes and mountains outside. Clouds had finally accumulated, breaking the streak of days with clear skies in the city. Even with the few clouds, the weather had still been perfect. It was the right balance between heat and coolness. Though I wanted to sit there forever, I knew I would be leaving in a couple of hours. I could see the bus station a few yards away, right below the gated hill on which my hostel sat. I had watched the buses come and go. Coming and going just like the passengers that occupied them. Coming and going just like I would be later that night.

When I arrived in Arica, the early morning hours still did not show any signs of daybreak. Streetlights lit the way as I risked safety, searching for my hostel in the dark. People had not begun stirring in the street, nor in their homes, from what I could tell. The hostel was located close to the beach, as I could smell the Pacific saltwater once I stepped off the bus. I had forgotten how good it felt to be by the water.

The hostel sat behind a locked red door, prompting me to press the doorbell. After a few unsuccessful attempts, I figured I would have to wait outside the door until it opened. It had been the only hostel I knew about nearby, and tiredness had already overtaken me, which prevented me from walking anywhere else. I sat down on the warm cement by the door with my back against the wall and my bags beside me. The nearby streetlight cast an orange glow on me and everything that it touched as I waited. Though I had limited vision from the night sky and surrounding parked cars, I felt a sense of protection from any other eyes.

Little did I know, I was not alone. A young dog dashed out from behind one of the parked cars on the side of the street, and startled me with its sudden appearance, making me leap to my feet.

My nerves eased a bit more when I realized the dog just wanted to play. It aggressively jumped up to put its front legs up to my thighs, causing me to stumble slightly as it wagged its tail. I rubbed the dog behind the ears, hoping it would somewhat calm her down. Then I pulled out an open pack of crackers and gave it to her.

A little over an hour passed before departing guests opened the door. "Socks" and I made our way to the hostel from the now dim morning streets. I named her Socks because all four of her paws were white, different from her light brown coat.

As we entered the hostel, I sat down on the lobby couch while Socks made her way into the kitchen, rummaging through the trash can. After finishing her chicken-bone meal, she explored the rest of the hostel, every so often jumping on the couch to check on me.

Eventually, the owner came downstairs, finding not only a new guest but also trash over the kitchen floor. Surprisingly, she laughed, grabbed Socks, and put her outside like this was not her first time making her way into the hostel.

People began stirring in the hostel, coming down for breakfast. I planned to stay only for a day, but I still asked around about things I might have wanted to check out while I was there. Someone recommended Morro de Arica, a steep protruding hill by the coast that you could see from practically anywhere in Arica. I did not need any direction; I walked toward the hill.

Once I arrived at the top of the hill, the setting reminded me of a larger-scale Huacachina with a desert surrounding all parts of the city. While standing there looking over everything, I questioned if I appreciated everything I had seen throughout my trip, or if I had taken everything for granted. I stood there overlooking a city I did not plan on visiting, just to have something to do. Just to waste time. Some people back home were excited to travel to Atlanta or Charlotte. And there I stood in Arica, Peru, doing things just to waste time, not thinking about the fact that I would never be there again in life.

Though there was not much to do in Arica, it made me think of other times when I may have been somewhere, not appreciating being there in the moment. There was no question that I had glimpses of it, but how much did I embrace it?

—

Upon my departure the next day, I ate breakfast and said my goodbyes. As I walked the streets in the dewy morning air, I also wanted to say goodbye to Socks, but I could not find her anywhere. As soon as I made it to the other block, there she appeared, running out of nowhere. I gave her some more crackers and patted her while she ate. She followed me until I came upon a busy intersection, and while I crossed the street, she sat on the corner watching me cross to the other side.

Out of all the stray dogs I had encountered, I felt attached to Socks. I am not sure why, but it hurt me to leave her behind. Even with our encounter being brief, it made my trip to Arica worth it.

Afterwards, I rode a colectivo to the border, got my immigration papers, and caught a taxi with four other people to Tacna, Peru, traveling across the straight flat land of dirt that looked like beach sand for miles along the cracked pavement. Upon reaching the town of Tacna, we unloaded at the bus station, and I immediately purchased my ticket to Arequipa. No longer did I feel the need to wear a jacket or long sleeves or my jean pants. The summer's warmth began carrying me for the rest of my trip.

While traveling to Arequipa, I struggled with the idea that my travel days were numbered, now returning to familiar places. With my hair wild and untamed, I carried under it memories of imperfect faces, cities, and towns with stories that gave me my own, and the unapologetic culture that forged my thoughts and ideas.

I sat thumbing through my albums on my iPod, thinking of the many times I had listened to them on rides, and how they had never gotten old to me. How each album—each song, even—reminded me of a moment from my trip. *To Pimp a Butterfly* reminded me of Mancora/Huanchaco/Lima, Peru. *Cadillactica* reminded me of Bogotá, Colombia, and Iquitos, Peru, and the live version of "Ready Aim" reminded me of Caracas, Venezuela.

Though I traveled alone, the music made me feel like I always had company. It connected me from one place to the next, keeping me in touch with home somehow. The songs I listened to did not reflect the people and places I explored, but more of what I felt like listening to while there. And now, revisiting Arequipa would reacquaint me with Donnie Hathaway and D'Angelo.

When I arrived back in Arequipa, I returned to my old hostel. Because they were already full, I walked over to the hostel next door and checked in. The last time I stayed in Arequipa, I prepared to go on the ayahuasca retreat. I instantly thought about everyone I met when I first came, as well as the crew from Colca Canyon.

My new hostel seemed livelier compared to my old one. Though it did not take long for me to meet people, I knew I wanted to move back to my old hostel as soon as possible.

After I settled in, back out into the streets I went like I never skipped a beat, knowing exactly where everything was just like before. And with that came everything else, even the uncomfortable stares of people that did not understand me, just like I did not understand them. Being back in Arequipa reminded me how hurtful it could be. Sharp memories of bewildered faces that would stare competing with smiling faces that would share conversation.

I visited the corner store near my hostel where I would get gummy candies when walking back from Spanish class. Further down, I had bought bags of fruit from baby bananas to orange granadilla fruit. All were still the same, from the plaza with its continuous flow of people and cars bending corners around the plaza's perimeter to my duck-off spot in the alley where I would go to sit and pick up food from one of my usual spots.

Striking up a conversation with two girls from Canada, Janet and Ele, I waited to check out and move back into my old hostel the next morning. Janet and I talked about our trip while Ele sat hunched over to the knee from an upset stomach, a feeling I knew quite well. Even though other people began stirring around the hostel, I knew this group of girls would be the ones I would hang out with for my duration in Arequipa.

As a traveler, when you clicked with people, you found your friends. No matter who you met after that, the first people you bonded with when you first arrived somewhere were normally the ones you looked for when going to do anything. And that we did.

When I finally moved back over to my old hostel, I instantly regretted it. While I remembered sitting in the eating area doing homework, standing out on the balcony looking out at volcanoes in the distance, or shooting pool with friends in the common area, this time it felt empty, figuratively and literally. No matter how long I sat at the table to write, gazed at the volcanoes, or shot pool with other guests, my friends had left. The initial bond I had with those select people was not there anymore. That time was gone.

—

Things back home were still tense with the recent Charleston shooting, as more discussions surrounded removing the Confederate flag at the State House grounds. Being on the outside looking in, watching people debate about what should happen was like watching a play I had seen before, a play where characters on both sides used history as their defense to support their argument. A play I knew all the lines to, just as I knew what the outcome would be. Simply put, the U.S. looked silly. And I was sure other places looked at the U.S. in the same way. In a couple of weeks, I would be back in the play as well, but with a new role, I hoped.

I chilled in the hostel and shot pool one last time before messaging Janet about my departure. Altogether, I had lived in Arequipa for close to three weeks, including when I first visited. Despite the ugliness I experienced at times, I had grown attached to it. And now, I was continuing further north, back to Lima.

33

Transition

Only the weather and the dates were different when I arrived in Lima for the third time. I returned to the same hostel but could only stay for the night, needing to find a new one in the morning.

While there, my grandma sent me a picture of my granddad barbecuing ribs for Independence Day. The only ribs I had seen since being on my trip were the ones attached to me. I had occasionally eaten good food, but I had undoubtedly lost weight while traveling. Remembering the sweet taste of Sweet Baby Ray's barbeque sauce, I stared at the pictures, hoping they would jump out of the phone. I went to bed holding my own ribs that night, realizing I had less than two weeks left before I was back home.

I moved a few blocks over to a new hostel the next morning. Just like my last hostel back in Arequipa, I no longer felt that feeling I once had. My adventurous spirit had now succumbed to the realization of my impending departure.

The eating area looked like a representation of how I felt. Leaks from the ceiling dripped on tabletops and into buckets as I sat down at a dry table to eat. I struck up a conversation while eating, still appreciating the fact that one could easily begin because we all knew we had traveled from different parts of the world.

When I found out that Ella, whom I had met in Salta, Argentina, had also arrived in Lima, we agreed to meet up. Ella and I strolled to the park and sat on a bench right by the cliff, as I had done on many other occasions. This time, gray clouds covered the sky, which seemed fitting as the end of my journey neared. Ella and I chatted as she smoked a cigarette, blowing out clouds like the ones in the sky.

Like myself, Ella, too, wondered what things would be like when she returned home. I connected with her immensely because we were both lost. We sat there for a long time, at times discussing thoughts, and sitting at other times in silence. We were both leaving for Bogotá, Colombia the following day, having the same flight and thus discussing plans for the next day. It was not long before we retired for the night.

Once back at my hostel, I met two new roommates. We all talked for a while, them in their bunk beds and me on the opposite side of mine. One guy from the Netherlands sat with his legs crossed and his back against the wall as he played a small guitar. Something had tinged the bottom of his feet gray as if he walked around with no shoes on. His stringy, sandy-colored hair swayed as he sang to his music, which sounded good enough for me to record.

I was not sure why, but I appreciated his singing, and the moment altogether. The sense of being free and not having worries. Only in a hostel could people accept a guy with dirty feet hanging off the bed, singing in a room full of strangers. There was liberation being around these people. A sense of self. Some magical understanding that it was okay to be whoever you are. *I will miss that the most when I leave*, I thought. After a while, he stopped singing, as my blinking eyes closed, drifting me off to sleep.

—

Ten days left. No longer thrilled about venturing to the next destination, I could feel my trip coming to an end emotionally. I prepared to return to reality instead, like a kid returning to school after summer vacation. I had spent a significant portion of my trip throughout Peru, about two months' worth, with all of its bittersweet moments. It was the place where I first noticed those strange looks and stares that seemed to follow me. I did not experience that in Colombia, or maybe I never thought to notice. Either way, I believed once I made it to Colombia, I would be in safe territory again.

Ella and I agreed we would share a cab to the airport to catch our flight. When we arrived at the airport, I ended up having to pay extra for purchasing the wrong ticket, my luggage, and a tourist fee, which all sounded dumb. Just when I thought the bullshit had ended, I got stopped when checking out to get my stamp at immigration. Though Ella and I had enough time to catch our flight, another hurdle ate away at the clock.

The official sat behind the glass, looking at his computer system with my passport next to his keyboard. After standing there a while, I knew something was not right because it took longer than usual to receive my stamp. Before I knew it, two more officials came over to assess the issue. Ella, now my translator, tried to figure out the holdup.

"They said it is a red asterisk by your passport number in the system. They are trying to know why."

As well I.

I checked in and out of every country I had ever been in, so it could not have been an immigration issue. I grew worried as the time inched closer for us to board our plane. So much so that I told Ella to go ahead without me.

During that time, they had pulled us over to another area so that we would not hold up other travelers. I thought back to when I lost my immigration paper when I first entered Peru and had to get another one. *Maybe that's it*, I thought. However, I would have gotten stopped much sooner when I left Peru or when I tried to reenter. There were four officials now looking at my passport, then looking at me.

"They are starting to question if you are who you say you are. They don't think you are the same person in the photograph," explained Ella.

"Damn, they can't see that's me?"

Over the time I had traveled, my hair had grown wild on my head and on my face, a hell of a lot different from the well-groomed man in the photo. But damn, they still couldn't tell I was the same person?

Was it an identity issue? Had I changed that much while I was gone? People began staring at us as they walked past with freshly stamped passports, and I wished we could be part of that number. The red asterisk, though? Why was there a red asterisk by my passport number? And who knows what they could have been thinking? I had already been mistaken for a drug dealer during my trip.

Suddenly, I felt red hot. My face went warm as my stomach dropped. I realized they could have marked my name in the system somehow when I tried to turn in that fake airplane ticket to the embassy in Buenos Aires. That the woman held my passport for that reason. I glanced at Ella, my face flushed with anxiety, not mentioning anything to her.

A few moments later, they pulled me into a back room as I left Ella out on her own. I did not need any translation to know what room they held me in. I sat down on a bench right behind a one-sided mirror as I continued waiting. It seemed like the closer I got to returning home, the more difficult it became. My stomach tossed and turned as I sat, looking back out the glass window to look for Ella. During most of my time in Peru, people looked at me unwelcomely, and now that I was trying to get the hell out, I was having a hard time doing so.

I remained there for about ten minutes, awaiting my outcome, when, suddenly, they waved me to go. I grabbed my bags and rushed out of the room, meeting back up with Ella and not looking back. Though I did not know what that red asterisk next to my name meant, I knew I did not want to stay any longer to find out.

—

Ella and I arrived in Bogotá at midnight, and it felt good to be back. We piled into a cab and headed into town, each getting dropped off at different hostels. I got dropped off at my very first hostel, Musicology. I could only smile as I approached the door, noticing they had installed a new doorbell.

As I stood there, I wondered if Samita would answer the door like she had when I first arrived, if she would remember me. Though it was not her who opened the door, the memories that rushed back to me were all too familiar. The worn green and white checkered tiles in the TV area. Photographs of music legends on the wall. Hammocks hanging from wooden pillars in the court area. Everything was still the same. I checked back into my room again, still with the black and white piano painting on the wall and thick wooden bunk beds.

Being transported back in time, I walked around for a moment, reminiscing about the breakfasts and salsa classes, and my friend Anna, whom I went head over heels for. I remembered that uncomfortable feeling of trying to play sleep while some guy was trying to have sex with her, of wanting to say something to her while saying nothing at all. I remembered everything. In some ways, having my journey end from where it began seemed appropriate. But like all hostels I had revisited, the magical essence that had once been there was now gone.

During breakfast, a small group invited me out with them to Lake Guavita, which I did not hear about the first time I visited. The weather was still cloudy and cool, like I had always known it to be. Before our hike to the lake, we stopped by a small ranch-like restaurant in the countryside, northeast of Bogotá. I felt elated to be out in the countryside, gazing at green hills and walking along wet dirt roads rimmed with wired fences. The only time I had remotely seen this side of Colombia had been in Silvia, but the beauty near Bogotá made me stop and pause.

While at the lake, my group schooled me about the myth of the lake, and how people said the lake had gold at the bottom. We stood atop of a hill, looking down into the lake below, letting our imagination wander about us finding the gold. We stayed for a few hours before continuing, still enjoying the walk now that the sun finally started beaming through.

Sunshine broke through parts of the dark clouds, casting shadows over the hills and green landscape. The yellow dandelions sprinkled about enticed the girls to pick some and place them in their hair. I noticed I enjoyed the small things more than anything else. Not being in the big cities or doing something crazy and wild, but taking a stroll in the countryside with good people. And I enjoyed every small minute of it, talking and walking as we passed the time.

Outside of Venezuela, Colombia had some of the most gorgeous-looking women. And though I had spotted a few who I would have liked to take back home, Samita stood out to me the most. She ran the hostel, had her own dog walking business, and attended school. On my second to last night in Colombia, Samita and I talked for hours as she lay swaying in a hammock while I sat on the edge of a broken water fountain in the hostel. We talked about life, religion, love, careers, and where we wanted to go. I wanted to stay there even longer as she smiled and spoke with her Colombian accent, saying my name with what seemed like an "H" in it: "Russhell." It sounded good either way.

Samita wore her long, brown, curly hair wrapped in a bun, with her brown eyes peering through her stylish black glasses. Her earrings draped down below her rosy-colored cheeks. We shared thoughtful quotes from Alan Watts, both having a love of deep conversation, writing, and the arts. Samita did not believe in God, but she believed in kindness and love and knowing right from wrong. Though I had gotten away from church and religion, I believed in a higher power, which made me feel more comfortable opening up to her. No longer concerned about feeling judged, I felt comfortable enough to tell her about the racial friction I had encountered.

"How have you dealt with feeling this way?" Samita asked.

"I just have to understand that I am not home," I began. "The people I've encountered in these other countries looked at me just how they saw me. I'm in somebody else's home, and where I have to accept their culture and beliefs for what it is. I have no control over what somebody else thinks, and I have to accept it," I admitted.

"I get the feeling you have grown more from this experience, yes? To understand you live in whatever world you perceive it to be," she replied.

Desiring to share more than just words with Samita, I wanted to ask her if I could spend the night with her, but I could not bring myself to ask. Even if my intentions were out of innocence.

—

On my departure day, Samita had already left for school that morning. I wasted time going out to eat, lounging around the hostel, and meeting up with Ella. The two of us seemed like retired world travelers as we sat atop the roof. We talked above Bogotá, sitting on the rooftop of a nearby restaurant, drinking cool beers. The weather had grayed, giving a light drizzle that tickled the flesh. We had both planned to leave that night, her heading to Medellin and me to Salento, but we agreed to meet back up in Cartagena, the place that would mark the end of my journey.

My fellow retiree and I agreed to meet back at my hostel so that we could take a taxi to the bus station. Because I could not see Samita in time, I sent her a message, saying how much I appreciated her and that I would love to see her again. She messaged me back sometime later, wishing me the best, and that she looked forward to the next time we would meet. Knowing she did not mind crossing paths again made me feel as if the thought of coming back to see her did not sound crazy. Maybe we could have some more stories to share later in life one day.

Later on, Ella and I hopped into a cab, and off to the bus station we went. I wondered if I would see Musicology again. I wondered if I would see Colombia again. When Ella and I walked into the bus terminal, we hugged and said our farewells. Then she headed to one end of the terminal, and I walked down the other.

As I prepared to head to Salento, darkness still covered the morning skies when I arrived in the town of Armenia. Because there were no direct buses from Armenia to Salento, I had to catch a colectivo to reach my destination. I sat alone in the colectivo for a short while until other passengers slowly began filling the minibus size vehicle. The day had broken by the time we pulled off from the still-sleeping town.

Something about Colombia comforted me. It could have been because I did not feel like I needed to be on edge, worrying about who would look at me funny. Or maybe because things just seemed to slow down there. Nothing felt rushed.

Countrysides began occupying the windows of the bus, with views of clouds that dipped down and around hills and valleys. The coolness of the air met me when I stepped off the bus. People were finally stirring as I beheld the small plaza of Salento.

A little less than a mile away, my hostel awaited me, a ranch-style hostel surrounded by green landscapes and mountains that poked through the gray clouds. It was the most incredible hostel I had visited. Even calling it a hostel felt disrespectful. The property spread across a massive piece of land, with a separate building for eating, a fire pit and shed area, the main area where guests would sleep, and a few areas for guests who wanted private rooms. And that did not include the land for the horses and cows. It was like a small, isolated community.

I sat on a wooden bench near the fence under palm trees, looking over the earth's vast hills and bumps. *An ideal seat for a writer*, I thought. I thanked myself for coming there, more confirmation of why I liked Colombia so much.

During my time there, my mom sent me pictures of the large gathering outside of the State House for the removal of the

Confederate flag. I did not think it would ever happen, but it did. I wondered how the racial tension would be once I arrived back home. Would I be able to feel the change? Would anything change at all? Either way, I would receive my answers in less than a week.

After a while, I strolled to town to roam and to grab some food. I enjoyed the long walk to town, walking the dirt, trench-like road, having green fields leading out to hills on either side. Then I sat and ate in the plaza for a while, feeling the way I did when I first began my trip. I tapped back into autopilot mode, going wherever my body would take me.

—

I traveled to Salento to see the wax palm trees—extremely tall palm trees that stood out from any other tree—in Cocora Valley. The following morning, I walked for about two hours on the trail, stepping around huge rocks that obscured the path every so often. I crossed bridges, passed streams of water that flowed around large stones, and watched herds of cows graze on the other side of barbed wire fences lining the trail.

Just before I made it to my first stop, I spotted it up ahead like an oasis to a thirsty man as wooden stomps led to an area with shacks and houses. Some people already occupied the bench tables and chairs, sharing the same relief of being able to sit down. The area provided small refreshments like cheese and sugarcane water.

The number of hummingbirds that fluttered around amazed me. These birds sported green coats that seemed to turn blue depending on how they moved. Their coats shimmered under the sun's radiance. They were not the only animals there, though. Horses, roosters, and chickens strutted nearby, urging hikers to pet one of them. But one animal caught my attention above the rest, one I had never seen before. An animal that had the body and tail of a raccoon but the face of an anteater. It walked around unafraid of people as it walked on its feet, sniffing for food.

On the way back, I thought about how this adventure was my last trek, and how much I enjoyed it. I realized seeing beautiful backgrounds of mountains, hills, and landscapes keeps me grounded. It reminds me of how I am a part of something much bigger than me, and how small my problems are in life. Despite whatever is going on, I know nature is real. Our individual worlds are just that, individual. And those worlds are just a part of an ecosystem that is the real one. The one that matters.

Having missed the bus back to my town, I hitchhiked a ride hanging on the back of a fully occupied vehicle. The wind hitting my face and rushing through my hair felt good as we returned to town.

Once back in town, I sat under a long tent with lines of wooden table benches under it. While traveling, I learned people did not mind sitting close to you when it was time to eat. A table could be full of strangers and considered normal. Back home, it was completely the opposite. We liked our privacy and space, especially when it was time to eat. We preferred to sit at the other end of the table, which signified peace and elbow room.

While I was under the tent, an entire family came and sat right beside me: a father, a mother, an older daughter, a younger daughter, and a young son. As time passed, the older daughter and I began conversing, since she spoke perfect English; and soon her family joined in. Gabriella and I talked about music and my trip. Her two younger siblings, who were around seven, seemed curious about me, especially the younger boy.

Shortly after Gabriella translated her brother's question about my interest in basketball, the young boy randomly pointed to my hair and shouted: "Animal!"

I thought to myself, *Damn, I know I haven't had a haircut in a while, but if a child starts calling me an animal, I know I must be fucked up.*

Unexpectedly, he reached into my hair and pulled out a bug. I realized he called a bug an animal, and that I had a bug in my hair. I definitely needed that laugh.

On my way back home, I walked that long dirt road back to my hostel, the streetlights illuminating my path. The night was warm and calm, and I was exhausted and weary. The once-lit pastures had now turned to darkness, with the blinks of lightning bugs poking holes in them. Though I could see a few bubbles of light from what I assumed were homes, I knew the gray clouds still lingered above from flashes of silent lightning. This phenomenon reminded me of summer nights back home when lightning would cause the skies to glow, with no thunder and no rain. I found beauty in the irony of that. With the thunder absent, it seemed like God putting on a show instead of something scary. It made me think of my trip and how beautiful my experience had been since I had chosen not to be fearful. While I do not know why, I felt like crying at that moment. I wanted to hold on to this feeling forever, fully appreciating my time traveling.

—

My last day seemed to fly by, filled with visiting a nature reserve park and chatting with others in the hostel before leaving. Now that it had gotten dark, I took that long dirt road back to town with a backpack on and a book bag across my chest, thinking about how much I loved making this walk. When I arrived in town, all the taxis were done for the night, which resulted in me asking around for a ride back to Armenia.

After the hassle of trying to find a local willing to take me, I asked a taxi driver who stood outside of a bar with some friends. Though I knew he was done for the night, he could tell I needed a ride, so, thankfully, he gave me a lift. At the bus station, I booked a ride to my last destination: Cartagena. The name of the end.

I stood in line waiting with a few others until one girl in front of me started talking to me, but I could not understand her. The girl looked close to my age, about shoulder height with braces, and she was an extrovert. She pointed to herself and said, "Angela." And I pointed to myself, saying, "Russell." She stuck with me the whole time as we sat together waiting for the same bus. We spoke through Google Translate on my phone getting to know each other. She had visited Salento to see family. She even flirted with me, asking if I had a girlfriend and if she could come back to the States with me. I guess she found it attractive that I could not speak Spanish.

278

Our bus arrived about 12:30 a.m., and we were off to what would be a twenty-four-hour ride. My new friend and I had different seats on the trip, her destination a bit shorter than mine. I arrived in Cartagena the next morning around 2 a.m., and I walked the streets shortly after being dropped off by a taxi, and not being able to get into the hostel I wanted. Though I walked the street in an unknown area at an extremely late hour, I was not afraid. The thought of this being my last destination weighed too heavily on my mind, the final day of a journey that had lasted six months.

34

Reset

As I searched for a hostel to take me in, the streetlights illuminated vibrant buildings, ranging from yellows and reds to blues and purples, with flower plants hanging over door frames and window seals. Once I found one, I wanted nothing more than a warm bed to sleep in.

When I awoke the next day, the skies were gray, and the weather felt warm and soothing to the skin. Knowing this would be the last day of a six-month trip seemed somewhat numbing. I was neither depressed nor excited but content that my trip had lasted this long.

After breakfast, I flipped through my journal, amused at the wildly drawn marks I called words, stretching above and past the margins of lines. I could tell when I was in a rush, where sentences were written recklessly, containing words that looked like an unknown language. Other times I could see moments that resonated with me, having chosen words carefully as I wrote more poetically. I made scratches and lines over words in my attempt to correct misspellings, with replacement words that may have still been misspelled. I even attempted to rewrite letters to make them look more legible, only making the ink thicker and some letters bolder than others. My writings served as a visual representation of my brain and thoughts on paper, being all over the place just like the body that had carried them for six months.

Ella had also arrived in Cartagena, and we agreed to meet up for lunch. The hostel itself had been quiet, with only a few stragglers walking around—including one who invited us to a small island just off the beach.

Once we arrived, we noticed white tents and plastic chairs lined up and down the beach. The number of people there had been so minuscule that if it had not been for the vendors, I would have thought we were the only ones. For the second time, I spotted groups of dark-skinned people, both times in Colombia. Some were out tending to the boats, others selling or working under thatched huts and stands. I could not have been happier to see dark-complexioned people once more. It delighted me to think that the next day I would be around my people again.

I could feel this chapter of my journey ending as we all sat under a tent drinking beers. Cartagena would inevitably close another chapter in my life. And with each hour, those last pages closed more and more. Ella and I spent about two hours there, conversing, drinking beer, listening to house music, and buying bracelets. Even one of the local girls agreed to braid a piece of string with rasta colors—green, gold, and red—into my hair. I sat there experiencing the same feelings I had once experienced in the days leading up to graduation. I felt at ease and carefree, knowing I had accomplished all that I could, and now I awaited the date, not caring about anything except waiting for time to pass.

Knowing this city would be my last destination in South America, I observed the skyline of Cartagena from across the water. I scanned the rising and falling of the buildings like they depicted an image of concrete mountains along the coast. And from within those concrete mountains, I would depart and make my way back home.

Ella and I met back up later that night and grabbed some pizza before hanging with a few of the friends she met at her hostel. The night could not have gone any smoother as we had drinks at a rooftop bar, but the thought of me leaving consumed my mind. I had mentioned my return home to my friend Bobby a few weeks earlier, and he had agreed to pick me up from the airport. It had been a blessing to reach all of my destinations safely. Now, I just needed to make one more trip to cross the finish line, one more favor to make it back home.

I glanced over the balcony and down into the plaza, watching people come and go. The world seemed so much bigger and yet still the same. One girl in our group noticed me standing off by myself and came over to talk, mainly about my heading back home after such a long trip.

"It's hard to believe this is it for me. The road stops here," I said.

"But you've enjoyed yourself, yeah? Not many people can say they've had an experience as you've had," she replied.

"I'm scared I'll fall back into the same routines. That all the progress I made or having a new perspective is all for nothing. This shit is going to feel like I'm back in the Matrix all over again." I leaned over on the railing of the balcony as I spoke, completely zoned out, reflecting on everything.

"It will be hard to not have perspective now. This is something that you will never forget. And quite frankly, when you think about it, the journey never really ends."

She was right; the journey never really ends. The people I met were real. The places I saw were real. And now all of that was a part of me and with me. Even if I never saw them again, I knew they existed. Everything. I knew I lived in the world I perceived.

Before long, most of the girls suggested heading to a club afterward, but I had had my fun for the night. Ella thought the same thing as we said farewell to the group.

After I walked Ella back to her hostel, I knew this would be the last time I would see her. We had met up in Argentina, Peru, and Colombia, in four different cities. We had traveled together more times than any other traveling partner I had, by taxi, car, plane, and boat. From looking over the Pacific Ocean in Lima to standing on the white-crusted surface of the salt flats in Jujuy, Bolivia, I would miss hanging out with Ella. We embraced each other and wished each other a safe trip. Then she went up to her hostel, and I went off to mine.

I fell asleep that night thinking the next time I opened my eyes, I would be on my way home. That my six months of dreaming would be over. I did not feel emotional. I did not feel happy or sad, nor did I complain or whine. Though I knew what the next day meant, I went to bed like any other night, anticipating some well-needed rest.

—

Graduation day. I awoke to a cool room with faint sounds of traffic seeping through the window. There had been nothing unusual about the day, nor did I feel any different from the day before. I did not think about what hostel I would book next. I did not think about what city I planned on visiting next. I was heading home. I did not think about what walking tour or day trip I could make. I did not think about making sure I exchanged more money. I was heading home. No longer did I think about who I was meeting up with that day, nor did I join my roommates on their trip to the mud volcano, El Totumo. I couldn't. I was heading home.

Cartagena had done exactly what I foresaw it would do: bring my trip to an end. When I spoke to other backpackers in the hostel and informed them that my last day had arrived, their reactions mirrored someone hearing about a respected sports player retiring. Travelers expressed mixed emotions of empathy and happiness when they learned a fellow traveler was heading back home. And now my time had come. They could now hang my backpacking jersey up in the rafters.

Cartagena is a popular city for tourists in Colombia, with the colorful styles of buildings in the old city being one of the more recognizable areas, especially its colonial-style balconies. Even though I wished I could stay longer to explore, I walked around for about an hour, taking pictures and videos before returning to the hostel to check out.

Shortly after, I found myself sitting in the terminal waiting to board the plane, thankful I did not encounter any issues coming in. I sat there drawing some graffiti as I had done in other cities before while listening to music. I did not let anyone know I had planned on coming home that day, thinking it would be a pleasant surprise. Bobby had still planned to pick me up from the airport, and we could still make the South Carolina Music Awards, for which our hip-hop group had been nominated.

I sat there in my tattered shoes, with the soles pulling away from the cloth. My unmanaged hair had grown down the sides of my face, across my cheeks, and around and under my chin. My mustache had grown so much that hair fell over my lips. My hair was tangled and matted, having not been properly washed in what seemed like forever. Colorful bracelets with unique patterns from different countries covered both of my wrists. And anyone who knew me could recognize the weight loss simply by looking at my face.

In each country I visited, I stitched the country's flag across the top part of my book bag, like a badge of honor. I had the Wi-Fi networks of all the airports and bus terminals I had visited still saved on my phone, like old contact numbers. In six months, I had traveled to seven countries and over thirty cities. Though I could not reach Brazil, I believed I had received everything I wanted out of the journey, something I could be proud of.

Over the past few days, I had experienced mixed emotions about returning home, confused about how to feel. I experienced moments of feeling excited about going home, and others feeling hurt that a beautiful experience would have to end. But the longer I thought about it, the more grateful I became. I now sat in a terminal surrounded by other travelers preparing to embark on their journey. And there were things I could look forward to once I got home. Outside of being with family and friends, I would have a story to tell and share with others.

With home getting even closer, I boarded my plane to New York for a transit stop. I had never been to "The Big Apple" before and while in the air, the city looked smaller than what I saw on TV. When I walked off the plane and saw the words "John F. Kennedy Airport" in English, I felt like Dorothy waking up at the end of *The Wizard of Oz*. "New York," "Welcome," and "Arrival" were words I did not have to think about when I read them. My brain took in words like water to a thirsty mouth, wanting to keep them a secret all to myself and to hold on to them like treasure. White people, Black people, Hispanic people, and Asian people wandered everywhere. I felt more of a culture shock now than when I had left six months before.

In the blink of an eye, everything had reset itself back to normal. No longer did I have to get my passport stamped. No longer did I have to check in with immigration. No longer did I have to exchange money. No longer did I have to worry about which direction I needed to go. From those profound words I now treasured, I knew where I was going. I was back home.

Strangely enough, it felt like my traveling had not ceased. Though I did not have plans to travel to any other country, it seemed like I constantly needed to move. I walked around seeing businesses like T-Mobile, Starbucks, and Chanel, ones I knew of that now seemed strange. The thought that I could speak to anyone now and they knew my language made me ecstatic. Yet, the only thing between me and my actual home was an eleven-hour layover, so I would have to spend the night at the airport.

I contemplated going out to get a feel of New York, but my exploring appetite had waned. Instead, I strolled over to Dunkin Donuts and purchased one chocolate-frosted doughnut and a strawberry-frosted one with sprinkles, laughing to myself that I could read the prices again. Then, I found a seat over by the wall and people-watched for the rest of the night. I sent Bobby a message saying that I had made it to New York safely. I was back home.

The following morning, I had a 7:36 a.m. flight from New York to Charlotte. I sat waiting after scarfing down a sandwich and some water, still in disbelief that I was back in the States. Once on the plane, I cued up the live version of Mali Music's "Ready Aim," just as I had when first preparing to take off. I landed at Charlotte Douglas International Airport around 9:45 a.m., met by the middle of July's summer heat.

I used the Wi-Fi to message Bobby, saying I had made it, and he messaged me back to say he had as well. I walked around anxiously searching for my friend, eager to see a familiar face to confirm that this was not a dream. Then I spotted his box haircut and silver-rimmed glasses coming through the doors. When we made eye contact, we both grinned and walked to each other to embrace. It felt good to see another Black face, a familiar Black face.

We both pulled out our phones to record the moment. I knew I looked like some wild man from the jungle with my crazy hair, but I did not care. I was back home and back with my homeboy. Even simply riding in a car again felt different as we both caught each other up on what had been going on. I honestly did not even know where to begin or what to say first. After riding in a passenger seat again, getting back to Columbia, eating IHOP pancakes, going to the library, going to Orangeburg and Blackville, and seeing other beautiful Black faces that I recognized again, I knew this was where I needed to be, around my people, around my tribe. It felt like a homecoming. And things were going to get better. I realized that night that nowhere in the world could compare to being home.

After devising a quick scheme to surprise my friend on his birthday weekend, Bobby and I rode over to where the gathering had been that night. My heart pounded as I waited outside the house, adrenaline pumping with excitement for Bobby to give me the cue. Once I got the signal, I buzzed through the door full of emotion.

"Turn up! Turn up!" I shouted.

The room exploded in a frenzy after registering who had just walked in. It felt like a shock of electricity circulated through the air, with sounds of "ohhhhhhhh" and "ohhhhh shit!" mixed with laughter.

Trembling with excitement, I made my way around the room, embracing my friends again.

"Russ, I'm not even gonna lie to you, you scared the hell out of me, bro," one of my friends said.

I could not blame her. Had I seen myself walking in looking like a mangy popsicle stick, I would have done the same. And I was sure my odor was working against me from traveling all day. But at that moment, no one seemed to care. They were just glad that I had made it back home. And so was I.

Words could not express the joy I felt being around my friends again, and finally taking a hot shower and sleeping in a comfortable bed. Even something as simple as getting my hair cut after six months felt like a luxury. The streets and roads I had driven so many times before felt like I was rekindling an old love once again. But all of this led up to the one moment that mattered the most: surprising my mother.

She had planned to represent me on my behalf at the SC Music Awards, just in case my group won an award. On the way there, I was anxious, understanding how big of a moment it would be. I even wondered if that was how soldiers felt when they returned home to surprise their loved ones at an event. I knew my mother would be worried about my safety and well-being the entire time I was gone. And now me being there with her, knowing I was back, would bring some great exhale from a six-month stint of held breath.

My mother had already been at the hotel preparing for the award show while Bobby and I pulled the same stunt we did with my friends. While waiting for Bobby to give me the signal, I only hoped my mother would not pass out when she saw me. The anticipation built up a knot in my stomach, as I was eager to see my mom again.

Once I received Bobby's text, I gathered my bags and headed to the elevator. Bobby met me outside of the hotel room and prepped his phone to record the moment. The door opened and there my mother stood, dressed up in a frizzled, tangerine ensemble. And when she saw me, she yelped and grabbed the wall to steady herself. Then she rushed over and flung her arms around my neck, releasing a joyous cry as we embraced.

Barely able to stand up straight, she cried out, "My baby! Ohhh, it's my baby!", as only a mother could. I could hear all the worry she had stored up inside of her for the past six months pouring out as she continued to bellow out with relief and joy. And though my group would win the 2015 South Carolina Group/Duo of the Year award later that night, nothing could compare to being back home and being reunited with my mom once more. I was home.

Section 7: Liberation

◆━━━━━━━━━━━━━━━━━━━━━━━━━━━━━━━◆

I see a child running freely in an open field, his arms stretched out like he's trying to hug a wall.

Light shimmers off of the grass from gentle breezes, creating green waves in front of him to chase.

He's out far enough; I can just make out the faint joys of laughter in the distance.

I imagine the wind is filling into his ears and passing between his small fingers.

Could he be imagining that he is a plane picking up speed to take off?

Or some brave eagle soaring the skies to get lost?

Or does it even matter?

Away and away and away, the world is his and nobody else's.

May his firm steps blossom the ground he walks so that every day feels like May.

And that his voice is strong enough that it makes a rip in the sky as beautiful as the Milky Way.

I catch a smile made from his adventurous heart, curious about what treasures he'll retrieve.

And like the weight lifted after a good cry, I'll watch on feeling relieved.

35

Soaring

Casting what shade they could, palm trees hovered above me as I reclined on a beach chair. The ocean breeze lightly brushed against my exposed arms as I scribbled words on paper right outside of my shack-type hostel. My body lay tired from helping a friend move to Alexandria, Virginia, while still having to work the next morning and also needing to pack to catch a flight the morning after.

I knew I would travel again, even if only for five days as a groomsman for a friend's wedding in Punta Cana, Dominican Republic. He and his bride had booked our resort for four days and three nights; however, I arrived a day before I could check in. A mistake that felt right, and one I deemed a treat. No resort could provide the excitement of feeling like a free-spirited backpacker again. Not only did I haul around my rental suite in my garment bag, but I also packed my clothes in my backpack, which did not seem as heavy as before. Even my book bag that now sported patches of South American flags felt lighter.

Pulled back into the memory of my backpacking journey, I recalled the minimalistic feeling of not having much and how calming and serene things seemed at times. The absent sounds of congested traffic and corporate businesses all around. This small tap back into the world of a backpacker felt refreshing, even when I got picked up on the back of a truck while heading to a hostel. Everything about it made me yearn for that feeling of being out again, out in the world.

Handwritten messages and signatures from travelers were sprawled along the chipped, blue-painted walls in the main shack of my hostel, marked with Sharpies and permanent markers. Each marking had its own style and personality on display for anyone willing to tilt their heads or squint their eyes.

The nostalgia of calling myself a backpacker for one more day rushed over me once more. Being able to speak a few Spanish words brought back memories of my efforts to navigate cities. Even knowing that I would sleep in a bunk bed again amused me.

A native of Bogotá, Colombia, the owner of the hostel, listened to me gush about Bogotá and its culture and how it was one of my favorite places. After a year since my trip, being able to talk to someone who knew about the world of backpacking and hostel living felt like finding a place of refuge from a hostile society. And at this refuge, you were either out swimming or trying to slackline between two palm trees, which introduced me to turquoise-colored water for the first time. Water so blue that it almost looked artificial, rushing up the soft sand, combing back whatever was light enough to come with it.

—

Since returning home, I realized not much had changed. Not like I had hoped, anyway. I was finally seeing the aftermath of backpacking and those daunting thoughts of not knowing what life would be when I got back home. And to be honest, it was not as horrible as I thought it would be.

Though I had hoped things would move more quickly than how they were moving, being back home had its pros and cons. As far as pros, I got a job at Edible Arrangements delivering fruit baskets and bouquets, which offered good hours. I also worked on more music with my group member, Bobby, and began writing my memoir about my backpacking experience, the one you are reading now.

The cons mainly involved me feeling stagnant sometimes, being a twenty-six-year-old man still living at his mother's house. I understood things could have been a hell of a lot worse, but I had hoped to have some traction by this point. It had been a constant struggle for me not to fall back into my old patterns, overthinking, having self-doubt, and wanting to have control. But as they say, old habits die hard. That once ambitious drive I had to start anew had now run out of steam. That laser beam focus I had before had now steered off course. However, I had gotten back into reading more. I explored books about business and marketing, trying to learn what I could, yet still at a loss for what I wanted to do.

—

It felt like paradise leaving footprints in the pale sand, deciding whether the water or the sky flaunted the better blue. Closer inland was a line of crooked palm trees, bent from what I assumed were previous storms, with half-dead leaves spread back in one direction like wild hair, just as my hair once was.

From time to time, I would hear from some of my old buddies from the trip, like Ernesto and Ruben from Venezuela, some of my peers from the ayahuasca retreat, my four girls from Ireland, or Samita from Colombia. Everyone carried on with their lives and continued their paths, all yearning to travel again. Though one or two were still out traveling, most of them were back home like me, reminiscing about how much fun we had.

About two months after I returned home, Tom from England, who I met in Baños, Ecuador, came to stay with me, en route to a music festival in Atlanta called TomorrowWorld. I thought it was dope that he dedicated a day to hanging out with me. Giving him a taste of Southern hospitality, I introduced him to some friends, shared drinks with him at a bar downtown, and introduced him to my mom, who treated him to Southern cooking. She got a kick out of him not being familiar with collard greens

While I no longer felt like I was still traveling, bits and pieces of those events reminded me I remained connected to that world. After the Dominican Republic, who knows when I will ever venture out again? Janet, whom I met my last time in Arequipa, and I flirted with the idea of backpacking together in Southeast Asia sometime, though I think she took it more seriously than I did. If ever I were to travel again, it would not be nearly as long as six months. And I think I would rather go to Africa the next time around.

Speaking of Africa, I also took the Ancestry DNA test, seeking answers to the question about my roots that still lingered in my mind. Primarily, I had the highest percentage of ancestry in Nigeria and Mali, so I had been trying to learn more about those areas, reading literature like *Things Fall Apart* by Chinua Achebe, a native of Nigeria.

—

The weather in Punta Cana felt delightful. As I attempted to slackline, trying to balance myself on the thin, wobbly, tense strips, the lessons that Meka, a worker at the hostel, demonstrated did not rub off on me well. Just trying to stand on the strap quickly landed me back in the warm sand. I looked on as he bounced, walked, sat, and even turned flips off the line with confidence, as if his techniques were fixed. Even though I was not good at slacklining, I enjoyed being out in the open breeze.

Back home, I started a routine of going to the park and walking nature trails on weekends, even taking a pen and paper with me to write sometimes. I got the idea one night while speaking to a deacon turned reverend who helped me look for a job. Of course, whether I attended church came up, which I had not done in years. When I informed him of my change in beliefs, I braced myself for a sermon, but he respected my decision and suggested that I at least find a place of my own to be with God. I ventured out into nature to find my sanctuary.

There is something about being outside that makes me feel like I am always involved and connected with everything. Walking the trails sometimes reminds me of the treks I used to walk, imagining I am still somewhere in the Andes, replacing the sounds of shuffling loose rocks under my shoes with the crackles and snaps of dry pine straw. Yet, the chirp of the birds, the sun's kiss on the skin, and the light touch of the wind all felt the same. I tried to bring as much of my trip back as I could, even cooking Lomo Saltado for my family. (They found it strange to eat fries with rice.) I also tried making Pisco Sour for my friends one night. Though the cocktail did not turn out as it should have, everyone enjoyed it because we were drinking.

—

When I returned from the beach, two more guests had arrived at the hostel, both of whom were both studying abroad. We stayed up talking about traveling, and they asked questions about my trip like I was a traveling guru, listening to every word and amazed at such an experience.

"Six months, bro? That's insane!"

"How was it living among the people?"

"I don't know if I could do all that."

Both of them were more advanced in speaking Spanish than me, because they had traveled to the Dominican Republic to help teach the children there. We chatted away for the rest of the night until we went to sleep.

Without skipping a beat, I was back to feeling like a backpacker, just as before. The nostalgia of it as I climbed up to the top of my bunk bed, and woke up to the crows of roosters and the grunts of cows. In a way, they were more pleasurable to listen to than being awakened by alarm clocks and cell phone notifications. I had taken a break from social media for a while to focus more on myself and creating, doing all that I could to find more time in the day.

At Allen University, I received an opportunity to hear Hip Hop legend KRS-One speak. He dropped so many valuable jewels and information that day, but what stuck with me the most was:

"The more words you know, the more things you can see." When you think about it, that makes perfect sense. The more words you know, the more you understand, and the more you can explain. As a result, I dedicated my time to working on myself more, trying to learn about myself and educate myself, reading any– and everything.

A few months prior to my trip to Punta Cana, my buddy Gary, a videographer, helped me shoot *Trigger*, the first short film I wrote while in Peru and Bolivia. Though it was something I had written on a small scale, seeing it come off the page and into motion touched me deeply.

As far as music, Bobby and I began working on a new project inspired by Marvin Gaye's album, *What's Going On*. I like to think that my trip contributed to this body of music we called *Kids of Tomorrow*. There is a song on Marvin's album called "Save the Children," and I could not help but think of my experience with skin color in the eyes of children. How they think. How they move. How we have to be mindful that our kids are watching us. How one day they could become a reflection of us. Maybe if we think about them first, and understand our own tendencies to be judgmental of others—which put our own insecurities on display—we will succeed in not indirectly teaching children to be self-conscious about themselves.

Looking forward to his own plans with music, my good friend who had gotten arrested while I was away was still doing time. I wrote letters to him, encouraging him to keep his head up. He assured me he was in good spirits, and I believed he would be just fine.

–

Taking in the moment, I sat at a table and smelled the fresh morning dew in the air and the moist grass that surrounded me. A handful of chickens strutted across the area, plucking the ground with their beaks for food, while a dog lay on its stomach gnawing at a bone. Aside from their company, there was the sunrise, as I began writing—as I had always done in the mornings.

I no longer had crayons to mark the pages with the flags and colors of the country I was in. Now, I just wrote the date and where I was. I continued writing in the same journal, but only from time to time. Tricking myself into the feeling that I was still traveling. I guess we never really stop the journey.

The past couple of months involved me watching Kobe Bryant play his last game, hearing about the passing of Prince, and just two months later, the passing of Muhammed Ali. Things I thought I would never witness, things I never even took the time to think about happening. I even experienced another loss in my family with the passing of my uncle, Alvin. I remembered when I worried about having holes develop in my life while I was absent. And in ways, even when I was absent, life continued to go on, whether I was there or not.

I delivered a fruit arrangement to my old job one day and saw my old coworkers still working there. It was a pleasure to see them again. Taking a moment to catch up with me, they surrounded me with their collared shirts, khaki pants, and ID badges hanging from their necks and belts, while I sported blue jeans, a khaki sun visor, and a light blue shirt with a fruit design printed on it. I did not feel embarrassed, though. I felt liberated. Proud of myself for following through with what I had desired to do. On the wall map displayed in the room, I pointed to the furthest place I had traveled, showcasing the bracelets that still hung from my wrist a year later. Though I had left my job, my spirit felt promoted, like I had achieved something.

I witnessed the achievements of my cousin and little brother's graduations. One of them leaving high school, the other entering high school. There was even a girl I worked with, whom I had taken an interest in, who was interested in me. Overall, one year back home had its ups and downs, but I tried my best to remain persistent through everything, working on my wellness and sharpening my focus. A never-ending battle that teetered back and forth between trying to be flawless and just being human. I worked to build and redesign my habits to become the person I wanted to be for the future I wanted to have. Exercising had even become a part of my routine, as I aimed to strengthen my mind and my body.

—

For the rest of the day, I returned to the beach with the crew for more slacklining and swimming. I wished life could always be like this, cherishing the late morning sunlight dancing off the turquoise-colored water. Toes warm from being dragged down in golden brown sand while drinking from a freshly cut coconut.

We stayed out for just a couple more hours before I prepared to leave for my resort. I had been receiving messages on my phone about the other wedding party members arriving and checking in. As I had done over and over and over again, I bid farewell to a unique group of people—goodbyes I never got used to saying. I hopped onto the back of Meka's moped with my bags and my black garment bag, and we were on our way.

After getting lost and having to go completely in the opposite direction, I appreciated my last bit of freedom of going in whatever direction I happened to be going in one last time. Just to land wherever I ended up.

We finally pulled up to tall, barred gates with security officers standing out front, checking all entries. Behind the gates, I could see the luxurious resort with uniformed greeters and doormen opening taxi doors while carrying luggage. I stepped off the back of Meka's moped with my garment bag still wrapped around my arm. And just like that, it seemed like I stood between two different worlds.

The security guard eyed me skeptically. "You have proof that you are booked at this resort?" he asked.

Once I scrambled to find the correct information to show him, he radioed in to open the gate.

—

Maybe there will be another opportunity for me again somewhere in my lifetime to seek another taste of freedom to just go. After all, I learned that the journey is the destination, not one particular place.

I looked back at Meka, and we exchanged nods.

"Safe travels," we spoke simultaneously.

That is all one can hope until we make it back home.

Epilogue

The small trinkets and souvenirs I collected on my trip are now kept somewhere in a dusty box that gets as much light as the dingy bookbag that houses my travel journal. I will occasionally spot one of the t-shirts I received on my travels, stuffed in the back of my dresser drawer or randomly mixed in with the clothes in my laundry basket. But I cannot tell you the countless times throughout the years I have scrolled through the many photos I captured, recalling faces with names and forgetting the names of others. Trying to relive moments by hanging onto each sound that emerges from the numerous videos I recorded.

I started writing this book in November 2015, four months after I returned from a six-month backpacking trip in South America. I would be remiss if I did not say the process was a journey in itself, outside of the tedious task of writing my story while referring to that now untouched journal and those nostalgic photos and videos of my trip, which now feels like a faint dream. Or how difficult it was to uncover the purpose of this memoir and why you should read it.

Initially, I thought this book would encourage you to step out on faith. Show you how beautiful the unknown can be. Maybe even show you that no matter where you go or where you are in life, you will always experience ups and downs. However, there is something about the word "gratitude" that keeps coming back to me. Gratitude for the moment. Gratitude for wanting to expand

and to grow. Gratitude for the situations and experiences that shaped my perspective. Gratitude for realizing how much joy can come from small things. How that gratitude can encourage us to move forward. How finding gratitude comes in different ways and different forms for different people. And how the process described in this book is mine.

But who am I? Who am I to learn anything from? I am just as flawed and imperfect as the next person, stumbling over life's obstacles. Making mistakes displayed by my marks and blemishes. Aware of my ignorance but not of my spaced teeth when I smile. Yet, all these things are a part of the raw undertaking of the human experience: we develop and strive to be better as we go. And the common thread that ties all who may or may not read this is, we all just want to get it right. We are doing the best we can with what we know and what we have endured— accepting growth in whatever form it comes. And this is merely a recorded moment in time in a story where I happen to be the main character.

One lesson I have learned along my journey is, to be grateful in all of life's moments no matter how grand or miniscule. This lesson is important because moments do not last forever. Just like a sunset. Therefore, we must be grateful for every second and remain hopeful for the next one.

I am hopeful that my journey will be of some service to you as you progress throughout your own journey. Maybe you will decide to travel the world. Maybe you will meet beautiful strangers. Maybe you will bungee jump off a bridge, witness breathtaking sights, or immerse yourself in an unknown place. Maybe you, too, will share what you learn one day. And for that, I will be grateful.

About the Author

Russell J. Earle Jr. is from Columbia, SC and a South Carolina State University graduate. His writing journey spans well over 20 years with a background in Creative Writing from Midlands Technical College. He engages audiences by weaving life experiences through songwriting, poetry, and screenwriting. Now, he embarks on his debut book, *Until I Came Home: A Sunset's Journal.* When not penning his latest work, Russell enjoys the soothing sounds of Lo-fi music, embraces his role as a part-time professional walker, and often visits YouTube when attempting to cook. Ask him if he's burned rice lately or learn more at www.RussellEarleJr.com.

www.ingramcontent.com/pod-product-compliance
Lightning Source LLC
Chambersburg PA
CBHW021216130626
46554CB00004B/1245

* 9 7 9 8 9 9 1 3 7 2 9 0 9 *